12/2/13
$25.00
B+T
AS

Praise for *Highly Recommended*

"Consumers are increasingly cutting through all the 'puff and fluff' of advertising to get to what's real. They are relying more and more on 'people like them,' especially online, to help make purchasing decisions. If you're a marketer, you need to create and nurture fans and make it easy for new customers to hear from others how great you are. It's a new world where the most *highly recommended* brand wins. Paul's book *Highly Recommended* is THE playbook learning why and how to make this happen."

—**BOB ARMOUR,** Chief Marketing Officer, Guaranteed Rate, Inc.

"More often than not, great relationships and transformative experiences begin with an impassioned recommendation. That's how I came to know Paul Rand more than 15 years ago—and the personal and professional return on that simple referral has been immense. I am privileged to have had the benefit of Paul's insight, wisdom, good humor, and friendship while working to build brands for market categories as diverse as semiconductors, mobile phones, zero-emission electric cars, travel and tourism, and a leading nonprofit global service organization. For anyone who doesn't have the benefit of a direct relationship with Paul, this book delivers a thorough and thought-provoking blueprint for enabling both the highly recommended business and the highly recommended life."

—**ALAN J. BUDDENDECK,** Chief Communications Officer, Rotary International

"It is critically important that companies understand the business value of word of mouth and how to harness the power of recommendations—not just *a* recommendation, but the millions instantaneously accessible right at one's fingertips anytime and anywhere."

—**CHRISTINE CEA,** Senior Director of Marketing Communications, Unilever

"Being a brand that is *highly recommended*, as Paul recognizes, is more than using social media well and even more than doing smart brand strategy. It's the consequence of an enterprise doing the right things. Paul's book beautifully reframes these ideas and adds examples and insights to achieve this genuinely higher order goal."

—**TOM COLLINGER,** Executive Director, Medill IMC Spiegel Digital & Database Research Initiative, Northwestern University

"I did not need a book to know I *highly recommend* Paul! As you take the time to read this book, you will feel the same way about Paul as I do. This book is an incredible guide, filled with great stories that will take your brand to the next level. Love it!"

—**FRANK ELIASON,** Director of Global Social Media, Citi, and author of *@YourService*

"Paul gives us a refreshing gift of insight. *Highly Recommended* shows us the possibilities of a deeper relationship between consumers and brands."

—**SCOTT ELLIS,** VP North America and General Manager, August Storck KG

"Paul's new book *Highly Recommended* provides an easy-to-follow road map for companies trying to shift from a monologue to a dialogue with their customers. His emphasis on using purposeful storytelling, authenticity, and transparency to shape consumers' relationship with a brand is spot on. I would recommend this book to any marketers looking to transform their organizations through the power of word of mouth recommendations."

—**PEPPER EVANS,** Vice President of Loyalty Branding & Marketing, International Consumer & Small Business Services, American Express

"Have you ever wanted to get inside one of the brightest minds in the agency world to learn how he drives success for his clients? This is your chance. You'll find solid examples, hear the latest research, learn the biggest mishaps, and get the formula for being *highly recommended* in Paul Rand's new book."

—**SUZANNE P. FANNING,** President, Word of Mouth Marketing Association (WOMMA)

"Too many business and marketing books are one-hit wonders—they have one point to make and you get it after the first chapter. *Highly Recommended* makes a strong business case for generating recommendations and then specifically shows you how to systematically generate recommendations for your business. Every chapter is full of ways to be a thriving social business today. It's no wonder Paul has built the largest social media business in Omnicom Group."

—**ROB FLAHERTY,** Senior Partner and CEO, Ketchum

"*Highly Recommended* is a MUST-READ!! Where was this book when I needed it a couple of years ago as I embarked on this Social Business journey? I would have avoided many bumps and bruises. Paul's concept of 'Living a Recommendable Life' is brilliant! Showing how this can apply to the individual as well as a brand and/or a business was really powerful. *Highly Recommended* is action packed with real-world case studies and a clear formula on how to put this into action for your brand or business. I walked away with pages of ideas on how to put this in play for my business, all inspired by this great book."

—**KIM HEALY,** Vice President of Consumer Products Marketing, Solo Cup Company (now part of Dart Container Corporation)

"There is nothing more powerful than a recommendation to drive purchase intent. It's the perfect complement to a strong brand campaign and essential to drive success in today's competitive marketplace. Yet few people have figured out how to harness word of mouth and seamlessly integrate it into the marketing mix . . . until now. *Highly Recommended* will make you think differently about how you invest your marketing dollars."

—**SHANNON JENEST,** Director of Communications, Philips Consumer Lifestyle, North America

"*Highly Recommended* is very resonant with my own beliefs and experiences. The succinct organizing principles and approach are great for anyone interested in getting serious about WOM and social media as a matter of strategy rather than old school stunts inspired by P. T. Barnum. Paul demystifies much of what many think requires a magic lantern and lightning in a bottle. I love the idea of aspiring to become 'recommendable.' Clear, simple, and sticky."

—**RUSS KLEIN,** former Chief Marketing Officer,
Arby's Restaurant Group and former CMO, Burger King

"Paul understands the real-world quirks and complexities of marketing today and offers insights and actionable strategies for businesses to have an immediate impact. *Highly Recommended* should be required reading for all business, marketing, and social media leaders . . . and their superiors."

—**ERICH MARX,** Director of Interactive & Social Media Marketing, Nissan North America, Inc.

"Nearly every one of our global clients recognizes the business value and power of digital and social media. *Highly Recommended* brings clarity and life to some of the most important lessons and best practices around. Every brand should strive to become *highly recommended*. Paul has cracked the code, and his book shows you can do it too."

—**JONATHAN NELSON,** CEO, Omnicom Digital at Omnicom Group Inc.

"*Highly Recommended* is an understatement. Paul has nailed the pain points, challenges, and opportunities a company or brand must address in order to become a Social Business. Packed with research, case studies, and practical insights, the reader comes away with ideas ready for action. *Highly Recommended* should really be 'Mandatory Reading!'"

—**GARY SPANGLER,** Leader, DuPont Social Media Center of Excellence

"Recommendations are key in the hospitality business—even more so in the age of the always on, connected consumer. What I really appreciate about Paul's book is that it is written in a manner that is easy for everyone to understand irrespective of their knowledge of the subject. Huge."

—**JOHN WALLIS,** Global Head of Marketing and Brand Strategy, Hyatt Hotels

"Today's consumer is more in control than ever about the future of business through the things that they say—both positive and negative. Digital and social media are making this commentary real-time, diverse, and highly impacting. *Highly Recommended* is a must-read for the success of any company that is serious about being a part of the story—and understanding the principles of becoming 'recommended.'"

—**TYLER WALLIS,** Senior Vice President of Product & Marketing, Cricket Communications

"If you want your business to be talked about—buy this book! Paul gives you tried-and-true formulas to becoming a recommendable brand."

—**EKATERINA WALTER,** former Social Media Strategist, Intel, and author of the *Wall Street Journal* bestseller *Think Like Zuck*

"Want some great lessons in how to make your brand and your campaigns more remarkable and more talkable? You're in luck! Paul is a proven veteran in the world of word of mouth marketing, and he's sharing excellent how-to examples from his work with some of the most loved brands around."

—**DAVID WITT,** Director of Global Digital Marketing and Brand Public Relations, The Hershey Company

"As far as this book goes, *Highly Recommended* is an understatement. How about 'Must Read!' Paul's a five-star thinker. His depth of experience gets 'two thumbs up.' His attentive understanding of word of mouth ethics and message integrity deserves a million Likes. When asked to recommend the industry's best thinkers in brand advocacy and word of mouth, Paul's always—I repeat, always—at the top of my list."

—**PETE BLACKSHAW,** Global Head of Digital & Social Media, Nestlé, and author of *Satisfied Customers Tell Three Friends, Angry Customers Tell Three Thousand*

"*Highly Recommended* is a great book—I have pages of notes and takeaways. Paul's book turns the traditional tenets of advertising on their end and empowers us through insightful case studies and commentary to rethink marketing for the social economy. I *highly recommend* this book."

—**ADAM BROWN,** Executive Strategist for Salesforce.com and former Executive Director of Social Media for Dell and The Coca-Cola Company

"The power of recommendations is immense. They are a business asset that is far too precious to leave to chance. In *Highly Recommended*, Paul reveals that there is a science to being a successful social brand and lays out a compelling blueprint that separates the winners from the rest. I *highly recommend* it!"

—**ED KELLER,** CEO, The Keller Fay Group, and coauthor of *The Face-to-Face Book* and *The Influentials*

"Honestly I find most business books boring or quickly obsolete as they chase what's new. I was delighted to find Paul's book interesting, applicable, and an entertaining read. It's the triple crown of what makes a business book interesting and relevant. The measure of a good business book is not whether I keep it on my office shelf but rather if I continue to reference it in the months and years ahead. While technology has permanently changed the economy, the lessons in Paul's book are timeless in many ways. *Highly Recommended* is one book that I will be looking at and learning from for years to come."

—**PETE MARINO,** Vice President of Communications, MillerCoors

"The question that everyone should be asking is not, would you recommend us to a friend, it should be, did you recommend us? Paul shows why, in a time of connected consumerism, recommendations are more powerful than ever. Earn them!"

—**BRIAN SOLIS,** author of the bestselling *What's the Future of Business (WTF)*, and Principal Analyst, Altimeter Group

HIGHLY
RECOMMENDED

Harnessing the Power of **WORD OF MOUTH** and **SOCIAL MEDIA** to Build Your Brand and Your Business

PAUL M. RAND

New York   Chicago   San Francisco   Athens   London   Madrid
Mexico City   Milan   New Delhi   Singapore   Sydney   Toronto

1 2 3 4 5 6 7 8 9 0   DOC/DOC   1 9 8 7 6 5 4 3

ISBN   978-0-07-181621-2
MHID   0-07-181621-6

e-ISBN   978-0-07-181622-9
e-MHID   0-07-181622-4

Library of Congress Cataloging-in-Publication Data

Rand, Paul.
    Highly recommended : harnessing the power of word of mouth and social media to build your brand and your business / by Paul Rand.
       pages cm
    ISBN-13: 978-0-07-181621-2 (alk. paper)
    ISBN-10: 0-07-181621-6 (alk. paper)
    1. Branding (Marketing) 2. Marketing—Management. 3. Oral communication.
4. English language—Business English. I. Title.
    HF5415.1255.R363 2013
    658.8'72—dc23
                                                                    2013014110

McGraw-Hill Education books are available at special quantity discounts to use as premiums and sales promotions or for use in corporate training programs. To contact a representative, please visit the Contact Us pages at www.mhprofessional.com.

CONTENTS

Foreword   v

Preface   ix

Acknowledgments   xiii

Introduction   xv

PART 1

Word of Mouth Recommendations: Marketing's Holy Grail

CHAPTER 1   Stew Leonard's and the 30-Minute Recommendation   3

CHAPTER 2   Why Angie and Her List of Recommendations Are Worth $1.4 Billion   9

CHAPTER 3   Fixing What Advertising Has Broken   21

CHAPTER 4   A Whole New Model for a Whole New World   29

CHAPTER 5   The Power of Positive Recommendations   39

CHAPTER 6   Why, Where, and How We Recommend   47

CHAPTER 7   Some Recommendations Are More Valuable Than Others: The Oprah Effect and the Influencer Ecosystem   63

PART 2

The Road Map to Recommendations

CHAPTER 8   Know: Understanding Where and How Your Brand—and Your Competitors—Are Talked About and Recommended   81

CHAPTER 9   Plan: Articulating Your Shareable Story, Boosting Your Search Ranking, and Formalizing Your Paid, Earned, and Owned Recommendable Brand Strategy   95

CHAPTER 10   Identify: Discovering Those People Whose Recommendations
              Influence Your Brand's Purchase Decisions   113

CHAPTER 11   Activate: Creating Compelling Content and Experiences
              That Engage—The 90/10 Rule   125

CHAPTER 12   Protect: Identifying and Neutralizing Determined
              Detractors: Hear Me's, Reputation Terrorists,
              and Competitive Destroyers   139

PART 3

Beyond Marketing: Operationalizing Recommendations

CHAPTER 13   Customer Service That Gets You Recommended   153

CHAPTER 14   Attracting and Keeping the Best: Becoming the
              Most Recommended Place to Work   169

CHAPTER 15   Creating Products and Offerings Your Customers
              Tell You They Will Buy: Product Innovation and R&D   187

CHAPTER 16   Tying It All Together: Becoming a Highly
              Recommended Business   201

              Endnotes   215

              Index   219

You and I Are Not the Same Consumers
We Were Just a Few Years Ago

We are living in a period of truly transformative advancement and change. Technology's impact is seen all around us. It affects how we live, work, socialize, and learn, and it has accelerated business cycles. As a result, things that once seemed incredibly futuristic are happening now. Self-driving cars, computers in glasses and in watches, in shoes, and in just about any other form of apparel—real-time translation: all of these impossible things are either here today or right around the corner. Moore's law—the 1965 maxim, coined by Intel cofounder Gordon Moore, which states that computer processing power doubles every 18 to 24 months—has held true for over 45 years, and it is making many things that once seemed impossible not only possible but normal.

This trend is having a big, permanent impact on the relationship between consumers and brands. We see this in a couple of ways. First, consumer expectations are rising as never before. When the impossible becomes possible, people get used to it! Instant answers, fast navigation, one-click ordering, same-day shipping, and personalized experiences have increased expectations and raised the bar for every business. Second, the balance of power has shifted in the consumers' favor. They have an enormous range of choices, since online shelf space is practically infinite, and they are empowered with superior information along the entire path to purchase. The Internet is teeming with reviews, price comparisons, and specifications, and it has created an entirely new way for people to talk about products they like (or dislike). Recommendations from friends and trusted experts are within everyone's reach, no matter where they are.

Shoppers Are Taking Advantage
of This Shift in Power

In this new normal, brands can no longer just talk *to* consumers and expect to be successful. They need to talk *with* them. What does this mean? Successful brands (whether business to consumer or business to business) need to understand their purpose and value to their customers, to their employees (if they want to attract and retain the best people), and to the many stakeholders in the communities around them. They get there by becoming social—conversing, discussing, listening—just like their customers, and by embracing real-time connectivity and transparency across all aspects of how they operate.

Taking this focus as a brand and business is a big change from the past, when companies could control the flow of communications and interactions with their customers. Brand building processes used to be fairly linear: start with a carefully researched positioning of functional and emotional benefits for a target audience, then bring the brand to life with a communications plan built largely on one-way media such as TV, radio, and outdoor and in-store displays. The focus was on precision, consistency, and tight control, with less attention paid to cultivating direct relationships. After all, consumers couldn't easily respond.

Today, they can. In fact, the consumer has more influence on the conversation about brands than the brand owners themselves: 70 percent of brand content is now created by consumers. Companies can shape the conversation by providing great products and experiences, but they can't control it. This is true for even the biggest companies. Do a search on any of the world's top 20 brands, and you'll find that more than 25 percent of the results are links to user-generated content. So companies and brands need to take a whole new approach, one that puts serving the customer at the center of everything they do. They need to think about the moments that matter for their customers and how they can engage and help them in meaningful, valuable ways. More often than not, those moments are happening online, so the smart brands are the ones who are the most easily found and recommended both online and off.

There Is a New Dimension to How We Build Relationships with Brands

The Internet hasn't changed the essential need for humans to socialize, but it has given us the ability to do it with widening circles of people as well as with brands that are part of our lives. Brands can now use the tools and insights of the social web to be more discoverable, approachable, and recommendable. This is what Paul Rand's

Highly Recommended is about, and it is why I was so excited when Paul invited me to write this Foreword. I have known Paul for many years and have tremendous respect for his intellect and wit and for the results he's achieved in helping companies build stronger businesses and brands.

Paul believes that many of the existing concepts used to measure brand differentiation aren't well suited for today's environment, in which we have so much data and real-time insights. It's not just about whether or not people recommend you. It also matters when and how they do it. Do they say things that differentiate you? Do they think that you matter in their lives, at the most important times? Paul's thesis is that we now have the information to shape the answers to these questions as they come up, and in *Highly Recommended,* he proposes a straightforward approach that any business can use to do just that. It's a smart way to establish meaningful differentiation for your brand and to use the Internet to take word of mouth marketing and the power of recommendation—both implicit and explicit—to new heights.

The Importance of Being the Most Highly Recommended Brand in Your Category

As you read *Highly Recommended,* I hope you stay true to Paul's core challenge. Do you have a story that is worth telling and that your customers will want to endorse? Do you understand the moments that matter for your customers, the times in their lives where your brand can make a difference? Are you present in the right times and the right ways? Is your marketing focused on engaging your customers and converting them into brand advocates? When they talk about you, is what they say aligned with what you care about? Are you always accountable for and transparent about your actions, especially your missteps?

These are not easy questions, and in fact for business leaders, today the pace of change and plethora of tools, metrics, and data can feel overwhelming. Yet, despite these challenges, we are undoubtedly in a golden age for marketers. We have more insights into what people care about, and more opportunities to be relevant, engaging, and useful, than we could have even dreamed about just a few years ago. Fortunately, the things that have always made great brands great—remarkable products and experiences that earn users' love—haven't changed. Brands such as Google, Nike, Starbucks, Coca-Cola, and American Express follow this relentlessly. When people love you, they want to tell others; they want to share your story. And in this era of ubiquitous information, always-on connectivity, and global reach, that story can reach the world in an instant.

This is the power of being highly recommended. It's why we are clearly not the same consumers we were a few years ago. We're better informed, and we can share our views much more quickly and easily than ever before. And this change is helping to drive better businesses and brands. We all win.

—**MARGO GEORGIADIS**, President of Americas, Google

Becoming Highly Recommended

A brand is no longer what we tell the consumers it is; it's what the consumers tell each other it is.

—**SCOTT COOK**, Intuit

While nearly every business and organization has been exposed to and has adopted some foundational social media platforms (Facebook, Twitter, maybe even Pinterest, Google+, or YouTube), even the most sophisticated brands are wondering "What's next?"

Highly Recommended answers that question and provides a sustainable and scalable business approach that brings everything together. And not just marketing and communications. Social media and recommendations are reshaping all aspects of business, including human resources, innovation and R&D, and, of course, customer service.

All businesses, no matter what their size, can become recommended. However, the bigger the organization, the more its moving parts need to become aligned. Social media has uncovered the fact that, today, it's not just your product or service that gets feedback but, in fact, the whole organization is open to and vulnerable to the need to become recommended.

Now everyone, on every team, in every silo, is a "spokesperson" for the company, and each department has to look at itself and also its relationship to other departments in an organization as well as to the company as a whole. This world of interconnectedness has brought about a stronger need to model your process—or at least try to.

For anyone desiring to learn, understand, and apply the new strategies for marketing success, *Highly Recommended* will provide the insight and support needed to accelerate business growth. Never before has this been so important, and that is what makes this book so important.

We all know by now the impact of a positive recommendation. However, it works the other way too: more than 80 percent of consumers report that a negative review or recommendation dissuades them from purchasing a product or service they are considering.

Think about the last time you bought a new product or service—large or small. Chances are someone proactively recommended it ("I had the best BLT and avocado sandwich at SUBWAY"), or you asked the opinion of someone you trust ("What do you think of the new Nissan Pathfinder?").

Social media has supercharged the power and impact of recommendations. Today's businesses can't just *use* social media; they have to become social businesses, inside and out and from top to bottom. Ultimately, that is the goal of this book: to harness the power of being a social business to become the most highly recommended organization in your industry, category, and/or niche. The ability to easily research online consumer reviews or see which brands your social media friends like is fundamentally shifting how people buy—and sell—nearly everything.

Today we have the power to clearly understand where, how, and why brands get recommended (or criticized)—and then to proactively shape messages and directly connect with those who matter the most. The best part is that you can almost immediately see how people are engaging with you—and if that engagement is leading to a recommendation and ultimately a sale.

Whether you are an independent professional (like an attorney or a real estate agent), a leading consumer brand (like Frito-Lay), an industrial manufacturer (like Caterpillar), or even a global not-for-profit (like Rotary International), how people talk about and recommend you is the most important key to your success in this new world of doing social business. To succeed, let alone thrive, you can't just be highly effective; you must come highly recommended as well.

Marketers know that they have to change how they do business in the realm of the social or connected consumer. Additionally, the majority of companies are aggressively working to adopt and integrate social media into their marketing plans. In fact, HubSpot (a leading marketing research organization) states that the average social media budget has nearly tripled in the last three years. In addition, inbound leads created from social media are 61 percent less expensive than push or outbound marketing leads. These statistics will only continue to grow and change the way companies market forever.

Meanwhile, the marketing world is still primarily focused on "push" marketing—pushing various marketing activities to get brand messages in front of potential and existing customers, essentially interrupting target segments, very seldom with success. Add to this reality the fact that a typical American is exposed to 30,000 advertising messages daily, the percentage of people even responding to direct mail, e-mail, telemarketing, and so on, in most organizations' target market segments are often under 1 percent.

Another nuance to note is that a company's marketing message—that is, tagline—is very different from a trusted friend or colleague's word of mouth recommendation.

There is a dramatic difference between current push marketing methods with cool advertising lingo and pull marketing methods that have origins in real conversations between friends and colleagues based on preexisting, trusting relationships. Knowing how to create pull marketing initiatives that both accelerate sales and decrease marketing costs is a huge asset that hits a company's bottom-line earnings as well as its top-line profits—a powerful double punch in the business world.

However, understanding why and how consumers talk about and recommend a product is a new concept to the marketing world. More important, these efforts require a very different skill set than having a one-way conversation.

In 2000, as social media was in its infancy, Malcolm Gladwell electrified the business world with his bestselling book *The Tipping Point*.[1] Still on the *New York Times* Best Sellers list, readers remain captivated with the concept of having their brand become the next "social contagion." But what Gladwell's book missed, and what remains missing from the ongoing discussion, is an easy way for marketers to understand and act upon making their brand eminently "talkable," shareable, and recommended.

This is where *Highly Recommended* comes in . . .

ACKNOWLEDGMENTS

First and foremost, I'd like to thank whoever recommended that you read this book. For without these advocates—and people just like them—life would be far less informative, interesting, or fun.

I never could have written this book without the unfailing love and support of my wonderful wife, Diane, and our three children—Elena, Trevor, and Mason. You guys make life truly meaningful. Same for my parents, Leon and Marian Rand, and my sisters, Debra Perelman and Marta Hexamer: "Write a book? Of course you can! And it will be the best book ever."

Now the hard part comes. How do I identify and acknowledge all of the people who shaped and guided my education, experiences, and career?

Let me, of course, start with the leadership team at Zócalo Group—Emily Bader, Erik Hesler, Rina Mallick, Hugo Perez, Ryan Rasmussen, Michael Stern, David Stone, Jeff Woelker, and Andrea Wood. This book is a reflection of the pioneering, insightful, dedicated, and passionate learnings and experiences that we create and share together. My other Zócalo colleagues make it real every day—discovering, perfecting, and measuring the best ways possible to ensure that our clients' brands become the most talked about and recommended in their category.

About six years ago I went to my colleagues at Ketchum—Ray Kotcher, Rob Flaherty, Rob Lorfink, and Dale Bornstein—and shared the idea for Zócalo Group. They quickly made the concept even better and became tireless advocates. The leadership of Omnicom Group—John Wren, Tom Harrison, Dale Adams, and John Doolittle—all took a chance incubating a business and launching it to the world.

Work never seems like work when you have clients who are friends and partners. You'll read a lot of their stories in the following pages. Particular shout-outs to Erich Marx of Nissan, Tony Pace of

SUBWAY, Christine Cea of Unilever, Kim Healey of Dart Industries (Solo Cup), Christopher Wyse and Kristin Walsh of Frito-Lay, Gary Spangler of DuPont, Shannon Jenest of Philips, Alan Buddendeck of Rotary International, Scott Ellis of Storck, and Tyler Wallis and Deborah Jordan of Cricket Wireless. You are forward thinking and confident marketers.

Highly Recommended went from concept to reality through the passion, insights, and efforts of my agent, John Willig, coaches Melissa G. Wilson and Rusty Fisher, and editors Donya Dickerson and Casie Vogel of McGraw-Hill.

To my past and current fellow board members at the Word of Mouth Marketing Association (WOMMA), the Council of Better Business Bureaus, DePaul University's Driehaus College of Business and Kellstadt Graduate School of Business, Northwestern University's Spiegel Digital & Database Research Initiative, and the Rural Education Institute of Mexico—thank you. Our collective efforts have shaped various insights and examples that come through in this book.

Living a Recommendable Life

I was dressed in full graduation regalia—stiff black mortarboard, flowing black gown, and a regal purple and white stole. And I was nervous.

In two minutes, I'd be stepping on stage to deliver the commencement address for Northwestern University's Integrated Marketing Communications (IMC) graduate program.

What in the world could I say of value to students (and their families) who had just completed two grueling years of learning from some of the best marketing minds around?

These students already knew that the world of business and marketing was fundamentally shifting—much of it happening while they were getting their graduate degree. When I delivered this address in late spring 2012, social media was clearly transforming where, how, and why consumers learned about, engaged with, and bought all sorts of products and services.

Clearly I wasn't going to capture their hearts with theory alone. Expounding on the newest platform would only make me sound like every other so-called social media expert. And I'd never ignite their passion with an "it's a tough world out there; let me tell you how to really succeed in this business" soliloquy.

So, I remembered why I had been asked to speak in the first place.

After years as a communicator, marketer, entrepreneur, and educator, I launched a word of mouth, digital, and social media marketing company called Zócalo Group. In six years, an extraordinary team grew the agency to represent some of the world's leading brands—and among the largest digital and social media agencies in the Omnicom Group.

We began Zócalo with the insight that 92 percent of all consumers report that a word of mouth **recommendation** is the "leading reason they buy a product or service"—a fact initially posited by Roper Research and later confirmed by Nielsen. We shaped our model to ensure that the companies and brands we work with become the most talked about and recommended in their category. In the age of social media, word of mouth took on a whole new level of significance, turning every consumer into a human media channel.

That story was good. But it didn't seem enough for a graduation speech—at least one that was going to have any sort of impact.

So I applied the idea of business recommendations to how students should think about living their lives. I called it "Living a Recommendable Life."

My 12-minute remarks seemed to hit their mark. At the reception, students, professors, parents, and business leaders let me know that the idea of guiding your brand and living your life to become recommendable was a big idea—it was clear, focused, actionable, and measurable.

And it touched a human chord. We all want to know that what we do and how we live our lives is meaningful, positively pointed to, talked about—and recommended.

Shortly afterward, the respected marketing consultant and blogger Brian Solis, posted the article "How to Live a Recommendable Life" on his website and referenced the video.[1] It drew some of the most shares, comments, and recommendations of all of Brian's posts.

I knew from the brands that Zócalo Group worked with that the idea of focusing marketing efforts on becoming recommended was market changing—one that could guide all aspects of how a multinational brand, small business, or organization shaped and guided its business.

And every time I shared these thoughts in a presentation, someone would say, "You really need to write a book." The encouragement I received from the Northwestern speech finally convinced me that this was the right time.

I hope you agree and, of course, recommend this book to others. Here, in its entirety, is the speech I gave that day:

Living a Recommendable Life

What an honor it is to be with you here today.

You are graduating from one of the world's leading universities with a degree that is recognized and respected in the marketing and communications industry—and beyond.

So, I know you have received a top-notch education and have the fortitude to make your career—and your life—really count.

But before you embark on this next journey, I'd like to share a simple, yet incredibly powerful insight with you.

If you follow this insight, you will never go astray personally. You will become one of the best and most sought after marketers around.

If you follow this insight, you will have a road map for your life. You'll save thousands of dollars in therapy. You'll have a clear sense of purpose.

If you follow this insight, you'll be able to develop precise and impactful marketing strategies. You'll shape brands. And guide organizations.

Quite a buildup, eh?

So, here it is: Live a Recommendable Life.

Let me say it again: if you want to succeed personally and professionally, live a recommendable life.

Let me tell you what I mean.

I am here with you today because of a recommendation. Five years ago, someone recommended me as a guest lecturer to Tom Collinger (associate dean of the IMC program). And when IMC was looking for a commencement speaker, Tom threw my name into the mix. Another recommendation.

About a month ago, Nielsen published a compelling marketing study. The headline? Ninety-two percent of respondents reported that a positive recommendation from a friend, family member, or someone they trust is the biggest influence on whether they buy a product or service. In comparison, only 42 percent said they trusted radio advertising, and 58 percent said they trusted editorial content.

Think of that: 92 percent.

Unfortunately, the opposite also holds true. In fact, 67 percent of consumers in another study reported that seeing as few as three negative reviews was enough for them to not buy a product or service.[2]

Recommendations and word of mouth, of course, have always been important. But in the age of social media, they are essential. One-to-one communication has become one-to-millions. Word of mouth is now on steroids.

This change, of course, is profoundly affecting the marketing world. How a product or service is talked about and recommended is becoming recognized as one of the most essential, if not the most essential, part of the marketing mix.

This change also affects our personal lives. Before you get hired, your prospective employer will review your Facebook page and LinkedIn profile. New friends will explore the people you know in common. And, if you are like most of your peers, that information will be readily accessible.

Today, you must think of yourself as a brand—a brand worthy of a passionate recommendation by your friends, family, and coworkers.

Some of the most brilliant minds in business can argue incessantly about marketing strategy. But ask them how they want their product to be talked about and they get focused very quickly. That clear purpose should drive all marketing strategies. It most certainly drives search. It drives product differentiation. It drives people to buy—or not to buy. And it is extraordinarily measurable.

I can tell you that from working with some of the world's leading brands that word of mouth success doesn't happen by accident. It's the result of a deliberate strategy and consistent day-to-day—and year-to-year—execution.

This same insight applies to each of our own lives. Chances are you counted on recommendations from professors and employers to get into the IMC program. Same thing for getting a job after graduation.

What's most compelling to me is that the proven foundations and principles of driving recommendations for brands are almost identical to those that shape personal recommendations.

So, after many years of learning how influence, recommendations, and word of mouth work, I'd like to offer five key lessons.

Lesson 1: Develop a clear and purposeful story of how you want people to talk about and recommend both you and your brands.

■ It's a simple question that needs to be answered: How do you want to be talked about and recommended—as a person, a son or daughter, *a parent, grandchild, friend, partner, spouse, employee, business leader—whatever the case?*

- *Same thing, of course, applies to any brands you are marketing. Buyers have a staggering amount of choices. Why would someone recommend your product or service over another?*

Lesson 2: *Live your brand.*

- *It's as simple as that. If you want to be recommended as a thoughtful and caring friend— make sure you are always a thoughtful and caring friend.*
- *If you want your brand to be recommended for having the most advanced features and design— make sure your energy and focus go into owning that role and not ceding it to any competitors.*

Lesson 3: *Be human, be transparent, and live up to mistakes quickly.*

- *Yes. We need to live our brands. But we are human beings. And our brands and organizations are run by human beings. So we and our brands will occasionally veer off course and make mistakes:*
  - *In this era of social media, consumer journalism, and always-on news, years of thoughtfully lived lives or well-managed brands can be undone in astonishingly short order.*
  - *Own it when you or your brand goofs up. Fix what you can, and ask for forgiveness when needed.*

Lesson 4: *Stay engaging and interesting.*

- *Ever been cornered by the party bores? They drone on about themselves, don't ask you any questions, and seem oblivious to anyone's needs or interests beyond their own.*

■ *Marketing success used to be defined by how well we could interrupt consumers and compel them to give us their attention. Success today is based on how well we engage our audiences before, during, and after the sale.*

■ *This doesn't happen by accident. We often talk to brands about following the 90/10 Rule. Spend 90 percent of your time on your social channels listening, paying attention, and engaging with your consumers on their terms. Spend 10 percent of the time talking about yourself. Not a bad approach for life either.*

Lesson 5: *Regularly evaluate and evolve—but stay true to your core.*

■ *People and brands must always evolve. Lives and markets change:*
  ● *Take time to be introspective and ensure that you are living the life—and being recommended—in the ways that you want to be. It's good—actually it's essential—to evolve, change, and grow. Same thing for the brands we represent.*
  ● *But don't let these changes happen by accident or get forced into them. Then it's often too late. Take ownership of your life and your brands.*

It's a few years old, but many of you may have seen the movie Saving Private Ryan. *As the story goes, all of Private Ryan's brothers have been killed in World War II. A team of soldiers, led by Tom Hanks, is sent to retrieve the private before he too is killed—and his mother has no more sons. After a fierce final battle, Private Ryan thanks Hanks for saving him. In his dying breath, Hanks looks at the private and says, "Earn it."*

In the poignant ending scene, Private Ryan is an old man. He and his adult children and grandchildren have gone to Arlington National Cemetery to pay respects to Hanks's character. The private looks at his wife and says, "Please tell me that I am a good man. That I'm a good husband and father. That I earned being saved."

In other words, what he really wanted to know was whether he had lived a recommendable life.

Being recommendable is a very commendable goal for ourselves. And essential for the brands we represent.

Congratulations, graduates. What you have accomplished so far is amazing. And I'm willing to bet you have just begun. Now go and create your own recommendable life.

PART 1

Word of Mouth Recommendations: Marketing's Holy Grail

CHAPTER 1

Stew Leonard's and the 30-Minute Recommendation

n October 2012, after weeks of careful planning, a couple colleagues and I made our way from Chicago to Stamford, Connecticut, for a series of meetings with the brand leaders at Philips Consumer Products Group.

We'd been working with Philips Norelco, and the director of brand communications, Shannon Jenest, wanted to introduce us to the other brands so they could consider word of mouth and social media marketing in their programs for the new year.

We had a busy two days' worth of sessions scheduled with all of the consumer lifestyle brands under the Philips umbrella—Avent (baby products), Sonicare and Zoom (oral healthcare), Philips Norelco (men's grooming), and Saeco (espresso machines).

Our first day of back-to-back sessions had gone very well. To celebrate our collective success, a group of us headed out to dinner. My team had booked a table at a local steak house, our default celebratory setting of choice, but our clients strongly recommended their favorite Italian restaurant. (You can guess where we ended up . . .)

After enjoying drinks and appetizers and, naturally, rehashing the day's conversations, we got around to talking about everyone's upcoming weekend plans.

One of our clients mentioned that she was taking her son to someplace called "Stew Leonard's" to buy his pumpkin and pick up a few Halloween decorations.

"Never heard of Stew Leonard's," I said, not suspecting I was about to be schooled, big time, in the art of recommendations. "What is it—an apple orchard or something?"

Both clients looked at me incredulously.

"Stew Leonard's is the most amazing, fun, delicious, and incredible grocery store in the whole world," one of them said to me, with the other nodding and smiling, eager to weigh in.

So, for the next 30 minutes (not an exaggeration), my two clients shared every detail of this dairy wonderland—each trying to outdo the other about who loved Stew Leonard's more.

The Disneyland of Dairy

Now, for the uninformed, like me, Stew Leonard's is a chain of four supermarkets—though that hardly begins to describe the full extent of their awesomeness—in Connecticut and New York. I have to admit that once I began researching the company, I felt a little neglectful for never having heard of it before.

Not only has Ripley's Believe It or Not! deemed the chain the "World's Largest Dairy" but none other than *Fortune* magazine lists Stew Leonard's as one of the "100 Best Companies to Work For."

The more I learned, the clearer it became that Stew Leonard's had purposefully integrated ways to be recommended into every aspect of its business: design, product selection, marketing, PR, customer service, advertising, product innovation, promotions, and human resources. In short, it had become what we all must become in this new Digital Age: a social business, integrating customer and employee feedback at the speed of sound and using it to craft our future. As a result, and as I'd just witnessed firsthand, the company came highly recommended.

This place has no right to be called a "supermarket chain." (In fact, the *New York Times* called it "the Disneyland of Dairy Stores.")

There is an ice cream parlor, naturally; a viewing area where you can watch your milk being processed, bottled, stickered, stamped, and rolled right down the line; a bakery; a catering operation; and an outdoor cafeteria or, as Stew's calls it, the Hoedown Area. Forget the small florist section you find at most grocery stores; Stew's has a full-on nursery complete with seasonal cuttings, floral arrangements, and more.

There are handmade, supersized, from-scratch potato chips made right in the store; grind-your-own-beans coffee stations; fresh sushi made right on the spot—the list goes on and on.

And even as impressive as all that is, Stew's has also found a way to add rich, interactive, added-value details to nearly every nook and cranny. The Hoedown Area doesn't just offer the usual burgers and fries but also lobster prepared freshly all day long. The ice cream parlor doesn't just add free sprinkles to your cones. It also offers a free cone for each $100 spent in the store. Stew's doesn't just juice its own oranges and bottle its own orange juice. The employees do it all behind plate glass windows where everyone can watch them all day long.

The website offers recipes for everything from appetizers to full-course meals. Stew's will send care packages to your kid in college. There's even a "cow cam" where you can watch the cattle where your milk comes from. An online suggestion box at the bottom of the home page reveals just how critical customer feedback, response, involvement, engagement, and interaction are to the company, as does its customer service policy, which is literally written in stone.

I'm not joking. There's a giant rock in the store on which the following policy is etched: "Rule 1: The customer is always right! Rule 2: If the customer is ever wrong, reread Rule 1."

The Vocal Majority: *Welcome to the Recommendation Age*

Have you ever been shocked to discover that a friend, family member, or colleague hasn't seen your favorite movie, read your favorite book, visited your favorite restaurant, or tasted your favorite Starbucks beverage of choice?

Now do you recall the zealousness of your explanation about said movie, book, restaurant, or beverage? The passion of your vocal advocacy? The sudden opportunity to share your love of a particular person, place, or thing with someone you care about or even someone you've just met? "You just *have* to read it! I know you. You'll love it, and the best part is, when you're done, there are six more books in the series!"

If so, then you can picture what it was like listening to these two women extol every virtue of the great and mighty Stew Leonard's over dinner that evening. Here is a representative sampling of the snatches of conversation from dinner:

> "I love it when they start sampling the seasonal specials all over the store!"
>
> "Have you ever had the lobster roll?!"

"It's the first place I take out-of-town visitors."

"I could spend a whole day in the bakery aisle!"

The only real debate about how great Stew Leonard's was came when one of the clients said she "thought their prices were a little bit high, but it was worth it." The other client said, "No. They aren't high at all; and they have great deals."

Amazing. When every grocery chain I know of sends out regular "can't beat our prices" inserts and runs full-page "we're the low price leaders" advertising, the issue of price was the last, and seemingly the least relevant, issue when it came to Stew Leonard's advocates.

I was already impressed with their advocacy when not one but both clients offered to pick me up early before the next day's meetings to see the nearest Stew Leonard's location for myself.

When at last the pep rally ended and both clients took a breath, I sat back and marveled aloud at the job they'd just done on not just Stew Leonard's behalf but my own. When they looked back at me quizzically, I explained that they'd just spent half an hour exemplifying the power of word of mouth and recommendations.

And they had. It was a microcourse, right there at that dinner table, about how the recommendation culture worked, the power of recommendations, the passion of advocacy, and the motivation behind helping others through suggestion.

So we sat there for another half hour, detailing the process and brainstorming why these two women were such passionate advocates and cheerleaders, really, about Stew Leonard's. Here's what we came up with:

- Stew Leonard's goes out of its way to make the shopping experience pleasant and fun for everyone involved.
- The company's employees are in on the game—which has also helped Stew's earn a Fortune "100 Best Companies to Work For" designation.
- The store has a carnival-like atmosphere that reflects local produce and personality, seasonal holidays, and the smells, tastes, and foods of the season.
- The company is committed to the community with various and regular outreach services like "Stew the Duck" and a variety of holiday and seasonal in- and out-of-store events.

- Employees actively engage consumers in a real and vital way, soliciting customer feedback both online and off, while in the store and out.
- Local ads aren't about "slashing prices" or "special offers" but about what is new, fresh, ripe, or now. It isn't just about pumpkins. It's about "jack o' lantern" pumpkins. It isn't just about ground chuck. It's about its "world famous" filet mignon, "fresh from Kansas."
- What's more, the store circulars regularly feature the owner, "Stew," posing with local or at least "real" farmers. There is a folksy, rather than corporate, feel to any and all printed, web, and other marketing materials.
- No one seems to associate the store with commerce but with emotions. Stew's is about family gatherings, celebrations, holidays, scents and sounds, and seasonal produce like pumpkins in the fall and flowers in the spring. It is, as one client mentioned, a place to go with family and friends, a place to take visitors and guests and out-of-town folks to "show it off."

This was, of course, all nonscientific, heart versus head stuff, but clearly the folks behind the Stew Leonard's folksy, familial brand were doing something right, and they knew how to keep doing it so that the customers become cheerleaders and the skeptics (like me) quickly become at first, devotees and later, willing and quite vocal advocates. (Here I am writing about them, for Pete's sake.)

Obviously, this didn't just "happen" by accident. Behind the folksy exterior, no doubt, the folks behind the Stew Leonard's "brand" are working as hard as the rest of us to do more of what works and less of what doesn't. The question comes to mind, if it is that easy to become recommendable, then why don't more businesses do that? Why are they still "push" marketing?

Although companies like Stew Leonard's and the rest of those we'll read about in case studies throughout this book make it look easy, it is complex. For us, the challenge is turning the recommendable part into a sustainable system of excellence.

Another challenge for most of us, big company or small, B2C or B2B, external or internal, is that we don't inherently feel like a Stew Leonard's. We may not have ice cream cones and fall pumpkins and sampling stations and "cow cams" to brag about.

You may be thinking that dairy stores and your brand or industry have little in common, but the fact is recommendations are recommendations, whether they're for running shoes, bestselling young adult vampire novels, blockbuster or indie movies, designer handbags, protein bars, sports drinks, widgets, or throw pillows.

Even in the B2B or nonprofit worlds, even within your own company, recommendations are vital to your success, growth, and survival in a world increasingly dependent on one-to-one, word of mouth marketing.

How do we make deodorant sexy? Old Spice and Axe have managed to do it.

How do we get folks talking about something as surface "boring" as car insurance? State Farm, Progressive, and Geico make it happen.

How do we turn a movie about kids killing other kids into the next blockbuster teen sensation? Ask the folks at *Hunger Games* marketing HQ, and they'll tell you it's largely due to recommendations, cheerleading, and advocacy.

I think the takeaway for me and my clients that night, and a most surprising one at that, was how to put ourselves in Stew Leonard's shoes and make it so that others want to recommend us, cheerlead and advocate for us, and spread the word in such a way that they're passionate, proactive, and prolific about it.

That, in a nutshell, is what *Highly Recommended* is all about.

CHAPTER 2

Why Angie and Her List of Recommendations Are Worth $1.4 Billion

Sometimes we make succeeding in business more complicated than it needs to be. Among the myriad buzzwords, metrics, analytics, white papers, articles, statistics, and strategies surrounding social media, it's easy to lose track of why all those tools exist in the first place. To clear away the clutter and focus on the takeaway, we need to return to the basics to remember what our customers think—and why.

Case in point: Angie's List, a website that aggregates verified consumer reviews of service companies as a way to capture word of mouth wisdom went public in November 2011 and currently has a market cap of nearly $1.4 billion. There's a very clear—and simple—reason why: consumers want, and are willing to pay for, **recommendations they can trust**.

Dealing with Information Overload

We've all seen the numbers. Each one of us is overwhelmed with commercial messages, channel choices, e-mails, text messages—and now Facebook updates, tweets, pins, and check-ins.

Of course, there are so many numbers about these numbers that no one can quite agree on the actual number. *Consumer Reports* tells us that the number of incoming messages we receive each day is as low as 247 while some of the more vocal anti-advertising antagonists tell us that it's anywhere from 2,500 to 4,000.

Add these messages to the extra push from the average 30,000 new products introduced each year (95 percent of which fail, according to Harvard Business School professor Clayton Christensen), and it's a wonder that any marketing messages actually make it through the clutter at all.

In the history of the world, there has never been a time when more information was available to the general public. Nearly any piece of data we need—from historical to educational to governmental to the trivial—is available in a few mouse clicks.

Want to know the gestation period of a water buffalo? *Wikipedia* has you covered. Want to know who the sound effects editor was for the 1986 John Hughes classic *Pretty in Pink*? Imdb.com has you covered. Eager to find out who the twenty-seventh president of the United States was? Just Google it, and you can spend the next two weeks getting to know everything and anything about William Howard Taft.

No fact is too trivial, no genre too niche, no statistic too archaic to avoid the nearly endless reach of the Internet. And more information is coming every day.

The first wave of this information overload came in one direction: from creator to end user. Someone posted something, such as a *Wikipedia* entry; we took advantage of it. But with each new factoid, photo, link, or reference, we needed more ways to deal with the information bits and to filter them, process them, and categorize them. The second wave of information overload included more social interaction; someone posted something, we took advantage of it, and **we let the person know what we thought of it.**

This second wave, or Web 2.0, or any of a myriad of names it's been called, eventually wound up under the general heading of "social media." Facebook, Twitter, LinkedIn, Pinterest, YouTube—take your pick; it was all about people connecting in ways they never had before.

Suddenly, we could control the content we saw. On Twitter, we could "follow" those like-minded individuals who "got" us or sounded like us or made us laugh or think or nod or even shake our heads in ways that were unique to us. So rather than following anyone and everyone, we could limit what we saw to those people we wanted to hear from.

It was the same on Facebook, where our walls were full of only those people we chose to "friend" or "like." If we ran across a blog that fit our lifestyle, needs, or personality, we could subscribe to it, join it, or follow it. We could subscribe to this newsletter or that person's updates or that company's news.

In this way we were able to stem the tidal wave of information overload. We were able to find dry land, catch our breath, and cherry pick what messages, images, input, and feedback we had received. And once we had drawn our veritable line in the social media sand, we could begin to assess all that information.

And that's when things got really interesting.

Why We Listen to and Act on Recommendations

Thirteen years ago, Dr. Robert Cialdini, currently the professor emeritus of psychology and marketing at Arizona State University, wrote the first edition of a book called *Influence: Science and Practice* (Prentice Hall, 2008). The book came out right around the time advertisers were realizing that information and commercial overload were endangering the way they did business and were looking for the next magic bullet.

Nearly 2 million copies and four editions later, Cialdini's insights are more relevant than ever—particularly when it comes to recommendations. And this is not just an American phenomenon. *Influence* has been published in 27 languages—and the people in each market think that the insights were written just for them.

Cialdini focused on what he called "the science of social proof." People determine what is correct by finding out what other people think is correct. As a rule, he points out, we will make fewer mistakes by acting in accord with social evidence than by acting contrary to it. Usually when a lot of people are doing something—and recommending something—it is the right thing to do.

Delving deeper into how we are influenced, how we listen to and act on recommendations, there is a kind of five act "arc" to the average social media users' learning experiences:

- In Act 1, they discover social media. They find a few old high school friends on Facebook, discover how hilarious actors Nathan Fillion (@NathanFillion) and Neil Patrick Harris (@ActuallyNPH) are on Twitter. They like a new flavor of ice cream that tastes delicious and wonder how they ever lived without it!

- During Act 2, they obsess over it. They gather as many Facebook friends as they can, follow all the Twitter users they are recommended to follow, and stay up late noodling over why that business associate on LinkedIn hasn't accepted their invitation. They check their page stats at work, multitask from screen to screen, and check in on their social media platforms several times an hour, every hour.
- In Act 3, they level out. They've hit their maximum of friends, can't keep up with what they are following, and they are finding that social media is beginning to interfere with their "real" life.
- In Act 4, they turn on it! "It takes too much time." "Everybody's trying to sell something!" "No one ever writes me back." These are the complaints I hear most often from Act 4 social media users.
- Finally, in Act 5, they learn how to master social media. This is where social media becomes the tool it was always intended to be: it is a dramatic, revolutionary, and useful platform across which to find information, content, connections, and, above all, recommendations.

Wherever you are on this social media arc, it should be clear that the only way to use social media effectively is to do just that: use it. And by "social media," I mean every form of media that enlists other people (the "social") to inform, educate, amuse, and enlighten your life. Why? Because it's what your customers—or your client's customers—are doing.

The world is now one big DVR. Where once upon a time paid advertising was the only source of information, now it's optional and far from optimal. Whether it's via a Twitter feed, our Facebook wall, a search feature, or our blog descriptions, we are more in control than ever of what media messages we see, respond to, empathize with, and act on.

Of course, social media is just one aspect of being recommended. While we'll be talking at length about social media and its power and impact on becoming recommended, not to mention being recommendable, let us never forget the fuel that powers social media: human interaction and the willingness of consumers to become your willing and vocal advocates.

Yelp, Yellow Dog, and Me

I am far from a food snob, but I have a kind of knee-jerk negative reaction to the forced fun, fixed menus, and rubber chicken that is so prevalent at most American resorts. And few resorts are as American or as rigid in their culinary standards as the Walt Disney World Resort.

Don't get me wrong: few places in the world offer as much variety, eye appeal, customer service, and family options as Disney, a corporation known for its cutting-edge work in all things amusement park, hotel, and even dining choices.

And choices there are: from Planet Hollywood to Wolfgang Pucks, from Ghirardelli's to the House of Blues to the Rainforest Café and beyond, they've got it, front and center. But sometimes you want something new, something adventurous, something off the beaten path. On a recent trip to Disney with my wife and kids, I was in the mood for just such an adventure. Unfortunately, I was the only one. I had had enough food court fries and brand-name cuisine to choke a horse, and one afternoon I suggested "an alternative" to my sunburned and happy family.

"But we haven't gone to the Rainforest Café yet," they complained.

"Can't we just stay here?"

"Why go somewhere else when everything we want is a bus stop, surrey ride, or sidewalk away?"

Talk about overcoming objections. I knew if my covert eating operation was going to work, I'd need to come fully armed and loaded for battle. Where did I go? Where every traveling social media savvy food lover goes: Yelp and TripAdvisor.

Entering keywords like "Orlando," "eatery," and "family," the same restaurant kept coming up with the highest of recommendations. Yellow Dog Eats had received a nearly five-star rating on Yelp with over a hundred reviews, dozens of user pictures of great dishes, and a quaint atmosphere. It had been ranked 17—not 77, not 700, but 17—out of 1,436 restaurants in Orlando on TripAdvisor.com.

It was sudden immersion in all things Yellow Dog Eats, and I knew it would be both a unique and unusual Orlando excursion for my family as well as an experiment in "becoming recommended" for me. So, armed with a GPS full of coordinates and a grumbling family, we headed off for our little Orlando adventure and wound up in the quaint and picturesque town of Windermere, Florida.

By the time we arrived at our destination, which looked more like a general store than a five-star restaurant, we had given ourselves over to the experience. My wife enjoyed the quick getaway from tourist central, and once the kids saw the gift shop, with lots of funky Florida-themed presents, they were hooked.

The food was terrific, the service excellent, the atmosphere as far removed from touristy and chain as you could get, and we all—each of us, individually—had a great time and raved about it the whole way back to Disney.

And why? Because in as few as three clicks, I used two of today's most popular social media sites—Yelp and TripAdvisor—to seek, and find, a recommendation.

The trip was a real-life lab rat experiment of what I share with my clients each day: how to get recommended early and often. Today's smartphones, downloadable apps, and immediacy of free and available Wi-Fi networks make this easier and easier every day.

Good or bad, customers can relate their experiences immediately. Once upon a time we had to wait until we got home to review a restaurant, hotel, or trip to a big box retail store. Today we can do it in the lobby, waiting room, or parking lot. That's why it's so important to become a social business—not seeing social media postings as just single events but as integral parts of the ongoing branding process.

There is no filter of time to color our experience. We can immediately lash out at an inattentive server, complain about an inadequate stay at a chain hotel, or lament the add-on sales of our latest cashier at Best Buy. You could tell that the folks at Yellow Dog Eats were acutely aware of this and lived and breathed it in their business model. It quickly became evident just why they had been so highly recommended. In addressing this "speed of Wi-Fi" phenomenon in his book *The Thank You Economy* (HarperCollins, 2011), social media and branding expert Gary Vaynerchuk relates, "The Internet, where the Thank You Economy was born, has given consumers back their voice, and the tremendous power of their opinions via social media means that companies and brands have to compete on a whole different level than they used to."

One can only imagine the pride that the owners, chef, servers, and staff at Yellow Dog Eats feel about their predominant status on Yelp and TripAdvisor, while at the same time they must also be fearing that a handful of one- and two-star reviews might adversely affect their unusually high rankings.

Such is the fine line we all walk now in this totally transparent, brutally blunt recommendation atmosphere. With a thumbs-up or thumbs-down mentality, our futures now depend more than ever on the whims, emotions, reactions, and verbosity of our clientele. It's more important than ever to get out in front of the conversation and steer it rather than sit back and react to it.

Word of Mouth: *The Holy Grail of Modern Marketing*

One of the ways I filter my own information overload is with Google alerts. Whether pertaining to my own edification or a client's, at any one time I can have a dozen or two Google alerts running that send me filtered, targeted, and useful information all day long.

One such Google alert is for the keyword phrase "word of mouth." It's one of my more active alerts because now word of mouth is truly the holy grail of modern marketing.

It may sound different because much of today's word of mouth is nonverbal, but whether you hear it over the backyard fence or on a site like Yelp, Angie's List, or TripAdvisor, word of mouth drives our modern decision-making process.

Comment boxes are the new watercoolers, where everyone can gather around one big, virtual office and heap praise—or rip to shreds—anything from their latest pizza delivery from Dominos to Donald Trump's new book on Amazon.com to a story on *Huffington Post*.

The time to respond to those comments isn't after the fact. Instead, you can build entire social media strategies specifically designed to court positive feedback and prevent, or at least derail, negative feedback.

And yet with company after company and client after client, it's amazing to me how few organizations truly understand the massive power—and potential—of online word of mouth or how to tap it for their own gain.

It starts with awareness. All of it, every ounce of my energy, is spent on helping companies increase their awareness of the power of positive feedback and how to get recommended.

It's not an either-or situation anymore. You have to know, going in, that the world of yesteryear—of even last year—no longer exists. You can't simply have a one-way communication with your audience anymore and expect it to predictably guide feedback in your direction unless you start with the basic understanding that con-sumers are no longer sheep to be led.

Are You Engaging Your Audience— or Interrupting Them?

How do you get consumers with a virtual DVR and their hand on the fast forward button to push "play" on your message instead? That's right, the message. And the message must be, "I'm not just trying to sell you something. I'm trying to share something with you." But what? What are you sharing?

Well, if it's Nike, you're sharing the love of athletics, sweat, exer-tion, excellence, challenge, and sports. Same with Gatorade and PowerBar.

If I'm the AMC or Regal or Cobb or RAVE movie theater chain, I'm sharing the love of film, of actors, directors, great per-formances, summer blockbusters, Oscar season, soundtracks, and beyond.

If I'm Bath & Body Works, Pier 1 Imports, or Crate & Barrel, I'm sharing a lifestyle of the four seasons, pleasant aromas, entertaining guests, lively accessories, and home styles.

Once upon a time, traditional advertising was nothing more than a series of interruptions. In many ways, for many companies, it still is. But print ads, billboards, TV ads, as engaging as they are, or can be, for many modern consumers used to interaction, feedback, and interactivity, are little more than interruptions.

We need to start engaging more with our audience and inter-rupting them less. How? Let's say I sell frozen food for Bertolli. I start with my message. What is it? Something about food: the love of food; the love of good food; fast, convenient, and affordable food. But, above all, the love of Italian food.

So maybe I start a Facebook fan page where folks of a like mind can Like me, my message, my product, and my posts. What should those posts be about? Food, obviously. Italian food, primarily. But in addition, all kinds of food. Mother's Day recipes, table decorat-ing tips, a comparison of cheeses and their tastes, textures, aromas, and consistencies. A wine chart for enthusiasts. Poems, quotes, sayings about food, contests to win food, or travel to Italy and taste food.

Day by day, fan by fan, Like by Like, I'm not just building a brand. I'm building something equally as important: a community. In this case it is a community of food lovers, Italian food lovers, foodies, wine lovers, cheese lovers, travel lovers, whatever. Suddenly I'm no longer just a staple in the freezer but a familiar, loved, trusted, and regular name in affordable, fast, tasty, and convenient dinners.

How? By finding a way—by finding a message—to connect with and be relevant to my fans.

And it all starts with engaging my audience, not interrupting them.

Recognize and Recommend

Interruptions are one sure way of becoming recognized. Call it "media impression," call it "buy-in," call it "brand recognition," call it what you will, but it's only one part of the Becoming Recommended equation.

Bertolli does plenty of print ads, even television commercials. That's a sure way to get recognized. But with the company's Facebook page and other social media interactions, that connection, that community, helps it become recommended.

The beauty, and danger, of online transparency and the rise of consumers as cheerleaders—or advocates—is that at some point the recommendation is in the customers' hands.

Be it Yellow Dog Eats, Wolfgang Puck, Hilton, or Days Inn, there is no active way for a company to control its Yelp or TripAdvisor rating other than to run a tight ship, control the media message, train all hands in the message, and consistently stick to it.

If you're an author with a book on Amazon.com, the only way to control your message is to write a great book. And even then, enough anonymous online haters can still find ways to sully that accomplishment with just enough one- and two-star reviews to tear down your rating.

That's why I say the goal and the messaging that follows start so far downstream. Becoming Highly Recommended is about being recommendable, at every turn of the consumer experience. Before they buy, while they buy, after they buy, the next time they buy, and when their friends buy, all cylinders in the marketing and service machine must be firing.

Advertising is just a reminder to me to check out a company and see if people recommend it or not. That's why it's recognize and recommend, not recognize OR recommend. You use traditional channels to help users recognize it, but before purchasing, they will look for recommendations. It's a one-two punch, not one replacing the other.

Why Angie's Is on My List

Back to Angie's List. Once upon a time my driveway had a few cracks. I wanted them filled. Should be a simple matter.

Like any homeowner, I needed a recommendation. I turned to my neighbors first, but either they were not as distressed by their own driveway cracks as I was by mine or they had simply repaved them so they weren't in a position to recommend someone for a touch-up job.

I next went to the local newspaper Classified section and the Yellow Pages. I found a few names, got in touch, and asked for bids. Those who responded were either astronomically high or comically low, save for one guy. We'll call him "Phil."

Phil gave me a very reasonable bid of $1,000 to repair my driveway cracks. I knew going in he'd probably want half down, and I was right. I gave Phil a check for $500, and he pledged to return with the materials he'd need and start the job later that week.

If you're nodding your head right now, you've been here before. If you can see where I'm going, well, you'll know I'm no great mystery writer. Fact is, I never saw Phil—or my money—again. I tried calling him, repeatedly, with no answer. I tried the bank, but it was too late to stop payment on the check; he'd already cashed it. I got in touch with a lawyer to take Phil to small claims court, but nothing ever came of it.

I'd been duped, completely and soundly. And what's worse, my driveway still had cracks. Enter Angie's List. For a small monthly fee, I could have access to personal, trusted, validated, individual, and firsthand recommendations of local contractors. Not just people in New York, Chicago, or LA but contractors who were 5, 10, or 15 minutes away.

I quickly got online and started searching, and within a week I had my driveway repaired, good as new. Since then I've had trees trimmed, lawn work done, and a variety of other home and garden repairs that have at best exceeded expectations and at worst been done adequately, on time, and for the price agreed upon.

It's the perfect microcosm of becoming highly recommended. Contractors know that they're on Angie's List, they know that they're going to be reviewed, and they work hard to keep their reviews up because the better their reviews, the more business they get, and the more money goes directly in their pockets.

As a consumer, part of the deal is that I'm encouraged to leave reviews around my experience using Angie's List and always do. I'm eager to point out which contractors were helpful, go above and beyond, and are experts or are simply proficient. Because I trust others to give realistic and impartial reviews, I give them as well.

Nobody likes being thought of as stupid. There's nothing worse than feeling you've been "had." In fact, we try to avoid that at all costs. When I got taken by Phil, I was embarrassed to tell my wife.

I vowed never to make that same mistake again, and I'm not alone. How many of us have bought a book that was no good, seen a movie that stunk, bought a car that was a lemon, or paid for a contractor that never showed up or never finished the job? Becoming highly recommended is as simple, and complicated, as answering that very basic question.

No one wants to get taken. And in this day and age, with all the tools available to us, we don't have to be anymore. Whether it's seeing reviewers' consensus on RottenTomatoes.com or checking out the customer ratings of your new computer monitor on Best Buy's website, we are now advocates and even activists around our own purchasing power. This is the current climate of our end users, our clientele, our customers, and consumers. And it's the mindset we must first understand and then control if we too are to become recommended.

Parting Words: *Why Do We Want People to Recommend This Book?*

"What do you want people to say when they recommend you?"

This is the question I ask every new client when we start working together. It's a little like writing a mystery; you have to know the end before you start at the beginning. *Highly Recommended* is about actively recruiting recommenders—those people who feel connected to you, familiar with you, impressed by you, and, yes, loyal to you.

Why does my uncle recommend Nissan over Toyota? Why does my aunt recommend Carrabba's over Olive Garden? Why does my accountant recommend Quicken over any other home financial software? What happened along the customer food chain to build that kind of loyalty, to increase consumers' awareness, solidify their satisfaction, and turn them into recommenders versus recognizers?

I can tell you from experience that it starts with the message and branches out from there. And yet, surprisingly, so few know the right message so that they can communicate with others effectively.

I'll never forget sitting in the boardroom of a leading casual dining chain and asking the heads of creative, marketing, promotion, sales, strategy, anybody, everybody who was a part of their media message the question: "What do you want people to say when they recommend you?"

With about a dozen different people sitting at the table, I got nearly that many different messages:

- "We're a great value."
- "We make everything from scratch."
- "We serve big portions that are meant to be shared."
- "Our president taste tests every recipe."
- "We've got an incredible variety—everyone will be happy."
- "Our staff and servers make you feel like family."

I almost said, "Well, which is it?" But after that exercise, I didn't have to. Once you understand what you want to be recommended for, you can then go about the simple—but far from easy—work of becoming highly recommended.

As the author of this book, as CEO of Highly Recommended, Inc., I want readers to say the following when they recommend my book:

- "The book was very readable and helped me understand what it means to have and how to achieve a highly recommended business. It's one of the best business books I've read."

I'm going to stay on point, on task, and on message so that you won't be lying when you, I hope, do recommend this book.

CHAPTER 3

Fixing What Advertising Has Broken

How are we to respond to news that "73 percent of CEOs think Marketers lack business credibility and are not the business growth generators they should be"?[1] And what's going on when two of advertising's brightest luminaries come out within weeks of each other stating that their industry is dead?

Bill Lee, president of the Lee Consulting Group and author of *The Hidden Wealth of Customers*,[2] was not the first pundit to trot out the "this is the end of marketing" trope that seems to be so trendy recently, but he was certainly one of the loudest, strongest, and most respected authors to do so. And in his article called "Marketing Is Dead" for none other than the *Harvard Business Review*, he certainly had one of the biggest pulpits to preach from.[3]

Lee wrote at length about the death of traditional marketing, and he led an online call to arms for embracing new, interactive, social media, relationship-based marketing ideas such as "community marketing," finding "customer influencers," and—coining one last business buzz term for the ages—building "social capital."

His message, thinly veiled under his inflammatory headline, was basically the memorandum that "what got you here won't get you there," and commenters, nearly 600 of them, were mostly quick to call him out on that fact.

But Lee wasn't alone in his trumpeting of the "marketing is dead" message. Recently profiled in the *Drum*, an online publication from the United Kingdom, Kevin Roberts, CEO of Saatchi & Saatchi Worldwide, went Bill Lee one further when he made the equally bold claim that "in today's crazy world, strategy is dead, the big idea is dead, management is dead, and marketing, as we know, is also dead."[4]

The point Roberts was making, I believe, was the same point Bill Lee was trying to make: selling that blockbuster tagline, or big idea, alone is dead. Simply handing money over to a crack team of pitch writers and graphic designers alone is dead, and ultimately, what we used to know as "traditional advertising" and the one-way system of interrupting instead of interacting are dead. In other words, today's successful marketing campaign will be an integrated, hybrid, and "holistic" (more on that later in this chapter) affair.

No one thing, traditional or modern, old or new, low or high tech, alone is going to win the recommendation age. Instead, the only way to win is to find that right "media mix" that fits your unique budget, company, brand, and customers.

Roberts said it best when he explained, "Don't just interrupt, but interact. Asking about Return on Investment is the wrong question today. You should be asking about Return on Involvement."

I love that phrase **return on involvement** because if social media and the recommendation age are about any singular, driving notion, it's about involvement: involving your customers, their imaginations, their friends, their voices, their actions, and their efforts to turn them from consumers to advocates.

At the heart of becoming a social business is the understanding of *social engagement*: that aspect of active and voluntary involvement that makes customers so eager to highly recommend you to one and all.

Cashier Confessionals

Once upon a time, every successful merchant knew the power of recommendations. In addition to goods, the earliest merchants, be they traveling salespeople, door-to-door peddlers, or general store owners, had the corner on another very valuable market: expertise.

Long before full-page magazine spreads and 30-second radio and TV spots, clerks were the original gateway to consumer goods and services. Yes, they read the product specs and bought the manufacturer's spiel, but they knew also that to survive on the ground, face-to-face with the angry or satisfied public, they had to push their customers toward what worked and away from what didn't. And who better to hear about the latest breakthroughs, upsets, disappointments, and pleasant surprises than the men or women who had more face time with consumers than any manufacturer or CEO: shop clerks.

From soap to detergents to headache cures to stain removers to shoelaces, consumers would come into their stores and ask the proprietors what product they would recommend to fill a specific need. Quickly, lest the customers doubt their expertise, the merchants would give a recommendation—either validated or not by other local shoppers. It was the system that worked for decades, in the first few colonies, on the frontier plains, in boom towns, and even in the earliest of industrialized cities.

Albert Lasker and the Advertising Renaissance

In 1898, Albert Lasker, regarded as the "father of modern advertising," came along. Smart guy. So smart, in fact, that as he was working to build the cigarette market among women, he convinced them that if they smoked Lucky Strike, not only would they look sophisticated but they would actually protect their voice and throat through the brand's unique tobacco "toasting" process. And he did this by enlisting some of the world's leading female opera singers to promote the brand.

The rest is advertising history. Brands began realizing that instead of simply reaching consumers one-on-one through local merchants, an admittedly painstaking and time-consuming effort, they could run ads—in print in newspapers and magazines, then later on radio and even later on TV—that simply **told** thousands of consumers what products could help them think, feel, and do.

By taking charge of the message, the world's first "ad agencies" effectively controlled the consumer conversation as well. But it was hardly that; Lasker and the "advertising renaissance" he invented meant a new industry full of preachers, teachers, lecturers, and interrupters. These new "stop sign" ads left no room for debate. They were only an endless stream of one-way information that flowed from the top down, with little to no room for interruption along the way.

This new form of broadcast advertising was great, at first. Images, slogans, taglines, and perceptions—great one-way forms of communication all—worked wonders and sold millions of products.

Sure, consumers talked among themselves. "BS on the Lucky Strike claim," they'd mumble knowingly over white picket fences and watercoolers and clotheslines. "We all know that cigarettes make your breath stink, and they make you wheeze and die early." But those messages had a limited audience—and zero ad budget.

Social Media's Seismic Shift

Then social media came along, giving voice to the masses with multiple venues in which to discuss their gripes, air their grievances, even send their thanks, well-wishes, praise, and compliments. And suddenly every consumer became a journalist, publisher, and critic.

And just as suddenly, the mystical, mythical curtain was drawn back on the great and mighty advertising wizards who, for years, had pushed the buttons and pulled the levers on an unsuspecting public without fear of feedback, complaint, or retribution.

This immediate sense of transparency, this empowerment of millions to complain about—or, alternately, praise—a company, brand, CEO, employee, or a simple meal had a ripple effect throughout the advertising agency world that we're still feeling to this day.

Today, if brands make false or misleading claims, treat consumers poorly, or have products that don't work, there's an almost immediate backlash. Call it an overexaggeration, but few who've ever felt the sting of an online whipping for their product or service would dispute that, for better or worse, social media has changed everything.

What's interesting is that, after decades enjoying a one-way relationship with the consumer public, today's advertisers are being forced to return to their humble roots as one-on-one communicators, finding advocates not just in store clerks or salespeople but also in consumers themselves. But to truly relearn what one-on-one recommendations taught us so many years ago, we'll have to unlearn how one-way advertising led us astray.

In short, we'll have to fix what advertising itself has broken.

The End of BS: *Relearning the Art of Recommendation*

What was interesting to me about the Bill Lee article, in particular, was how quickly readers' "BS meters" went off and how vocal they were in expressing their intolerance of the author's obvious "come on" tactics and in disputing the title of his article in relation to what the article actually said. Comments ranged somewhere along the continuum of the opinions paraphrased here:

- "Marketing is not dead. Only certain types of old, outdated marketing strategies are dead."
- "This is just old news disguised as new news."

- "Since when is marketing about selling?"
- "Your 'interrupter' headline proves that traditional marketing isn't dead!"

And, oddly enough, one of the most salient points to come out of Lee's "Marketing Is Dead" article wasn't written by its author but appeared farther down the page in the lively, diverse, and largely argumentative comments section where, to paraphrase, one reader amended Lee's title to read: "I would say that BS-ing the consumer is dead, not marketing itself."

Additionally, I would amend that reader's comment further to conclude that, frankly, there is no such thing as BS-ing the consumer anymore. Consumers are, we are, far too sophisticated for that at this stage of the game. What used to be only groused about between neighbors and coworkers is now fair game for the entire Internet, hence the entire online world, to read.

One need only to revisit a recent, high-profile example to see how even some of the world's biggest, and one would think smartest, companies can be so quickly burned by the online backlash that is the flip side, but also part and parcel, of recommendation marketing.

Consider the strange cautionary tale of the Hollister stores, the hip, chic clothing apparel giant that got burned online after several of their male models mocked Asian reporters, fans, and shoppers at the grand opening of a Hollister outlet in South Korea.

As news spread of several of Hollister's male models taking insensitive pictures showing themselves flipping off crowds, making "squinty eyes," and mocking Asian speech patterns, Hollister corporate was quick to post the following apology on its Facebook fan page: "Hollister Co. and its parent company Abercrombie & Fitch value diversity and inclusion. In a recent incident in South Korea, a couple of associates did not adhere to these values. As a company, we do not tolerate inappropriate or offensive behavior. We terminated the associates involved as a result of their actions."

The sentiment was clearly too little, too late for many online commenters, over 300 of whom posted their largely negative reaction to the pat corporate speak with such representative (paraphrased) comments as "Maybe we'd buy this apology if you actually showed some diversity in your advertising," and "You could have avoided this debacle altogether by simply hiring Korean models in the first place," and even "Why not hire models who can think for themselves—and about others—rather than just look good."

The case is another example of what would, once upon a time, have been a nonissue. Not because no one would have cared about the racist implications of a few male models insulting Asians but because very few would have known about it pre-Internet.

Today, it's all instant, it's all fair game, and above all, it's all transparent. It's challenging and costly to "spin" a negative, control the damage, or try to undo a marketing scandal. On paper, Hollister did the right thing; the company quickly and effectively owned up to the issue, made a declarative and decisive apology, and even fired those employees who messed up. But clearly, in the eyes of their customers past, present, and future, it simply wasn't enough.

Diversity is clearly a hot button issue in this evolving, changing world, and the feeling of many who commented, or simply read, Hollister's Facebook fan page can be stated thus: "Stop trying to BS us." The company's statement concerning how much it valued diversity clearly didn't jibe with its very purposeful public perception, that of young, attractive, mostly blond and blue-eyed models.

The Next Danger Zone: *Creeping Your Customers Out*

When it comes to collecting consumer data, no matter how high the quality or relevance, the fact is that there *can* be too much of a good thing. Chris Babel, CEO of privacy management company TRUSTe, recently said something that has really stuck with me (and likely will with you as well): "Marketers are beginning to creep consumers out."

Babel pointed to research he and his firm had conducted stating that "94 percent of consumers were concerned about online privacy, with 54 percent more concerned compared to this time last year."

This jump in concern may not be surprising when you consider how often we all experience the following. Say you're online, looking at a website for a new seafood restaurant. You spend a few minutes there, maybe bookmark it, and then on the very next website you visit, you notice all the ads are about seafood, or raw bar, or fishing poles, or bass hats. You visit your favorite search engine, and amazingly enough, even more ads show up for seafood restaurants or aquariums or other keyword-related businesses.

It gets very Big Brother very fast, and you know that some company, somewhere, has gained access to your computer's "cookies," those little random nuggets of stored information, and it is using them to "target" you in a very persistent, obvious, and predictably creepy way.

The fact is, this is traditional marketing masked with a little high-tech wizardry. How is this any different from, say, buying a deep sea fishing magazine and finding, surprise, ads for lures and bait and charter boat companies and outboard engines? Or reading a women's magazine and finding ads for clothes, shoes, perfumes, jewelry, and other accessories?

The only difference is that with "creepy advertising," you're being involuntarily targeted. You buy a fishing magazine, and you expect to get those ads. When you visit a seafood restaurant on Monday, you don't expect to be seeing seafood-related ads all week. You also don't expect your computer to spy on you, or others to spy on you via your computer, without your permission.

When marketers use this method involving cookies, they cross the line from passive advertisers to active stalkers, and few who truly appreciate the interactive nature of social media respond favorably to such manipulative tactics. So ask yourself, "Is my marketing too creepy?"

You may just be surprised by the answer.

Parting Words: *Our Big, Fat, Scary Marketing Reboot*

So, what have we learned? Hopefully a lot, but more specifically we've learned that marketing—true, interactive marketing—is not dead but merely coming back online after being "interrupted" by traditional, one-way methods of interrupting consumers.

Hopefully by now you can see the promise of holistic marketing, of integrating the best of the old with the promise of the new. Frankly, whatever gets people talking about you, among themselves—to friends and family over the backyard fence, or to random strangers, connections, fans, or followers via social media—is the marketing mix that works for you.

We need to "reboot" our way of thinking about how we market, why we market, and to whom we market. One concept emerging during this big, fat, scary marketing reboot is that of coauthoring with consumers.

I've seen companies invite their blog readers to help design a new e-book cover, or even pick the name of the blog, or even write for the blog. I've seen reader polls on all types of company websites that ask questions of the week or otherwise engage readers to participate, actively or passively, with real decisions that may one day impact them.

Whatever you do, evolution must be part of the program. Don't merely throw out traditional advertising simply because everyone is headed in social media's direction. We've seen how powerful and positive a healthy media mix can be as we grow and evolve into the recommendation age.

However, you must evolve quickly. Everywhere around us, new technologies, new avenues, and new opportunities are popping up. We must get in the habit of observing our competitors, and their success stories, in a way that is daily and dynamic.

Many companies make the mistake of "getting social" as a one-time event, but truly social businesses know that active engagement must be a daily event and that, to be truly effective, it must become habitual behavior in every department. (More about that later in the book.)

Urgency is an issue. Things are changing so quickly, technology is evolving so fast, that those who can't adapt are falling behind, including chief marketing officers (CMOs) and even entire companies and brands who simply can't adapt fast enough to this holistic way of approaching marketing.

Don't be one of them.

CHAPTER 4

A Whole New Model for a Whole New World

Long before advertising's Mad Men era, an American marketing executive named E. St. Elmo Lewis concocted a model to illustrate a customer's journey from the moment a brand or product attracts his or her attention all the way to the point of action or purchase.

Lewis's approach is often referred to as the AIDA model, an acronym for Awareness, Interest, Desire, and Action. It's a pretty straightforward approach:

- **Awareness.** The customer is aware of the existence of a product or service.
- **Interest.** The customer actively expresses an interest in a product group.
- **Desire.** The customer aspires to a particular brand or product.
- **Action.** The customer takes the next step toward purchasing the chosen product.

Then in 1923, a fellow marketer by the name of Edward K. Strong published what became known as a seminal advertising tome: *Psychology of Selling and Advertising.*

He credited Lewis with the Purchase Funnel model, and it has been taught in every marketing and advertising class ever since. The impact of Lewis's model was thought to be so great that he was posthumously inducted into the Advertising Hall of Fame in 1951.

Embarking on the New Consumer Decision Journey

Lewis's model stood—with some tweaking and refining—until 2009. At that point, every marketer knew that the model didn't reflect the new age and impact of the explosion of product choices, the Internet, and social media. But it took the venerable blue-chip consulting firm McKinsey & Company to propose a new model after examining the purchase decisions of almost 20,000 consumers across five industries and three continents.

McKinsey's model, known as the "Consumer Decision Journey" and shown in Figure 4.1, brought to life the new reality: the shift away from one-way communication—from marketers to consumers—toward a two-way conversation. It meant that marketers needed a more systematic way to satisfy customer demands, to manage word of mouth, and to harness the power of recommendations.

Today, you can see how every aspect of the Consumer Decision Journey is affected by the Internet, which has essentially changed one-way communication into two-way communication. As shown in Figure 4.1, there are four phases in the journey:

- **Initial consideration set.** In this phase, the consumer reviews an initial set of brands, based on brand perceptions and

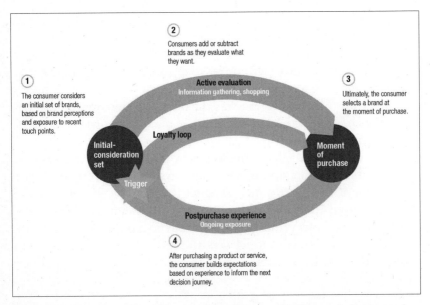

Figure 4.1 Consumer Decision Journey. (Source: McKinsey & Company.)

exposure to recent touch points. Today, these touch points include a variety of online sources, including consumer blogs, forums, e-tailers like Amazon.com or BestBuy.com, and the company's own website. Consider the selection of a new laptop. A consumer might visit Dell.com directly, where she can read about the product specs, see a variety of pictures, and possibly read consumer reviews. Or she might visit BestBuy.com where she can see a more random and openly critical set of consumer reviews, or visit a "Dell" forum where she can ask questions, get answers, or read earlier threads.

- **Active evaluation.** Here, consumers add or subtract brands as they evaluate what they want. In our fictional search for a laptop, our buyer may have been swayed away from Apple or Hewlett-Packard by a great offer from Sony. Or a friend might have shown her his own laptop from Sony that had all the bells and whistles she needed. Now focused on a Dell Inspiron model, she purposefully searches out the best deal for herself.

- **Moment of purchase.** Ultimately, consumers will select a brand at what McKinsey referred to as "the moment of purchase." For a laptop, this could mean walking into an Office Depot, Best Buy, or CompUSA store, ordering it online from Amazon.com, or using a combination of the two.

- **Postpurchase experience.** After purchasing a product or service, consumers build expectations based on experience to inform their next decision journey. For instance, let's say that buying a laptop in a brick-and-mortar store has always been vaguely problematic for our laptop purchaser. She has always felt bullied and intimidated by the more knowledgeable sales staff, and she has often bought more than she wanted or needed, including buying a variety of warranties or service plans she'll never use. Consequently, if during her initial laptop consideration set and active evaluation, she was able to research most of the laptop's specs online, compare them, and contrast them through unbiased reader reviews and even use her friend's computer, all without ever entering a store, she may never buy another big-ticket item in a retail store again.

- **Loyalty loop.** What's more, if she particularly enjoyed the online ordering process via, say, Best Buy's website, she might become a loyal customer. She may have even taken advantage of a financing plan offered at the time of purchase, or she may have applied for a Best Buy card midway through purchase, and, once approved, she may come back later to use it on the laptop. She may even join a "rewards program" at the store and use the points from this purchase to get an accessory, like a fiber optic laptop mouse or a set of portable speakers, for free.

Postpurchase: *It's Not the End. It's Just the Beginning*

Many companies focus on the prepurchase aspects of the Consumer Decision Journey, and rightfully so. You can't run a company without appealing to, finding, and ultimately selling to actual consumers. But those who ignore postpurchase behavior are literally leaving money on the table.

What's more, those who truly believe that marketing is dead are missing the fundamental opportunities provided by the last two items in the above scenario: the **postpurchase experience** and the **loyalty loop**. If anything, here is where modern marketing and the recommendation age are enjoying a glorious and active rebirth.

If we are to take part in this marketing resurrection, however, we must learn to engage consumers postpurchase—not as just a one-time event but every time, as a habit.

One of the earliest industries to note the power of the postpurchase experience and fully invest in the loyalty loop was actually the auto industry. In particular, Lexus and Acura were both early adopters. What likely began as a way of differentiating their luxury cars from those built by Mercedes and BMW became an active and profitable business practice aimed at gaining not just one-time car buyers but Lexus and Acura buyers for life—true advocates who lived and "cheerleaded" for those distinctive brands.

Those early forays into postpurchase customer service encouraged customers to come in not just for an oil change every 3,000 miles but also for a car wash and tire pressure check, all accomplished while the customer waited in a low-key waiting "lounge" complete with a coffee bar and soothing refreshments. Today, of course, most dealerships come complete with waiting lounges, and they work just as hard as Acura and Lexus did back then to ensure consumer loyalty.

To ensure that your own marketing never dies, it's critical for you to believe that the postpurchase sale is really the beginning of the relationship, not the end. To ensure the loyalty loop is indeed a never-ending circle instead of a finite line, your job is not just to keep your customers satisfied but to make them active advocates by providing feedback and improving your relationship so it continues to their next purchases.

Again, this postpurchase experience is not unique to the auto industry, nor does it require converting your waiting room into a waiting lounge, though that probably never hurts. Here is what could contribute to the postpurchase experience in a variety of industries:

- A dry cleaner that helps you recycle your wire hangers and rewards you for doing so
- A shoe company that matches your purchase by giving away a pair of shoes to needy people
- An electronics retailer that updates you on a new software download that will make your Blu-ray player work even better

I'm reminded of a local chain of tire and auto repair shops that recently entered the gas station business in a very significant, real, and telling way, indicating that the company was not only aware of the loyalty loop but also eager to have customers join its loop.

Duxler Tire has been in business in Illinois since 1926, opening four branches over time and maintaining hundreds of thousands of cars. Now, I could write reams about how the company treats its customers with respect, runs free car care clinics, and celebrates a customer's 400,000-mile mark with cake and a party, but Duxler's attention to postpurchase details recently hit a high water mark when it decided to start selling gas.

Not only did Duxler debut with gas prices 5 cents below its nearest competitors but it also made all of the pumps full service, something many in the younger generations may not have ever experienced in their lifetimes. What's more, when the attendants appear at your driver's side door to collect the money, they're there with a basket of candy, popcorn, or if you've got a pooch, a dog biscuit.

Since I get gas nearly every week, I've become very familiar with the folks at the local Duxler. So when my daughter's brakes started squeaking, Duxler was the first place I thought to bring her car. And since she was treated so well, it was the first place she thought to bring it back when the air went out of a tire and Dad was traveling for business.

So, in this case, Duxler's loyalty loop included me and my daughter. And it included how many other countless families due to the company's unwavering commitment to postpurchase customer service. What's more, Duxler's business practices—attention to detail, customer commitment, going the extra mile, and so on—can be applied to the marketing practices of businesses large and small.

Interrupting Versus Interacting

In the last chapter, I introduced you to the concept of "interrupting" as a popular form of marketing. While this may sound old-fashioned, the fact is, it's very much a part of the traditional marketing method employed by companies big and small.

Even young, so-called hip or modern media-savvy companies still engage in this "look at me, look at me" method of marketing. Even those same authors, bloggers, pundits, and consultants who tout the "marketing is dead" bait and switch—*see my sensational headline! click on my blog! read how marketing isn't actually dead after all! just foolin'!*—are basically interrupting your morning, afternoon, or evening routine to stop what you're doing and look, listen, and pay attention, even if it's all smoke and mirrors.

Which is not to say that interrupting consumers can't be effective. Whether it's "Flo" from Progressive Insurance, Kia's dancing hamsters, or the Aflac duck, those commercials, mascots, or icons everyone loves to hate are obviously quite effective, or how else could the companies who create them afford to keep producing them?

The radical transformation that is occurring in marketing at the moment really centers around this old method of interrupting you to make a point and sell you something to one of interacting with you so that you'll feel involved, like you're part of the movement, group, or family, and ultimately not only purchase from them but recommend them.

Again, interrupting your normal routine with a funny visual, an arresting image, a controversial billboard, or a statement à la "Marketing is dead" is still an incredibly vital aspect of marketing. The challenge, the shift, the transformation comes when you go from interrupting—which is an event more than a habit, an occur-rence rather than a trend—to starting to interact on a serious level with your consumers.

The People's Burger Meets "Do Us a Flavor":
The Gold Standards of Interaction

"It's a burger for the people. By the people. Eaten by other people. That's the People's Burger." Such was the bold claim made by the Red Robin restaurant chain upon announcing the creation of "the people's burger," perhaps the first "create your own burger" ever to see an actual menu.

It was a contest, one emboldened by the creation of a separate website, www.peoplesburger.com, and it was shared daily on the Red Robin Facebook page. It got a lot of play in the Internet searches, fea-turing prominently on contest, game, and sweepstakes sites. And of course, what casual fans with a few minutes on their hands wouldn't want to create their very own hamburger and then . . . have other people eat it.

While many companies run contests, few have the nerve to serve the winner of the contest's creation in their stores and on their menus for better or worse. That was not just a promo item. That was a menu item and a conscious business decision.

It was also marketing gold. It was a hands-on, interactive request. It called for customers to manipulate menu items, combine them, and add or subtract them. Then they had to submit the creation and wait for the judging, voting, being judged, being voted on, a hundred times, a thousand times, however many participants there were, all of whom urging their friends to vote for them—and everyone, all the while, was looking at pictures of delicious Red Robin burgers and talking about Red Robin burgers.

Ultimately, the winning burger was called "The Dictator," and it featured a host of Red Robin's trademark offerings, including "angry onions," an onion bun, bacon, a fried egg(!), mayo, and, of course, an all-beef patty. Not only that, but dozens and dozens of runners up, including the "Caliavacado Burger" created by Shirley McNeill and the "Big Ben Burger" created by Adam Pellegrino, got a full profile page on the People's Burger website, bringing fame to participants who were also likely to become fully engaged in the loyalty loop for years to come.

Similar to the interactivity of Red Robin's "People's Burger" contest, Frito-Lay held a contest inviting consumers to help "Do Us a Flavor" and create a brand new flavor of Lay's potato chips. PepsiCo has activated this global program in more than a dozen countries around the world. The winner of the U.S. "Do Us a Flavor" contest wins either $1 million or 1 percent of the chip's net sales for one year, whichever is deemed the larger amount.

As of this writing, the Lay's "Do Us a Flavor" Facebook fan page had 6.1 million Likes, as well as a Facebook app to make it even more convenient for users to submit their flavor ideas.

Many posts on the page had upward of 18,000 comments, some offering flavors like "chicken fettuccini Alfredo" or "Nutella" flavor, others offering recipes to sweeten up current Lay's flavors, such as melting chocolate on top of the chips in the microwave.

Naturally, the Facebook fan page is fully interactive, and Lay's is making full use of user recommendations to collect not only priceless data but also promote current flavors, as the company did with this recent post: "17 percent of your submissions include bacon. Which reminds us, have you tried our new BLT flavored Lay's potato chips? They're incredible."

In case you're wondering, by the way, Cheesy Garlic Bread was the winning flavor. Yum.

Parting Words: *The Seismic Shift in Marketing*

Obviously, holding contests to name your restaurant's menu items or throwing up an entire section of your website to chronicle where your farm fed beef comes from is slightly more complicated than throwing together some clip art and clever slogans for a quarter-page newspaper ad in the Sunday circular, but unfortunately what worked then simply won't work now. At least, not in isolation.

The goal of becoming a truly top-down social business is not for you to mimic any of the companies or case studies you'll read about in this book but to simply adopt the same tone of interactivity, two-way conversation, and advocacy that make those companies stand out and so easily recommendable.

Likewise, recommendation marketing in the age of advocacy, loyalty, and cheerleading is emerging and evolving by the day. At its heart, recommendation marketing is really about trying to understand where and how and why people are talking about you and, ultimately, why they'll recommend you—highly.

What will they say about you, and how can you craft that message? How loudly will they say it and where, and what can you do to get them to say it more often, more loudly, in more places? The fact is, we are living in a world where everything—good, bad, or ugly, online or off—is part of our universal brand. We need advocates more than ever, and my hope is that in this book I'll guide you toward finding more than ever.

CHAPTER 5

The Power of Positive Recommendations

magine the following scenario, if you will. The setting? A Hollywood movie studio. The scene? A typical pitch meeting between creatives and executives. The subject? Next summer's tent pole blockbuster event.

And, action . . .

"Okay, gang, we're going to launch a movie about children killing children as a form of futuristic televised entertainment. And the fans of the book on which this movie is to be based are going to drive so many recommendations that it will become one of the decade's hottest movies."

Crazy, huh? It'll never work, right? But it did. It worked and then some. *The Hunger Games* (in case you hadn't guessed) drove $155 million in ticket sales its opening weekend, and as of this writing, it is well on its way to garnering over $700 million worldwide in sales.

In reporting the film's blockbuster success, the *New York Times* commented that *The Hunger Games* team "used social media and a blizzard of other inexpensive yet effective online techniques to pull off what may be the marketer's ultimate marketing strategy: persuading fans to persuade each other."

The movie could just as easily be a poster child for *Highly Recommended*, a distinct and beautiful universe unto itself that, more like a black hole, sucked both loyal fans and those "turned loyal" by other fans into its tightening grip.

Sure, it had a bestselling young adult book in its favor already, but so did previous adaptations like *Percy Jackson and the Lightning Thief*, *Beastly*, and *Cirque de Freak*, and none of those movies managed to cross over into worldwide phenomenon blockbuster territory.

What turned the tide, clearly, to launch a popular book into a worldwide phenomenon was more than just the "stickiness" of a book series. It was a tidal wave of advocates, which we'll learn about in this chapter on both the power of positive recommendations and the danger of negative recommendations.

Speaking of the latter, the opposite occurs as well. For every word of mouth blockbuster—be it a movie, book, sports drink, dollar value menu item, candy bar, or cookie—there are dozens of failures that fizzled out before they even got off the launch pad. By some estimates, nearly 70 percent of consumers report that they will not buy a product they are considering if they read "three or more" negative reviews. (Much more detail on managing negative word of mouth is in Chapter 12 on protecting your brand.)

In this new and challenging recommendation age, word of mouth cuts both ways with very little room for error. Positive word of mouth can't be appreciated and rewarded enough while negative reviews or recommendations can no longer be ignored.

The Science Behind the Scores

Marketers may spend millions of dollars on elaborately conceived advertising campaigns, yet often what really makes up a consumer's mind is not only simple but also free: a Word of Mouth recommendation from a trusted source.

—"A NEW WAY TO MEASURE WORD OF MOUTH MARKETING," *McKinsey Quarterly*

While there has always seemed to be universal agreement on the importance of recommendations, no one successfully found a way to meaningfully and simply quantify this impact until 2003.

That year, a fellow by the name of Fred Reichheld of Bain & Company and Satmetrix introduced the "Net Promoter Score," a concept that debuted in Reichheld's 2003 *Harvard Business Review* article "The One Number You Need to Grow."[1]

Reichheld discovered that the real test of customer loyalty was whether customers would recommend a product or service to a friend.

While you may be happy with your new HTC smartphone, would you actually recommend it to someone who trusts you?

Reichheld's model is quite simple, actually. By asking customers the basic "Would you recommend?" question and asking them to rank their score from 0 to 10, the customers can be categorized as *promoters*, *passives*, or *detractors*:

- **Promoters** (people who answer 9 or 10) are highly likely to recommend your company, brand, or service.
- **Passives** (people who answer 7 or 8) are somewhat likely to recommend your product or service.
- **Detractors** (people who answer 0 through 6) are highly unlikely to recommend your product or service.

The Net Promoter Score formula is itself surprisingly straightforward:

Percent of promoters – percent of detractors = NPS

For example, if 60 percent of your customers answer 9 or 10 and 20 percent are detractors (answering 0 to 6), your NPS is 40 percent. An NPS of 50 is considered very positive.

By analyzing companies' NPSs and their revenue growth rates, Reichheld and Satmetrix uncovered a clear connection between advocacy and revenue growth.

According to Reichheld in his book *The Ultimate Question: Driving Good Profits and True Growth*, "A 12 percent increase in Brand Advocacy, on average, generates a 2× increase in revenue growth rate plus boosts market share."

In another example, the London School of Economics (LSE) and the Listening Company found that word of mouth (WOM) advocacy and recommendations are powerful components in driving business growth.

They found that word of mouth advocacy (as measured by net promoter scores) and negative WOM were statistically significant predictors of annual sales growth:

- A 7 percent increase in word of mouth recommendations unlocks 1 percent additional company growth.
- A 2 percent reduction in negative word of mouth boosts sales growth by 1 percent.
- Companies with above average positive word of mouth and below average negative word of mouth grow four times as fast as those with below average positive word of mouth and above average negative word of mouth.

■ Dr. Paul Marsden, at LSE's Institute of Social Psychology, said: "These findings suggest that businesses seeking year-on-year growth may be overlooking their most powerful growth-generating asset; existing clients, customers or consumers. With a range of turn-key solutions for optimizing word of mouth advocacy, businesses can transform satisfied buyers into vocal advocates who become part of a volunteer sales force."[2]

Other companies have dug into this as well. The team at MotiveQuest, a social research group based in Evanston, Illinois, put out a white paper entitled *Beyond the Dashboard: The Correlation Between Online Advocacy and Offline Sales*. In the publication, the authors state: "The best metric of a brand's health in online conversation . . . is advocacy—the number of individuals actively promoting the brand."[3]

The researchers at MotiveQuest refer to themselves as "online anthropologists," and they study online chatter, social media sites, and forums to learn "what motivates groups of consumers and what you can do to turn them into your advocates."

What many brands have discovered, and what companies like MotiveQuest and their research support, is that you can now study, analyze, assess, and even measure the sound of the "buzz" surrounding your company. Until recently the concept of measuring buzz has seemed an almost magical, mystical, ephemeral idea. However, increasingly, findings indicate that buzz can, in fact, be measured, and what's more, it can be used to drive influence, recommendations, and sales.

The authors of *Beyond the Dashboard* go on to explain, "People's willingness to advocate for the brand online is a leading indicator of the brand's new-customer acquisition. . . . What people say online allows us to predict shifts in consumer behavior offline."

Time and again, studies have shown that increases in positive word of mouth recommendations portend future increases in sales.

A Whole New World Beyond the Net Promoter Score

As compelling and effective as the NPS is at capturing the intention of advocacy, it was conceived well in advance of the social web, so naturally it does not measure actual advocacy or detractors that occur on social channels.

New clients to Zócalo Group always ask us if we use the NPS in our measurements. "Of course," we tell them. But the NPS simply asks the question, "Would you recommend?" We now have the ability to also ask and answer so much more, including these:

- *Did* you recommend?
- Where, how, and why did you recommend?
- Were those recommendations from someone of influence in the category?
- How did others recommend?
- How do these recommendations compare to competitors and the industry?
- Did those recommendations make an impact? If so, where and how?

To generate useful information from the answers to those questions, the team at Zócalo Group created what we call the Recommendation Index, which provides insight into the positive and negative keywords and/or phrases used to trigger recommendations as well as the drivers of word of mouth.

The implications of this research are profound. If brands know where, how, and why recommendations are driven in their category, they can shape their products, offerings, and marketing messages to become the most recommended brands in their category.

Let me give you an idea of how the Recommendation Index works. While we've analyzed many different brands and industries, one of the more interesting—and relatable to a larger number of people—studies concerns the coffee chains.

Buying coffee to drink on the go is an American tradition and a $20 billion per year industry.[4] With more than 75 percent of U.S. adults consuming coffee[5] and more than a million conversations about the category occurring online over a period of 30 days, the Zócalo team uncovered, at the time the survey was done, the country's most recommended coffeehouse chains—and how they got that way.

Not surprisingly, Starbucks was the most talked about coffee chain online. But despite being the leader in online conversation volume, the brand was recommended in only about 1 in 200 conversations—while Caribou Coffee earned a recommendation once in every 20 conversations. Dunkin' Donuts and McDonald's followed Caribou in the Recommendation Index rankings of the top 10 largest coffeehouse chains operating in the United States.

The Recommendation Index found that top themes associated with positive coffeehouse chain recommendations included product quality and freshness, brand loyalty, and brew consistency. Primary drivers of negative word of mouth pointed to poor product quality, unskilled baristas, and brand detractors—all of which further illustrate the value consumers place on great taste and service when choosing where to buy their coffee.

Recommendation Index Results

The top 10 coffeehouse chains (of those operating in the United States) ranked by conversation volume during a recent 30-day period included those shown in Figure 5.1.

The Recommendation Index also evaluates the percentage of the conversation that is actually a positive recommendation. The top 10 coffeehouse chains (of those operating in the United States) ranked in this study by the level of positive recommendation included those shown in Figure 5.2.

In addition, the Recommendation Index provides insight into the positive and negative keywords and/or phrases used to trigger recommendations as well as the drivers of word of mouth. Top drivers of positive recommendations in the coffeehouse chain conversation included the following:

- **Product quality and freshness.** Good taste, always fresh, and delicious flavor

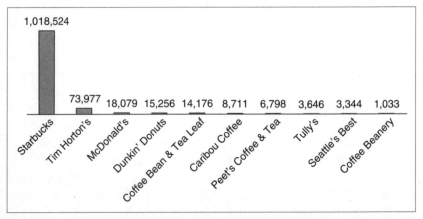

Figure 5.1 Conversation Volume (Number of Mentions).

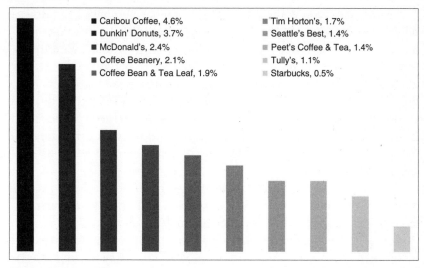

Figure 5.2 Percentage of Conversation with a Positive Recommendation.

- **Brand loyalty.** An unconditional affinity for a particular brand
- **Brew consistency.** Getting the same good cup of coffee time after time
- **Skilled baristas.** Friendly servers who create delicious specialty drinks
- **Physical location.** The best place to hang out, relax, and meet with friends

Top drivers of negative recommendations included the following:

- **Poor product quality.** Bad taste, poor flavor, and old or burned coffee
- **Unskilled baristas.** Servers who often "mess up" drinks
- **Brand detractors.** Overall dislike, contempt, or hatred for a particular brand
- **Exaggerated comparisons.** Tastes like dirt, tanning oil, and other substances
- **Physical side effects.** Complaints of discomfort associated with the coffee

Marketing Changing Insights

Imagine the implications. With these insights, what would you do if you were the marketing leaders of Caribou Coffee?

Chances are you'd keep doing a lot of what you have been doing, while also dialing up communications around those elements people love and talk about ("Our coffee is always fresh," "We hire for skilled and friendly baristas," and "We ensure product consistency at all costs"). You would also proactively ensure the marketers keep minimizing attributes known to drive negative recommendations (making sure coffee is never burned; ensuring that more pronounced flavors are clearly marked and communicated to avoid surprises; and increasing training and monitoring to ensure barista levels of skill and friendliness).

And if you are Starbucks? You'd have to decide if being recommended is important to you as a brand—and then you'd want to experiment with making the changes that will help evolve the high "volume" of conversations about your brand into a higher degree of recommendations. Or at a minimum, you'd make sure you are proactively addressing the high number of negative recommendations by helping consumers better understand your product attributes so they don't see them as negatives.

The best part? Marketers don't have to wait to conduct focus groups or ask consumers to fill out surveys. Nearly real time listening through social channels will let you know if you are succeeding or not in evolving your business into a social business and your brand into one that is highly recommendable.

CHAPTER 6

Why, Where, and How We Recommend

My career and my company changed the day I realized that people recommend paper towels.

In the earliest days of Zócalo Group, we were asked by Kimberly-Clark to help market their Viva brand of paper towels. Now, I must admit, I was hesitant about working with this brand at first. I just couldn't, for the life of me, understand why or how people could get excited by or recommend paper towels. Not in my home life and certainly not in my work life.

To me, paper towels were those things you got once a month, in bulk, at the cheapest rate possible at Costco or Sam's Club and forgot about for the next 30 days. Yes, it took a forklift and two neighbors to get them in the garage, but that was it—no more worrying about paper towels until next month.

It may not surprise you to discover that my wife had an entirely different theory about paper towels altogether. She, in fact, was a big fan of Viva towels—a brand loyalist to the nth degree and, not surprisingly, a vocal advocate. I quickly found out that she wasn't alone. In fact, she was in very good company.

Kimberly-Clark brought us in because they had heard we were doing good things with influencers and word of mouth marketing. I was excited because I always love a new challenge, but likewise intimidated by, again, the driving thought: "How are we going to get people excited, talking about and recommending paper towels?"

Well, it took me only about five minutes with the team to realize that the Viva towel brand was about more than just paper towels—a LOT more. And I quickly learned this other new fact as well: I was in the minority of folks who scrimped on paper towels.

One of the first things the folks at Viva did was show me the stacks of fan mail they got every week. (Yes, actually, paper towel brands do get fan mail. I have to admit, I was just as surprised as you may be right now.)

This was not just the same person writing over and over again to anyone who would listen. These were mothers, daughters, sons, husbands, wives, and anyone and everyone who had ever felt strongly enough about Viva paper towels to write to the company:

- "Love your brand!"
- "Don't change a thing."
- "I never use anything else."
- "You can use these towels over and over again."
- "Viva spells quality."
- "It's a staple of my kitchen."
- "I never scrimp on my paper towels. Glad to know you don't either!"

These comments convinced me that not only could the Viva brand benefit from the power of recommendations but also that it was already running under that very same steam. What strikes me as I recall the story was that, even then, as little as five or six years ago, social media was still in its infancy.

Yes, there were a few online groups sharing recommendations and awareness built around various brands and topics, but there was nowhere near the kind of platforms, networks, and groups that exist today. And yet here were people—we even toyed with calling them "Viva Divas"—at one point, who were vocal advocates for anyone who would listen.

No doubt, whether online or off, over the backyard fence, in the grocery store aisles, at work or on play dates, or anywhere else they could be heard, these Viva Divas were already influencing their own powerful networks with constant and reinforced recommendations.

What I saw then, at the crossroads between offline and online advocacy, was not just the power of influencers but the power of the Internet to enable influencers to spread their advocacy over a much wider reach. I knew then, on my way out of our first day of meetings with the folks from Viva, that the power of recommendations was only going to grow with each passing day, and I've been fortunate to have had a front row seat for that growth since the very infancy of social media on the web.

Why Do People Recommend?

You will probably be, at first, mildly surprised—and then strongly encouraged—to discover that, according to eMarketer.com, most people recommend a product or service because they **genuinely want to help.**

Whether it's "just" paper towels or something more major like a brand of car or a favorite restaurant, at least half of consumers list a "good experience with a product or service" as the reason why they recommend it. Meanwhile, a full 37 percent genuinely "want to help others."

And while "incentives and rewards" are often used to encourage advocacy, only 1 percent of consumers list this as a reason why they recommend any product or service to anybody (see Figure 6.1).

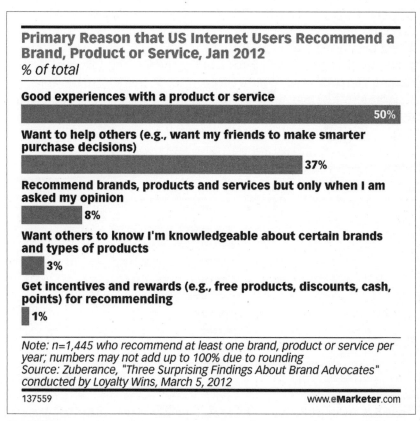

Figure 6.1

Researcher Ed Keller has, along with Brad Fay, written a new book called *The Face-to-Facebook: Why Real Relationships Rule in a Digital Marketplace.*[1] In it he states that "the average American talks each day about roughly 10 brands" and that "the typical brand conversation lasts between three and five minutes." He continues, "More than two thirds of these conversations involve a recommendation to buy, consider, or avoid the brand."

Imagine that: 10 brands a day, for three to five minutes. Consider the power of those minutes, of those face-to-face recommendations, whether they're being made over miles of DSL cable or the back fence.

Other researchers have come to even more sanguine conclusions: the average consumer in the United States makes 17 recommendations per week, according to a 2009 study.[2]

The idea of what is considered an online "recommendation" today by the average consumer is also quite surprising. Zócalo Group recently fielded the *2013 Recommendation Study* and learned that consumers actively consider YouTube reviews (46.5 percent), a friend Liking a brand page of Facebook (46.1 percent), and an online positive brand review (45.5 percent) as the leading forms of online recommendations (see Figure 6.2).

If you're like me, you wonder about what makes people tick. Why do they become loyal to brands in the first place, and why

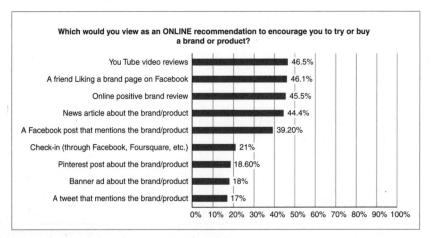

Figure 6.2 Different Forms of Online Recommendations. (Source: Zócalo Group, "2013 Recommendations Study," April 2013.)

do they stay loyal to the point of reviewing them online and often writing to the companies directly, providing feedback, support, and even ratings?

Earlier in this chapter I said you'd be encouraged by why, exactly, people recommend. Here's why I, personally, feel encouraged by this news: when you get to understand why people do what they do, when you realize that, statistically speaking, people make recommendations because they genuinely, sincerely want to help, you can get excited about how your product or service helps them.

Then again, not everyone is out there cheering your name simply to help make the world a better place. There are a variety of other reasons why we recommend, but few sum it up as well as the work of Pete Blackshaw, Nestlé's global head of digital and social media, who offers **five different reasons** why people recommend products and services for friends beyond the obvious (for example, we like and value the product):

1. **"First to know and first to tell."** A form of self-validation, letting others know that you are an "early elite product tester" or otherwise more knowledgeable about a product or service
2. **"Favor banking."** Trading currency or sharing with others who share back with you
3. **"Credibility rub-off."** When a brand has a particularly good reputation, knowing that its products can be recommended before they are even tested
4. **"Projection."** Recommending something to project a desired image of oneself onto others, generally one not earned
5. **"Genuine brand love."** Brand fans, generally 100 percent sincere[3]

One thing that should fascinate leaders of any company, big or small, is the mentality behind why people Like something on Facebook. Since a simple Facebook fan page is so easy to set up, maintain, and integrate into a social media campaign, it's generally a part of most, if not every, company's social media campaign.

But understanding the mentality of Facebook users is key to finding success on what is arguably the world's most popular social media platform. Furthermore, by virtue of its so-simple-it's-brilliant Like feature, Facebook is the leading proponent of recommendation culture.

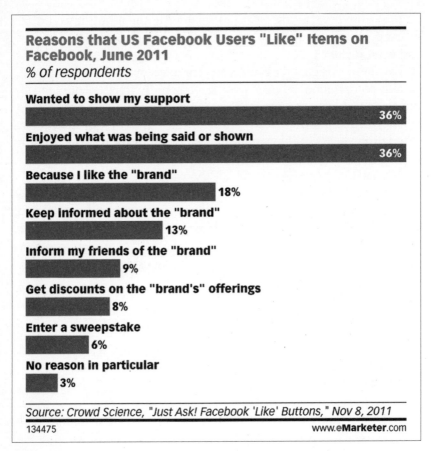

Reasons that US Facebook Users "Like" Items on Facebook, June 2011
% of respondents

Wanted to show my support
36%

Enjoyed what was being said or shown
36%

Because I like the "brand"
18%

Keep informed about the "brand"
13%

Inform my friends of the "brand"
9%

Get discounts on the "brand's" offerings
8%

Enter a sweepstake
6%

No reason in particular
3%

Source: Crowd Science, "Just Ask! Facebook 'Like' Buttons," Nov 8, 2011
134475   www.**eMarketer**.com

Figure 6.3

Why do Facebook users Like what they like? Several reports have established a pattern of likability that should definitely inform our *why* conversation.

For instance, in June 2011, 36 percent of U.S. Facebook users told Crowd Science that they Like an item on Facebook because they want to show support (see Figure 6.3). Other reasons included that they "enjoyed what was being said or shown," they "like the brand" or want to "inform [their] friends about the brand."[4]

There also continues to be plenty of debate about the value of a Facebook Like, a Twitter Follow, or a Pinterest Pin. While the debate will likely rage on, recent studies indicate that consumers are far more likely to purchase, talk about, and recommend a product

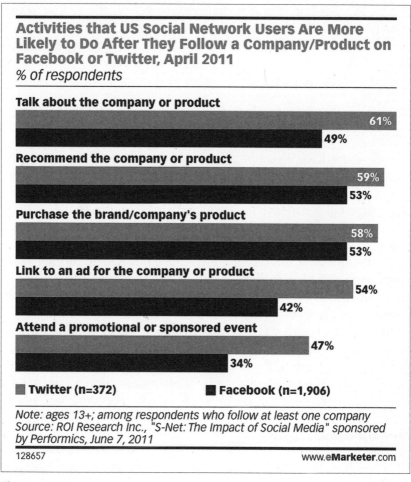

Activities that US Social Network Users Are More Likely to Do After They Follow a Company/Product on Facebook or Twitter, April 2011
% of respondents

Talk about the company or product
- 61%
- 49%

Recommend the company or product
- 59%
- 53%

Purchase the brand/company's product
- 58%
- 53%

Link to an ad for the company or product
- 54%
- 42%

Attend a promotional or sponsored event
- 47%
- 34%

■ Twitter (n=372)   ■ Facebook (n=1,906)

Note: ages 13+; among respondents who follow at least one company Source: ROI Research Inc., "S-Net: The Impact of Social Media" sponsored by Performics, June 7, 2011

128657   www.e**Marketer**.com

Figure 6.4

once they have become engaged with the brand on a social network (see Figure 6.4).

Of course, getting people to talk about you, even Like you, is all well and good. But the real goal of social media and recommendation marketing is to get them to say what you want them to say about you. Unfortunately, this is easier said than done.

Case in point: in 2011, 64 percent of social media marketers worldwide told Microsoft Advertising that it was a challenge to get people to talk about their goods and services on social media in a way that matched their desired brand attributes. Nearly 70 percent of respondents said it was a challenge to get people to talk about their goods and services on social media "at all."

Which brings us to our next point. If we can better understand why people recommend a brand, product, or service, we can then discover where they do so.

Where Do People Recommend?

We all know that Amazon.com has been at the forefront of this recommendation age since its inception. From user reviews to "list-manias" to sharing likes or dislikes on Twitter and Facebook, this dynamic e-tailer has taken great pains to stay on top of the cutting-edge ways its customers can recommend products to and with each other.

A recent report by Trevor Pinch and Filip Kesler entitled *How Aunt Ammy Gets Her Free Lunch: A Study of the Top-Thousand Customer Reviewers at Amazon.com*[5] begins to shed some light on Amazon's recommendation machine.

State the authors, "Given that Amazon is the world's largest online retailer, why is it that so many people work, in effect, for free for Amazon by providing content for the website for no remuneration? Is this even true? Our study holds an assumption and asks a question: the assumption is that there are no free lunches. So how come Amazon has managed to persuade so many people to give them the morsels from which they have built one of the biggest free lunches ever? That is the question."

What the researchers discovered was that one reason Amazon .com has found such a wealth of unpaid recommenders was its system of ranking reviewers. As one might imagine, Amazon.com has millions of products to sell and nearly that many people to review those products. By using a ranking system, those who rate and review the most books naturally rise to the top of the rankings.

It turns out that reviewers are rather protective of their rankings, which give them a sense of recognition for their work, as well as a sense of accomplishment and reward. Altruism was also a featured benefit, tying back to our intrinsic reason for *why* people recommend anything, anywhere.

The report is critical because Amazon is the first *where* for many would-be recommenders, who can review everything from books to movies to CDs to children's toys to shoes to dresses to gardening tools to, yes, even Viva paper towels.

Amazon may have started the "reviewing" trend, or at least been integral in making it acceptable worldwide, but today the *where* of reading, rating, and recommending is almost endless:

- Corporate and company websites like BestBuy.com where consumers can make recommendations and ratings based on past purchases to, again, help other consumers make wise buying decisions
- Online e-tailers like Amazon.com where users can rate, discuss (through forums), and otherwise endorse or warn against various products, services, and brands
- Entertainment websites, like RottenTomatoes.com where user rankings, both from recognized movie critics and everyday viewers, consort to give films various percentage ratings
- Thousands of special interest communities or forums where consumers talk about everything from household cleaning products (CleaningTalk.com) to running shoes (letsrun.com) to chemotherapy nausea therapies and medications (CancerCare.org)
- Global communities ranging from Cloob (Iran) to Cyworld (South Korea) to Fotolog (South America and Spain) to Grono (Poland) and literally hundreds of others

Where in the World Are People Recommending?

While it's easy to view the recommendation age from our own unique, U.S. vantage point, the fact is that word of mouth marketing is a global phenomenon.

Moreover, much as the United States itself has certain populations of citizens that are more likely to recommend products than others—teens or housewives or college students or seniors, and others—various countries are more likely to recommend than others. A recent study conducted by Jack Morton Worldwide found that the Chinese are "far more likely to be brand advocates and/or recommenders than [people] in the United States."[6]

In fact, the study found that "80 percent of Internet users indicated that when they are passionate about a brand or brands, they become active advocates for them; [this was a] larger percentage than among Internet users in the United States, Brazil, or India."

"Chinese netizens are more vocal and like to be in the know or be the expert among friends when it comes to recommendations," notes Scarlett Lok, head of digital for the agency TBWA/Tequila/ Shanghai when asked to explain the study's results.

Offline Is Where It's At

What's extremely powerful to note, particularly in a world seemingly obsessed with social media and developing an online presence, is the number of recommendations that take place offline. According to the Keller Fay Group's TalkTrack data, "90 percent of all word of mouth conversations happen offline, while 10 percent are online."[7]

The data further reports that there are upwards of "15 billion word of mouth impressions" about brands in the United States every week. Surprisingly enough, with all its hyperactivity, social media accounts for only "1.2 billion impressions" per week.

Viewing the chart in Figure 6.5, it's encouraging to see that some things, in fact, never change. It is hard to imagine that in a world in which so much time is spent online, most recommendations are still made "face-to-face," via a lunchtime chat, a carpool to work, an idle dinner conversation, or a simple phone call.

Don't be misled, though, by the seemingly overwhelming preponderance of offline recommendations. While the majority of word of mouth most certainly occurs offline, online information, opinions, and data are increasingly the most important fodder to allow these offline brand conversations to occur.

How Do People Recommend?

We've discussed *why*, and we've discussed *where*. Now it's time to talk about just *how*, exactly, those endorsements are made.

The Two Types of Endorsements: Explicit and Implied

Although people endorse all kinds of products, services, brands, and companies in a variety of locations, there are basically two types of endorsements:

- ■ **Explicit.** Explicit recommendations are direct and purposeful with the intent of sharing information and encouraging action. An example of an **explicit** recommendation is a review on Yelp, where a user explicitly offers advice to visit a particular restaurant, hotel, or some other place. This is an

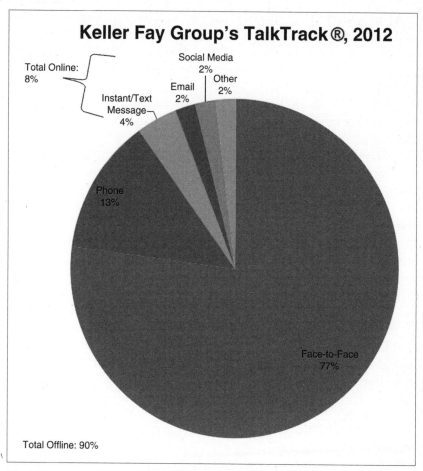

Figure 6.5 Where Word of Mouth Impressions Are Taking Place. (Source: Keller Fay Group's TalkTrack, December 2012.)

active, verbal, and purposeful statement. It takes time to log onto Yelp, rate an establishment, and then, further, to write up a quick one- to two-paragraph blurb.

- **Implied.** Recommendations don't have to be explicit to be effective. An example of an **implied** recommendation would be a check-in on Foursquare, where it is implied that, because a friend is visiting a particular restaurant or other venue, it is more highly recommended than those *not* visited. We can also imply a recommendation when we Like a certain Facebook page.

What's interesting is how often we recommend things without even realizing we're doing it. How many times a day do we implicitly recommend a product, service, movie, book, CD, artist, or something else by Liking it on Facebook or retweeting our opinion on Twitter?

Or when our friends see us on Foursquare eating out at Five Guys Burgers three times a week or when they see us posting an awesome looking book cover or movie poster on Pinterest? Even wearing an Old Navy or American Eagle or Hollister shirt emblazoned with the company logo is passively recommending those stores to anyone and everyone we see that day.

Thumbs Up or Down

Long before Amazon.com made one- and five-star ratings commonplace or even RottenTomatoes.com appeared with its algorithm for rating movies based on the percentage of critics' reviews, Gene Siskel and Roger Ebert made recommending literally as easy as a thumbs up or down when they began rating movies—with a thumbs up or down—on their national TV show *At the Movies*.

This simple pass-or-fail, yes-or-no approach made being a movie critic a spectator sport, something we could all engage in wordlessly, with one digit! Today, of course, many companies take positive and negative recommendations quite seriously, and with good reason.

Many businesses think that the majority of brand talk and recommendations are negative. TalkTrack has found, however, that it is just 8 percent. However, that doesn't necessarily mean that the other 92 percent are all positive. In fact, 66 percent of all brand word of mouth is described by respondents as "truly positive"; another 11 percent is "neutral" about the brand, and 15 percent is a mixture of positive and negative.

People exposed to positive opinions assign greater credibility than those exposed to negative ones. When people hear something positive about a brand, 66 percent assign a "very high credibility" to it, rating it 9 or 10 on a credibility scale ranging from 0 to 10. That compares to only 47 percent who give the same credibility to negative opinions about brands. Also, negative WOM is less viral than positive—with 56 percent saying they are highly likely to tell others about something positive compared to 41 percent saying they are highly likely to tell others about something negative.

A Case Study in Fandom: *The Frito-Lay Fan Program*

I want to end this section on how we recommend with one of Zócalo Group's case studies, which will show you how advocates are discovered, nurtured, and encouraged.

Many consumers LOVE Frito-Lay products and regularly share news and information about the snacks with their friends and social networks. Frito-Lay's motto, "good fun," captures the essence of its entire portfolio of snack chips, including best-loved brands like Lay's potato chips, Fritos corn chips, Tostitos tortilla chips, and SunChips multigrain snacks.

For more than two decades, the company has been giving "good" even more meaning by making its snacks more wholesome through a number of corporate initiatives: converting to better oils, voluntarily removing trans fat from snack chips years ahead of other food companies, and focusing on the simple, farm-grown ingredients it uses to make many of its snacks.

To help Frito-Lay fans share their love for the products and the positive messages about how the snacks are made, the brand launched the Frito-Lay Fan program. The objectives were straightforward:

- Increase sharing among Frito-Lay's most socially active brand evangelists
- Equip fans with "the truth about chips," helping to correct any myths and misperceptions
- Celebrate fans and their love for Frito-Lay snacks

The Insight

Through digital monitoring, our team discovered thousands of online conversations occurring each month among socially savvy consumers who were recommending Frito-Lay and its brands. With 6.2 percent of digital consumers driving 80 percent of online impressions about products and services,[8] Frito-Lay recognized the opportunity to leverage its most socially active, passionate brand advocates to drive positive online dialogue and help change brand perception among "Joe and Jill Consumer."

Frito-Lay realized that these fans—if armed with the right messaging—held huge potential in preserving, protecting, and elevating the reputation of Frito-Lay and its brands. Additionally, Frito-Lay understood that there was a big opportunity to educate those who had misperceptions about the brands. Why not encourage those who already love your brand to advocate with the right messaging?

The Solution

To activate its vocal advocates, we worked with Frito-Lay to launch the Frito-Lay Fan program, through which we initiated a relationship with the company's most socially active consumers. While other corporate reputation programs in place at Frito-Lay covered top-tier bloggers, influencers, and media, the Frito-Lay Fan program targeted **real fans**, active in the social media space, redefining "media" and "influencers" for the company.

Frito-Lay leveraged the following process to build and activate the Frito-Lay Fan network.

Find

As a first step, we worked with Frito-Lay to formalize the list of potential fans. This list was developed in two ways. First, we listened to conversations online for positive chatter about and advocacy for Frito-Lay and its brands to identify and engage chip lovers.

Second, we identified brand advocates interested in further communications with the company and vetted this list based on social influence. Throughout the program, Frito-Lay also monitored for negative comments to find opportunities to educate and correct misperceptions.

Gather

Frito-Lay then invited these consumers to join the Frito-Lay Fan program, gathering their information into a database for ongoing engagement. The outreach process involved initiating relevant conversations about the snacks these consumers love and creating unique opportunities to share the brand's key messaging around its products, great flavors, simple ingredients, wholesome snacking, and environmental sustainability.

Feed

We then seeded "registered" fans with relevant and exclusive content and inspired them to share fun facts and giveaway offers with their own audiences, and we educated these fans about applicable disclosure requirements.

At random, we distributed "fan packs" complete with product samples, Frito-Lay–branded merchandise, as well as information about Frito-Lay's nutrition and sustainability initiatives.

To keep fans connected with the company and at the forefront of company news, product launches, and events during relevant moments in time, all fans received *Frito-Lay FanFare*, a quarterly e-newsletter, which further drove conversation.

Grow

Frito-Lay inspired fans to share this information with others and talk about their passion for Frito-Lay snacks by offering fun and exclusive engagements that inspired them to proudly evangelize on Frito-Lay's behalf. For example, the brand hosted an "Ode to Chips" poetry contest in which fans expressed their love for Frito-Lay chips for the chance to be featured in an Ode to Chips poem posted on the company's *Snack Chat*[9] blog and to win a Frito-Lay Fan T-shirt. Additionally, advocacy was rewarded through Fan of the Week features on *Snack Chat* and via Twitter.

Below is a sample of Frito-Lay Fans' quotes, showcasing how these consumers began advocating on behalf of Frito-Lay:

- "I especially love Frito-Lay chips. . . . Frito-Lay offers a large variety of tasty snacks made with farm-grown ingredients, and many of their chips are made with just three simple ingredients."
- "Making great tasting snacks and helping to make the environment better? Yeah, I will be a fan of Frito-Lay for a very long time!"
- "Frito-Lay starts with farm-grown ingredients . . . potatoes or corn, oils, and salt."
- "The Lay's Lightly Salted Chips were also nice to snack on. . . . I cannot wait to add these chips to our holiday gatherings."
- "I never realized that Frito-Lay carried products with 50 percent less sodium than the originals until I connected with your program. They taste just as good as the chips with more sodium."

The Frito-Lay Fan program changed the way Frito-Lay conversed with consumers by allowing the company to build solid relationships with the right fans and share accurate, fun information in a manner appealing and exciting for fans. Frito-Lay continues to engage its fan community to further drive key messaging and share news about big initiatives, offer "fan-exclusive" opportunities, as well as foster further evangelism with the continually growing fan base.

The Results

A Frito-Lay Fan survey demonstrated the program's success and achieved the objective of increasing positive perception:

- 94 percent of fans recommended Frito-Lay and/or its snacks to others after joining the program.
- 82 percent of fans felt more informed about the nutrition of Frito-Lay snacks after engagement.
- 78 percent of fans felt more enthusiastic about the company thanks to the fan-specific programming.

Through the Frito-Lay Fan program, the company successfully built a network of consumer advocates to engage with online and to help shift perceptions about its snacks. The team recruited more than 1,300 socially active brand advocates during 2010, the first year of programming, each of whom, on average, posted publicly about Frito-Lay six times and reached 10,000 people. The Frito-Lay Fan program caught early momentum, with *Fast Company* highlighting one of the "inside look" videos produced as part of the program. After the first year of activation, the Frito-Lay Fan program generated twice as many positive social media impressions than planned for Frito-Lay.

While other programs focused on top-tier bloggers, influencers, and media, the fan program built an army of real consumer advocates who increased positive conversations and peer recommendations for Frito-Lay and successfully helped improve perceptions about its snacks.

CHAPTER 7

Some Recommendations Are More Valuable Than Others

The Oprah Effect and the Influencer Ecosystem

After years of sending samples of his book lights to the *Oprah Winfrey Show*, Lightwedge CEO James Bennett was told by producers to "stop sending" his free product samples to the show. Bennett jokes, "Their exact words were, 'We have plenty of samples, thank you very much.'"

However, a few weeks after the last rejection, Bennett noticed a distinct spike on the company's website: from an average of $3,700 in sales per day to $90,000 in sales in a single afternoon.

Bennett later discovered that a sleep expert named Dr. Michael Bruce had recently done a segment on *Oprah* about products that help people get a good night's sleep, and he had brought with him a reading light made by Bennett's Newton, Massachusetts–based company.

During one part of the segment, Oprah simply took the light out of Dr. Bruce's hands and said, "I have to get one of these." As a result of that brief declaration, sales exploded. Even after the spike, sales continued at more than **five times the usual rate** straight through the holiday season and well into February. Meanwhile, retail sales of the product at major bookstores also increased by a factor of five.

The Oprah Effect

What I know for sure is that what you give comes back to you.
—**OPRAH WINFREY**

Now, *that's* influence. In fact, the "Oprah Effect" has been credited with all kinds of unprecedented success stories, everything from helping elect President Barak Obama in 2008 to reinvigorating book sales for authors like Mark Nepo, who's *The Book of Awakening* was featured, to launching previously little known beauty products, like those of Carol's Daughter, into the sales stratosphere.

The Oprah Effect was a game changer not just for companies like Lightwedge and Carol's Daughter or even Old Navy, which sold out of a particular clothing line the week it was featured on the great and mighty *Oprah* show, but for many individuals as well, people for whom it was a *life* changer.

The unprecedented influence of Oprah on her 42 million viewers meant that a single five-minute appearance or a quick blurb in her magazine or a link on her website would create unlimited potential for a company, author, or individual willing to, as Oprah always so succinctly put it, "meet opportunity with preparation."

Of course, there is only one Oprah. But there are thousands of other "persons of influence" out there in the world, whose recommendations can help launch and sustain your business. The key is finding the right ones and actively engaging with and maintaining them.

Who's More Powerful: *An Influencer or the Average Joe?*

In 2000, Malcolm Gladwell wrote his powerful tome *The Tipping Point.*[1] Clearly, Gladwell hit a chord with his timely book, which promoted the concept that "ideas and products and messages spread like viruses do." The messages resonate so well that *The Tipping Point* continues to hold a spot on the *New York Times* Best Sellers list as well as top rankings in the Amazon top 100 list. (In fact, it was number 1 in Amazon's "marketing" books category the day I checked it, over a decade later.)

In his book, Gladwell promotes the idea of "the law of the few," arguing, "The success of any kind of social epidemic is heavily dependent on the involvement of people with a particular and rare set of social gifts."

What is the Oprah Effect, I would ask, other than a kind of "social epidemic"? Gladwell goes on to describe these people with "a particular and rare set of social gifts" in the following ways:

- **Connectors** are the people in a community who know large numbers of people and are in the habit of making introductions.
- **Mavens** are "information specialists," or "people we rely upon to connect us with new information."
- **Salespeople** are "persuaders," charismatic people with powerful negotiation skills.

The power of Gladwell's perceptions wasn't as much in his presenting something new as it was in his presenting it in a new way. As evidence, as you were reading the above descriptions, you no doubt were nodding your head, putting a face with each name.

The **connectors** are always in the thick of things, treating life like one big cocktail party, introducing everyone to everyone and following through to make sure a connection was made.

The **mavens** always have the latest cell phone, tablet, movie recommendation, or tip for getting in at the best restaurant, and they always keep their finger on the pulse of a select number of products or even niches. And, finally, the **salespeople** in your network can always easily convince you that such and such is the must-have item, the must-see movie, or the must-eat place.

Of course, as we've seen throughout this book, the power of influence is nothing new. What *The Tipping Point* did so effectively was give those interested in marketing (and aren't we all?) the science behind epidemics and a name for those powerful influences we needed to target to create our own.

But Gladwell wasn't alone in studying the significance of tipping points or the phenomenon of social epidemics. Plenty of researchers have weighed in on the subject as well.

Beyond the Tipping Point: *The Power of Influence*

According to Forrester Research published in April 2010, people in the United States are generating more than **500 billion online**

impressions on each other each year. I suppose this shouldn't really be shocking considering how much we talk about our favorite products, movies, CDs, tires, software programs, and the like.

What *was* interesting was how the research found that a **dedicated few** were influencing a majority of **the whole**. Forrester found that a mere 6.2 percent of online consumers were generating 80 percent of these 500 billion impressions.[2] At Zócalo, we call this passionate vocal minority **brand fans**—people like football fans or movie fans or book fans or any other type of fan who proudly, prolifically, and passionately root for their "team," that is, their brand.

Borrowing some of Gladwell's groundbreaking terminology, Forrester researchers broke these brand fans down into two segments—what they called **mass connectors** and **mass mavens** (see Figure 7.1):

- **Mass connectors** (MCs) are the 6.2 percent of the U.S. online population that generates 80 percent of all the impressions about products and services within social networks.

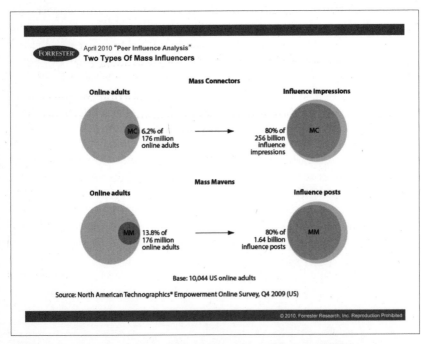

Figure 7.1 Mass Connectors (MCs) Versus Mass Mavens (MMs). (Source: Forrester Research, Inc., *Peer Influence Analysis*, April 2010.)

■ **Mass mavens** (MMs) are the 13.8 percent of the online population that creates 80 percent of all opinions about products and services in blog posts, blog comments, discussion forum posts, and reviews. (There is an overlap of 7 million individuals, 3.7 percent of the online population, between the two groups.)[3]

Not surprisingly, given the breadth of its exposure for over a decade now, there have been a number of detractors to Gladwell's influencer-based model, the most prominent being an ex-Yahoo! research scientist and author (*Everything Is Obvious, Six Degrees: The Science of a Connected Age*, and other books) named Duncan Watts, who contends that there really is no such person as an "influential."

Instead, Watts argues about the power of the "average Joe" and rails against the concept of single individuals who are capable of starting trends. "A rare bunch of cool people just don't have that power," Watts notes in a *Fast Company* interview.[4]

Another organization, which sells a highly promoted "brand advocate platform," goes so far as to rail against "influencers" as being overrated and having "their own agenda" while pointing out that "true influence drives action, not awareness." As in most cases when you have polarized views, either for or against, both perspectives have elements of truth. There are, in fact, individuals whose knowledge and influence are critical to supporting an idea—and then there are those individuals, many celebrated and many not, the "average Joes" if you will, who are essential to driving large-scale adoption and recommendation.

The Influencer Ecosystem

At Zócalo Group, we have organized this confluence of influencers, adopters, recommenders, and fans, even detractors, and it looks something like the diagram shown in Figure 7.2. Think about all of the people that influence the things you talk about, consider, and even purchase. They range from your friends to "experts" to pundits and even to detractors of a brand.

Let me give you a recent real-life example. I love music and have accumulated more than a terabyte (thousands and thousands of tracs)

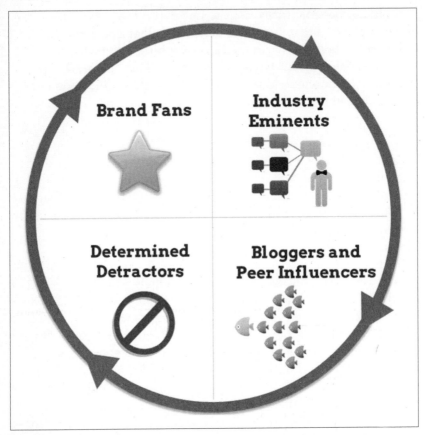

Figure 7.2 Zócalo Group's Influencer Ecosystem: Engage Influencers to Drive Sustainable Recommendations. (Source: Zócalo Group.)

of digital songs. I was looking for a new way to easily store, access, and play all this music when my buddy Joe recommended the Sonos music system. Joe's a real audiophile, and he gladly brought me into his home to show and tell just how wonderful Sonos worked for him. He's a true Sonos brand fan.

I'm glad Joe's a sincere advocate. But I'm not willing to make such an investment on just his advice. I want to know what the pros think. So I go to Engadget.com (one of my favorite sites) and read a review by Terence O'Brian. It gets high marks: "Sonos is for people who have embraced the digital music revolution but don't want to be stuck sitting in front of the computer or tethered to an iPod when the mood to groove strikes."

So far, so good. Joe the brand fan loves it. And so does the professional audio expert. Now, what about everyday consumers or peer influencers? And who doesn't like the product and why?

Naturally, I check some online review sites. "PeteTechGuy" in Woodside, California, gives Sonos 5.0 out of 5 stars and says, "Sonos is a dream come true." But another reviewer does not like the product at all: "What they promised was easy set-up was not, and I contacted customer service three times and received apologies but zero solutions. I will instead purchase an iPod, which will work just great. I should have done that in the first place." This reviewer goes beyond giving the product just a negative review. He becomes a determined detractor: "Sonos is all about $ales and not about recommending appropriate solutions."

We call this collection of voices the **influencer ecosystem**. All those sources work together to impact the perceptions and buying behaviors of entire audiences. The influencer ecosystem comprises the instigators and shapers of word of mouth and recommendations. It is important for every brand to know who is in its ecosystem, what is driving them, and how to successfully interact with them:

- **Brand fans.** The most potent and influential advocates a brand can have. Brand fans are excited to talk about and share their love for a brand.
- **Industry eminents.** Influencers and thought leaders—often in a professional capacity—who have broad reach and impact over the perceptions and buying decisions of a category or industry.
- **Peer influencers.** Everyday people who have gained social credibility through their networks and have voiced particular interest or passion for a product, brand, or category.
- **Determined detractors.** People who—for whatever reason—criticize, attack, or are just vocal about their dislike for a brand. We will dig deeper into how this specific group can challenge any company and, in Chapter 12, how to combat their negative influence.

Truly successful and sustainable word of mouth and recommendation programs engage each element of the influencer ecosystem in ways that are relevant, compelling, and ultimately sharable—both online and offline. Negative word of mouth is significantly more damaging than the upside of positive word of mouth. Managing detraction is a huge issue moving forward and carries as much, if not more, influence than the first three categories.

Let's dig deeper into each layer of the influencer ecosystem and discover what we need to do to attract these influencers, interact with them, engage them, and more.

Brand Fans

"Twihards" are just one example of some very extreme brand fans, so named for their rabid loyalty to the *Twilight* series of books, films, and paraphernalia. Their loyalty is not only very vocal but very visual; Twihards are the ones you see camping out weeks in advance of a new *Twilight* movie, featuring homemade "Team Edward" or "Team Jacob" T-shirts.

Likewise, "Parrotheads," the ubiquitous fan base for living legend Jimmy Buffet, are just as vocal and have been around for decades, following their fearless troubadour from town to town, concert to concert, decking themselves out in fancy parrot hats and tropical shirts and tailgating in the parking lot of each concert venue much like football fans before a big game.

Despite how powerful, vocal, and omnipresent they may seem, brand fans typically only make up 4 to 7 percent of a company's consumer population. So while 95 percent of folks who've seen a *Twilight* movie may have enjoyed it, told a few people or not, they're generally not brand fans in that they're not necessarily vocally supportive, let alone visibly. Rather than becoming brand fans, they're more like "brand mehs," collectively shrugging their shoulders and moving onto the next consumer experience.

So it's critical that you not only identify your brand fans but actively engage them in a variety of promotions, contests, rewards, and mentions. Keeping your brand fans in mind is an important aspect of brand management, and since they are the most receptive to influence—unlike, say, our next three quadrants—they should be the first in line for your ear, your attention, your attentiveness, and your affection.

Industry Eminents

Marion Nestle runs a food blog called *Food Politics*. She is the Paulette Goddard Professor in the Department of Nutrition, Food Studies, and Public Health (the department she chaired from 1988 to 2003) and a professor of sociology at New York University. She's written a number of books, from *Why Calories Count* to *Safe Food* to *Feed Your Pet Right*. Her column appears monthly in the *San Francisco Chronicle*.

And yet, despite her glowing résumé, esteemed CV, and very public persona, you've probably never heard of her. But as someone who works with a variety of food-centric clients, I can tell you that every one of them has heard of her, is concerned about what she has to say, and consciously covets her endorsement.

Not that she gives any. Marion Nestle is a fervent individualist and she is in nobody's pocket. Yet she recognizes the reality of mass-produced foodstuffs and consumer marketing and speaks frequently about a variety of companies, CEOs, and products and services that either earn her scorn or tacit endorsement.

In a very real way, in a very big industry, Marion Nestle is an industry eminent: a high-placed, highly vocal, and highly esteemed voice that, much the same way as the Oprah Effect could make or break a product, can in her own unique way endorse or discount a food product, service, company, or initiative.

She is a great example to use for this tier of your influencer eco-system because while not exactly a household name, in her particular niche she is a very, very big deal. Believe me, whether you're dealing in tires or sneakers or sports drinks or cancer treatments or wigs or books or movies or super glue, every industry has its handful of eminents.

As one might imagine, it takes quite an impressive pedigree to become an eminent, which is why there are only between 300 and 500 of them in any particular industry at any one time. Here at Zócalo Group we have amassed a database—called ZócaloNet—of tens of thousands of top-tier experts listed on a global level, in nearly every category, including photography, sports, food, and software and technology.

Peer Influencers

As important as brand fans and industry eminents are, many consumers listen to no one other than their peers, and only their peers, be it in person or online.

In a survey of more than 1,300 people conducted by the CMO Council and Lithium, 80 percent of consumers said that they are more likely to try new things based on friends' suggestions made in social media, and 74 percent are more likely to encourage friends to try new products.[5]

Attitudes Toward Brand Advocacy Among Internet Users in Select Countries, Oct 2011
% of respondents

	US	Brazil	China	India	Total
I only advocate brands when I have had great personal experiences with them	79%	74%	78%	78%	76%
With all the media and information available to me, if a brand wants to get my attention it has to do something special	65%	71%	84%	78%	75%
I feel so strongly about a certain brand, or brands, I am an active advocate for them	62%	51%	80%	74%	66%

Note: ages 18+
Source: Jack Morton Worldwide, "New Realities 2012," Jan 26, 2012

136517   www.**eMarketer**.com

Figure 7.3

In the Forrester word of mouth survey "How European Consumers Share Opinions," the researchers discovered that "European consumers prefer advice from their peers when making purchase decisions. And they trust this advice more than advertising messages or marketing communications." The authors of the study added, "More than 90 percent of online Europeans share information and opinions with their friends and family."[6]

Figure 7.3 provides an informative slide from eMarketer.com that shows the attitudes of various countries toward brand advocacy, showing who is more vocal, or more likely to be vocal, across the globe.

Clearly, peer influencers are a HUGE component of the influencer ecosystem, but so far we've discussed only the positive WOM that can serve to help companies. Now it's time to delve into the opposite end of the spectrum and discover how a small number of "determined detractors" can do as much harm as the other three groups combined can do good.

Determined Detractors

With the good always comes the bad, and nowhere is that truism more true than when dealing with the general public, particularly when trying to ask them for money or trying to sell them something. Irate customers, naysayers, doom and gloomers, and general malcontents have always been a presence on the consumer landscape, but never have they been given such a wide and public voice as with today's opportunities and reliance on social media.

Before the Internet, determined detractors had to be really determined to have their voices heard beyond their own backyards or see their occasional letter of complaint to the company in question achieve wide circulation. Today, in two clicks or fewer, they can spread their messages to hundreds, thousands, even hundreds of thousands, depending on their "reach."

Between message forums and blogs and consumer review sites and even a company's own website, these determined detractors can now do real damage to companies unwilling, unprepared, or simply unable to handle them properly.

One shining light in dealing with negative online chatter was the way Domino's Pizza embraced critics to actually improve their product. Says the American Management Association, "Domino's Pizza could have just promoted its new and improved product, communicating the positives without acknowledging the critics, but it chose a different route.

"The company built its entire campaign in 2010 around its 'pizza turnaround,' with television ads featuring focus group critics expressing their dislike for the product. The reworked recipe and self-deprecating communications campaign fueled a 14.3 percent jump in same-restaurant sales in the United States. Domino's Pizza used the power of online interaction, where transparency and authenticity are rewarded. In kind, the pizza giant was rewarded for its candor and attention to consumer input."[7]

Today, anyone who orders a Domino's pizza can see that evidence literally plastered all over the pizza box, whether in the form of quotes from satisfied customers or admission that their crust "used to taste like the box!" Customer satisfaction ratings are plainly evident under every item on the menu with little to no filter. Marketing strategy or not, few public companies are as transparent in their customer satisfaction ratings as Domino's Pizza. Then again, it's easier to get good ratings when you've put in the effort—and expense—to earn them.

It can be continually frustrating to discover that you not only have determined detractors but in addition, they are forceful, frequent, and focused on tarnishing your reputation by any and all means possible. It can even be costly in the manpower and hours it takes to combat, control, and undo the damage they create. However, in terms of nipping such behavior in the bud, the time you spend now is far superior to the costs if this behavior is left unmatched.

Once again, prevention is key. Domino's clearly saw the writing on the wall pre-reformation and chose to do something very drastic about it. In a very similar way, finding itself faced with new competition all the time in the "freshness" market, our client SUBWAY recently took active, even aggressive, steps to put a positive face forward, as the following case study will present.

SUBWAY: *A Case Study in Freshness*

Beyond the catchy "$5 FOOTLONG" jingle and its affordable food offerings, SUBWAY continues to maintain its slogan promoting health, "Eat Fresh." In 2012, we worked with SUBWAY to more fully embrace its entire influencer ecosystem around the promotion of wellness.

The Background

To kick off 2012 and encourage consumers to stick to their New Year's resolutions about health and wellness, SUBWAY launched a multitiered social advocacy program through its Facebook and Twitter communities.

The Challenge

The sandwich franchise, which for the last decade has focused on its healthy "Eat Fresh" message, sought to find a way to leverage its relationships with wellness bloggers. The restaurant chain wanted to inspire a more engaging conversation with its brand fans and most outspoken consumers on SUBWAY's social networks.

The Strategy

SUBWAY identified women between the ages of 18 and 24 as its advocates for the month-long initiative, which occurred in January 2012. This demographic views health as a primary focus, but it is a focus they are still forming opinions about, according to Tony Pace, SUBWAY's chief marketing officer.

"Fresh Fit Fridays" featured a weekly wellness tip posted on Facebook by SUBWAY's fitness trainer, Monica Vazquez, and various personal fitness bloggers, creating ongoing conversations with brand fans, industry eminents, and peer advocates.

"In this particular program, our brand advocates served as content contributors and participants in the ongoing dialogue," said Pace. "We saw a significant amount of engagement from commenting, sharing, and recommending tips and posts on Facebook, and we encouraged our brand advocates to participate and share with the bloggers and each other on a regular basis."

In addition, the sandwich chain hosted a live cross-platform chat with Vazquez at the end of the month, during which fans had their personal health and fitness questions answered. A tab was created on SUBWAY's Facebook page to host the chat. CoveritLive, a live-blogging tool, enabled the multiparticipant discussion. Participants were also encouraged to tweet their questions using the hashtag #subwayfitchat.

The Results

Fresh Fit Fridays posted a "healthy" month of engagement, said Pace, with 85 percent of the conversation having a positive or neutral sentiment. More than 2 million people were reached by the effort. In addition, it garnered a total of 320 comments and 4,186 likes, according to Facebook Insights.

For the one-hour chat with Vazquez, 440 consumers participated, and 926 comments were posted. The average participant remained signed in to the conversation for 19 minutes, according to CoveritLive. The chat also organically became a trending topic on Twitter, and 266 comments were picked up via the hashtag, added Pace.

"Overall, the good outweighed the bad," Pace said, "and in many cases we had advocates jump to our defense or provide a different suggestion if necessary. While we didn't actively seek and deploy our brand advocates to step into that role, it was nice to see it happening on its own."

The Key Takeaways

"Based on consumer response and participation on Facebook, we definitely recognize the power of giving our fans access to credible professionals that can provide personal recommendations," Pace said. "We actively seek ways to continue to provide fans with this 'insider' experience and access on a regular basis."

Pace also noted that it's important for SUBWAY to not only create ongoing friendly dialogue but also to leverage a brand voice that is transparent. The franchise's brand fans and advocates demand honesty, responsiveness, and fairness on social media.

Parting Words: *The Sliding Value of Recommendations*

In the final assessment, it's important to understand that everyone's opinion of your product, service, company, brand, image, or even CEO counts, but the fact is, **some opinions count more than others**.

Whether you're the author of the *Twilight* novels or the CEO of Domino's Pizza, you understand that every customer is critical to your success. However, the squeaky wheel *does* get the grease, and when you have folks who, for whatever reason, go out of their way to sing your praises, or even ring your bell, it's only natural to give them a little extra consideration.

Whether it's a vocal blogger, a food or movie critic, or just a group of women who really, really, REALLY love Robert Pattinson, knowing who they are, what to say to them, how to keep them happy, and what's more, how to include others in their fandom is critical to your present and future success.

Becoming a social business is about being social through and through, top to bottom, at every level. It is a philosophy that becomes a mission that becomes a habit. Understanding how your influencers think is as critical as understanding who your influencers are, and why they recommend you so highly.

You must learn to understand and engage with those influencers in each area of your influencer ecosystem so that you're able to use them when you need them. Crisis management is too far after the fact. You have to have crisis prevention through management and engagement of each of the various groups in your influencer ecosystem, constantly, all the time.

The more diligently you focus on these four groups, the fewer crises you'll be likely to have, and you'll lessen the need to have to do something drastic the way Domino's did to reinvent its image. Or, as I like to say, "Better to reallocate a few resources now than reinvent your entire brand later."

Knowing that each branch of your ecosystem requires a different type of TLC is crucial when finding, and addressing, peer influencers. For instance, brand fans are looking for a unique way to experience your brand. Unique engagements, special offers, anything "exclusive," or any value added can help keep them happy, engaged, and spreading the word to entice, enlist, and recruit other brand fans to join them.

Industry eminents are doing this as part of their job. They have made a career out of gathering and sharing what is valuable information, and they will always be more loyal to their fan bases than yours. You simply can't "sell" these people. However, you can gather and share information with them in an ongoing effort to strengthen your relationship. And finding the right industry eminent to endorse you rather than chasing the wrong one is not only a time-saving but also brand enhancing measure.

Peer influencers have less "buy-in" for your brand or any other brand. They are simply looking for passion points to connect with you, so they require a different kind of hand-holding than the three other groups. And no one requires more hand-holding than determined detractors!

Oprah may no longer have a show reaching 42 million viewers, but her influence still lingers as we study her "effect" long after she chose to leave her popular talk show format. What Oprah taught us, among so many other valuable lessons, was that there is power in one, but there is power in two, three, four, four dozen, and two thousand as well.

If you can't nab the Oprah Effect, if you can't impress an industry eminent like Marion Nestle, perhaps you can still be a brand fan favorite and share the love of a few thousand, or a few hundred thousand, peer influencers.

Remember, there is no rule that says your influencer ecosystem must flourish with all four types of inhabitants. However, you must tend and care for the delicate relationships that exist within it.

PART 2

The Road Map to Recommendations

CHAPTER 8

Know

Understanding Where and How Your Brand—and Your Competitors—Are Talked About and Recommended

Let's say you have a dog named Franklin. He's a wonderful black Labrador retriever—a genuinely loved member of your family. One day, while you are giving Franklin a belly rub, you notice some lumps underneath his skin. You take him to your vet and learn that Franklin's got cancer—canine mast cell tumors. It's curable, thank goodness, but you need to see a specialist.

You get your vet's opinion, of course. But you also check around online. What's going to sway you that one canine oncologist is better than the others?

This is the type of question that came up when we were doing some work with one of the leading chains of animal hospitals.

This particular chain is on the cutting edge of everyday veterinary medicine as well as specialized services in areas including cardiology, neurology, oncology, ophthalmology, and surgery. In fact, the advances in animal care are in many ways as evolved as they are in human medicine.

We were brought in to help this company launch a campaign designed to tout its modern technology and cutting-edge approach in the hopes of extending the company's reach and bringing clients in to experience such care for themselves. (Or, more specifically, for their pets.)

This client told us that more than 80 percent of their new clients came from word of mouth and recommendations. So, of course, we wanted to know who, why, where, when, and how often people were talking about and recommending veterinarians and animal care. Our expectation, and hope, was that "pet parents," as owners are affectionately called in the industry, would be impressed with, looking for, and talking about taking their pets to the most advanced care centers available. After careful and intense social study, we found a host of information that surprised both the animal hospital group and the Zócalo team.

We learned that when people talk about their pets and their vets, what they tend to talk about becomes very personal. We heard a lot of "I" language and ownership conversation.

Clearly, the respondents wanted vets who . . .

- "Knew and cared about my pet"
- "Were knowledgeable about my pet"
- "Had a staff that was professional and cared about my pet"
- "Listened to my concerns about my pet"
- "Created an environment in which my pet and I both felt comfortable"

The research revealed that what was most important to people were the relatively "soft" items as opposed to technology: touchy-feely emotional issues like concern, listening, empathy, and bedside manner.

Way down the list, at numbers 8 and 9, in fact, were concerns about modern technology or veterinarians' being up to date on the latest surgical procedures, which were, after all, the main concern of our client.

Naturally, the clients were surprised to find that their potential customers weren't as interested in new technology and cutting-edge procedures as they'd hoped, and so they began a concerted reshifting of the message. Lower down were the references to new technology and procedures, and sooner in the message came discussions of customer care, friendly staff, nurturing environment, and other soft items.

It was a great example and a true education in how every segment in any industry can benefit from **social listening**—that is, a careful analysis of the target audience before preparing a message to appeal to what it's really talking about.

 **Google It!**

Why is it that Google is, according to Alexa.com, the number 1 most visited website on the planet? Do people really value its search results that much? Or is there something else going on here? The answer is that there is a LOT going on here, and Google has worked consciously and relentlessly to manage what people use the Internet for the most: information.

Clearly, there is no shortage of Internet search engines to choose from. From Yahoo! to Bing and everything in between, you can find the same information regardless of which box you type the question into. What Google offers are features that go beyond the search.

Simply put, if you want to know more about what your customers are saying about you, where they are saying it, and how often, Google can help you not only find it but stay abreast of this information on a daily basis.

Website results not graphic enough? Search images.

Need to find the latest news story written about you? Drill down and search specifically in the "News" category.

Need to set up a free blog and capture the latest analytics on where folks are coming from to find it? Google now has Blogger .com at your fingertips.

Want to search just blogs to drill down on which bloggers are praising, or dinging, you? Google lets you do just that.

Need to find the full text of patents your competitors might be filing for? Now you can search for that as well.

You can even set Google Alerts for specific keywords concerning a new product launch, a favorite product, or promotion to get daily, even hourly, reports on who is talking about you, where and when.

Google groups list special interest forums in nearly every industry, topic, interest, or niche known to man, from Dr. Who fans to home brew aficionados to diabetes support groups.

Google has made information its number 1 priority because Google knows it's yours, and everybody else's, number 1 priority. Every acquisition, every development, every button on their growing "more" list allows users to drill down deeper and deeper, to search as light or as heavy as they wish and, of course, make Google their one-stop knowledge shop. I guess that's why, according to SearchEngineLand.com, Google processes a staggering "34,000 searches per second"!

In the Know: *How Can You Find Out What People Are Saying?*

Today's Internet is truly an embarrassment of riches. With the amount of information at your fingertips, it's daunting to start the hunt for who, what, when, where, why, and how often people are talking about you and your company.

In the following section, I will introduce you to a variety of free and paid tools to help you sort through the clutter and master the art of social listening as you evolve into a highly recommendable social business.

The Free Tools

There are a variety of free tools to help you explore what people are saying about your company, including these:

- **Google Alerts.** Google Alerts are so effective, so simple, and so helpful I'm surprised they are still free. Simply type in a search term, like your company name, your CEO's name, or a product name, include what sites Google Alerts should look at—like only in blogs, in the news or media, or in graphics or videos—and also include how frequently—like daily or weekly—and Google will deliver the information right to your e-mail address.
- **Twitter Search.** Twitter Search is a great means of hands-on data gathering because the results you get are real time and real specific, and they aren't sugarcoated. Simply use the search box and type in a term and see what comes up. You may, or may not, be surprised at what you find.
- **IceRocket blog search.** When it comes to social listening, few sources are as rich and bursting with discussion as blogs. IceRocket lets you search not only blogs but also Twitter, Facebook, images, and more to find the latest on who's talking about you and where.
- **Compete.com.** Your free Compete.com analytics account allows you to see traffic data for over 1 million websites, discover related sites and competitors, and get monthly updates on your site and more.
- **Technorati.** One of the, if not the, first search engines devoted to blogs, Technorati "tracks not only the authority and influence of blogs, but [it is] also the most comprehensive and current index of who and what is most popular in the Blogosphere."
- **HootSuite.** HootSuite is a great free tool for measuring not just your reach but also a whole lot more. According to the company's website, "With HootSuite's integrated, custom social analytics, you'll be able to measure your campaign performance to help improve your social media communications."

- **Yahoo! Small Business Advisor.** Helpful for knowing and growing, Yahoo! Small Business Advisor offers a variety of resources like articles, trend watches, columns, and more. In addition, it offers website hosting and a marketing analytics dashboard.
- **BrandMonitor.** When it comes to social listening, monitoring is the name of the game. Simply checking in with Facebook and Twitter every now and again isn't good enough. BrandMonitor helps you monitor both your social media reputation as well as that of your competitors, which, as we all know by now, can be just as important. Basic (and free) tools include a social media dashboard, brand sentiment analysis, and daily and weekly e-mail alerts so you can "set it and forget it."
- **SocialMention.** SocialMention is a social media search and analysis platform that aggregates user-generated content from across the universe into a single stream of information. It allows you to easily track and measure in real time what people are saying about you, your company, a new product, or any topic across the web's social media landscape. SocialMention monitors over 100 social media properties directly including Twitter, Facebook, FriendFeed, YouTube, Digg, and Google.[1]
- **SimplyMeasured.** This website has quite a few free reports to download as well.

The Paid Tools

I am never one for throwing money at a problem when a free service will suffice, but in the field of social listening, it's important to have a no-stone-unturned approach to what people are saying about you online. While not every paid tool is worth the money, a few that I've found extremely useful are as follows:

- **Radian6.** Acquired by Salesforce in 2010, Radian6 is one of the leading social listening platforms available today. The company provides a full "fire hose" of data for more critical and analytics needs.
- **Crimson Hexagon.** Instead of delivering large volumes of conversation for quantitative analysis, Crimson Hexagon's focus is on identifying qualitative trends through its semiautomated text analysis algorithms. For activities in which capturing every mention matters (for example, crisis

monitoring and campaign measuring), an aggregator like Radian6 or Sysomos is best. For activities in which speed-to-insight and trend analysis are concerned, Crimson Hexagon provides a unique solution for brand marketers seeking an automated alternative to hands-on analysis.

- **Sysomos.** Sysomos is another option to consider along the lines of Radian6. Sysomos provides much of the same in terms of data, but it differs from Radian6 in the visual display of information. Both serve the role of data aggregators—behemoth tools with a focus on collecting large volumes of conversation for quantitative analysis.

The Power of Human Synthesis

What's important to remember in the rush—even "crush"—of tools, data, and analytics offered by the above processes is that nothing can take the place of good old-fashioned human observation. What these tools do is help *gather* information. Your team needs to actually sift through that info to find the real insights.

Not all of it, of course. What we typically do at Zócalo Group on any given campaign is sift through a statistically significant hand sampling of the data that's coming in.

What's critical to understand about social listening and a company's or brand's ultimate reach in real conversations that are taking place both online and off is how social media results—Twitter, Facebook, blog, and forum mentions—are turning up as search engine results. We discussed earlier how Google makes it easy to search blog content, as well as other social media avenues, and you can see in the monitoring and analytics tools we just discussed how vital social media conversations are in defining your brand.

What we're learning through online WOM analysis is how thoroughly social media is blanketing *how* others hear and find out about you, *what* they hear and find out about you as well as *where*.

"Keyword monitoring" becomes critical in these online discussions because those keywords that are actually being used by consumers about consumer brands wind up rising to the top of the search engine results. Through careful monitoring and measurement, brands can master these keywords and use them to drive online discussions rather than merely follow them.

Which, of course, is what knowing is all about.

Listening Command Centers: *The Wave of the Future?*

One of the first companies to recognize and master the art of social listening in a concentrated and even physical way was Dell out of Austin, Texas.

We've worked with Dell in a number of capacities and have seen the power of what they call "Ground Control," which is just what it sounds like: a formal listening command center where expert staffers monitor, measure, and analyze the online chatter concerning the company.

The company launched Ground Control in 2010, and its vice president of social media and community, Manish Mehta, explained: "Ground Control is about tracking the largest number of possible conversations across the web and making sure we 'internalize' that feedback, good or bad. . . . It's also about tracking what you might call the 'long tail'—those smaller matters that might not bubble to the surface today but are out there and deserve to be heard."[2]

One can immediately see the potential of rich information gathered at such sites and its intrinsic value in determining not just one's reach but the online perception of a brand and its collaterals. Not just hearing the good but internalizing the bad, working to rectify it with a dedicated team well versed in how to manage negative chatter. The benefits, and ramifications, in this online recommendation age are nearly boundless.

How extensive and rich is the data that Dell's Ground Control mines? Staffers analyze over 20,000 daily posts mentioning the company, enabling Dell to take social listening to the next level—and beyond. Perhaps as a rallying cry to other businesses or merely to support its theory of the benefits of its own Ground Control, Dell has done additional and important work on the importance of listening. In fact, a Forrester Consulting study commissioned on behalf of Dell shows that "companies that launch listening and digital engagement initiatives are rewarded with improved customer satisfaction scores, loyalty, and brand metrics."

The study, which surveyed 200 medium and large United States–based marketers across three key industries, apparently paid off. "Nearly all the companies surveyed," stated the report's findings, "have specific plans to increase their social media investments, with 73 percent planning to add employees focused on listening and engagement initiatives in the coming year."

Karen Quintos, senior vice president and chief marketing officer at Dell, summarized the groundbreaking findings: "Listening and responding to customers is so basic and fundamental. The emergence of social media elevates how companies can act on the feedback they get from customers."

Despite Dell's leading the battle cry for a dedicated force devoted solely to monitoring online chatter and social listening, businesses are still lagging behind their customers, 80 percent of whom use social media:

- 50 percent of companies surveyed say their social media efforts are serious but not a core function.
- 16 percent reward customers whose ideas they use.
- Only 6 percent claim that their companies' listening and engagement initiatives are very integrated.

But companies' investment in listening is on the rise, and the benefits are tangible:

- 64 percent of respondents are incorporating customer feedback into products or services.
- 76 percent distribute customer feedback internally.
- 31 percent are enhancing sales by offering incentive programs for customers who engage online, including deals and discounts.[3]

The IBM Listening for Leads Program

At the heart of Dell's success with its groundbreaking Ground Control center is, of course, the art of listening. I say "art" because many who say they listen don't, and many companies who want to listen tend to go about it the wrong way. One company who is listening the *right* way—by making it a top priority—is none other than the tech giant IBM.

One aspect of the company's social media program is called *Listening for Leads*. This initiative relies on volunteers they call "seekers" who, according to the *Corporate Eye* blog, monitor "social media conversations happening on key websites where the company's target audiences spend time."

As the program's name implies, seekers aren't just on the lookout for online chatter to determine IBM's "reach" but instead are actively listening to "identify conversations that could generate leads." Potential leads are passed on to representatives from the company who can then follow up and initiate conversations that will hopefully result in new customers.

IBM's own Ed Linde, senior marketing manager at IBM Inside Sales, "attributes IBM's success from its Listening for Leads program to two primary factors":

1. Using enough employees as seekers who voluntarily spend a couple of hours per week listening to social media conversations to uncover a good amount of credible leads
2. Knowing where to look for conversations (that is, where target audiences spend time on the social web) and what keywords to search for in order to find relevant, actionable discussions[4]

A Brief History of Listening to Consumers

Well before social media garnered all the attention, focus groups were the name of the game when it came to social listening. While the use of focus groups didn't really pick up until the 1980s and 1990s, "focus interviews" were used all the way back in the 1950s. They started out as more of an academic pursuit, but they were modified to become more synonymous with market research.

Robert K. Merton is often named as the "father of focus groups." According to his obituary in the *New York Times*, Merton's "adoption of the focused interview to elicit the responses of groups to texts, radio programs, and films led to the 'focus groups' that politicians, their handlers, marketers, and hucksters now find indispensable."

Why did focus groups shift from mere academic exercises in the Mad Men era of 1950s advertising to the marketing tactic du jour of the 1980s and 1990s? For one, it gave companies a "bird's-eye view" of what their target consumers were saying about their brands, live and in person.

From children playing with the latest toys to people discussing a new toaster pastry or dish soap, researchers could guide healthy discussions through a series of leading questions and provide brands with at least a margin of opinion, for better or worse. Broken down into its simplest form, "the focus group methodology offers the researchers 'a way of listening to people and learning from them.'"[5]

Sound familiar? Long before the Internet, focus groups were a way of social listening, of eavesdropping on everyday citizens to get a clearer picture of what your product looked like on the ground and in their hands. Not everyone believed in the power of focus groups, however.

Skilled moderators were often hard to come by, according to the *Houston Chronicle*, leading to brand or product "cheerleaders" who effectively guided feedback to the positive. It was also hard to find objective focus group participants since many told focus group leaders what they thought they wanted to hear.

Of course, yesterday's focus groups are today's "Ground Control" centers and "Listening for Leads" programs. What used to be conducted live and in person, for better or worse, is now conducted online in a hundred different ways.

You may not know it, but those ubiquitous 100-calorie snack packs you see in vending machines, convenience stores, and grocery store shelves were actually the result of Kraft Foods' tapping into the online "focus groups" built by a company called Communispace, which would build online "communities" tailored and designed for each specific client, be it a community of foodies for Kraft or pet lovers for PetSmart.

Gary Arena, CFO of Communispace, recalls the advent of those snack packs: "One of the things that Kraft did with its community was to study what consumers want when they reach for snacks in vending machines or quick-serve facilities. They discovered that most consumers wanted tasty 100-calorie snacks just to tide them over between meals, and there was little concern over how many of the calories came from fat."[6]

Both methods, offline and online focus groups, sought the same *know* information: the *who, what, where,* and *why* of social listening.

To Truly Know, You Need to Understand the Four Ws

At the Zócalo Group we perform what is known as a "Digital Footprint Analysis." For any brand (and its competitors), we want to know the following:

- How much online conversation is there about you and your competitors?
- How are your consumers or customers talking about and recommending you versus competitors?

- Where are those conversations occurring in relation to competitors?
- What are the key themes driving recommendations in your category?

The First W: *Who—Who's Talking?*

To pinpoint the origins of any social listening exercise, you first want to explore *who*, specifically, is talking about your brand, your product launch, or your latest promotion or special.

- **Gender info.** This can be hard to find unless people are self-identified, but it can be important to know what sex is talking about you the most.
- **Demographic information.** Knowing the income, housing, and even employment status of who is talking about you can help you target not only where to find them more often but how to talk back when you do.
- **Personal information.** The more information you can glean about people—their beliefs, opinions, and so on—the better you can categorize who is saying what.

The Collective *Who.* With the above information, it's important to synthesize and understand how the *who* behave as a group. Do they meet up with each other in local areas? Do they attend category events together—auto shows, electronics shows, home expositions, and so on? Do they appear likely to WANT to engage with your brand, product, launch, or executives?

The Second W: *What—What Are They Saying?*

After you discover who is talking about you, you next want to explore *what* they are saying about you:

- **Keywords.** What keywords are they using? Are there keyword clusters, and, if so, are they worth exploring?
- **Overall volume.** *Volume* refers to social listening for how loud the online chatter is about your company—that is, the more people are talking about you, the more often, the higher the volume.
- **Brand and/or product attributes.** Outside of keywords, how do consumers recognize—or ignore—the attributes that are most critical to a brand or product? To what degree do the actual attributes of your brand, product, or service

get discussed, and does this align with your objectives and strategy? Do people talking about the brand or product in online conversations associate the tenets that a brand perceives as critical to be the key decision factors *against competitive brands or products?*

■ **How people are engaging with that volume.** *Engaging with volume* refers to how content from the brand—or even generated by other individuals—is acted upon by the prospective customers or general consumers. Are certain discussions being shared? How are those discussions being shared? Are reactions short-lived, or is there a long-tail impact of one piece of brand content or one consumer experience? Once the answers to these questions are determined, it's then important to consider similar characteristics to aid in creating future success. For example, what are the characteristics of content or comments that elicit sharing and enthusiasm, and how can those elements be implemented by the brand to facilitate future engagement?

■ **Tone.** Tone is a biggie because your volume can be "loud," but more damage than benefit can be done if it's more negative than positive.

The Third W: *Where—Where Are These Conversations Taking Place?*

Understanding where the social discussion is taking place will enable the brand to determine if brand content—as well as organically developing consumer conversations—are reaching the target audiences and are accessible to those who are searching for information online. The objective in determining *where* is to make sure that the conversations most relevant to your brand are happening on the channels most relevant to the target audience. Here are some good questions to ask to get that conversation going:

What platforms do your consumers use the most?
Do you have a presence there?
How can you get one?

What Type of Discussion Is Occurring? Is the type of discussion unique to where conversations occur? For example, is there more customer service–oriented discussion on Facebook or Twitter? Is the discussion on forums and communities composed more often of category enthusiasts or brand advocates? Understanding the different types of conversations that occur on different channels representing the determination of *where* will facilitate how social outreach and content can be tailored to the specific needs of those various channels.

The Fourth W: *Why—Why Does This Matter?*

Finally, you want to examine one of the most important Ws: *why* all of this matters so much. This is a key point for clients and for anyone searching his or her own personal brand. Once you've got all this information, what are you going to do with it? We'll explore more about what to do in our next chapter, where we move from knowing to planning.

Filling the Void

Now that you know where to look for these online conversations, what are you looking for? Look for something we call *the void*. As the name implies, the void is someplace you can fill, a place you belong but also where you can stand out. You can find the void by answering two specific questions:

1. **Which brands own what in your particular industry?** For instance, if you're in the running shoe business, you need to know the niche Nike fills, as well as Reebok, New Balance, and Sketchers. Knowing your competition as well as you know yourself is critical when knowing which void to fill. This leads to our next question.
2. **Where can you differentiate yourself?** Perhaps your running shoes are made from all recyclable materials and 10 percent of each sale goes to improve the lives of the factory workers that make them. This allows you to differentiate yourself from the hardcore athlete that gravitates to the Nike brand as well as the recreational athlete who typically buys New Balance.

Parting Words: *Go Forth and Do . . .*

Now that you've collected all this knowledge, what do you do with it? You plan your strategy on how to keep the positives going, deal with the negatives, and keep consumers on the path to recommendation. But wait, we're getting a little ahead of ourselves. That's what we'll discover in the next chapter.

CHAPTER 9

Plan

Articulating Your Shareable Story, Boosting Your Search Ranking, and Formalizing Your Paid, Earned, and Owned Recommendable Brand Strategy

'Ve got a topic that everyone should be talking about: home and small business safes.

As interesting as I find this subject, I'm willing to bet that it has been a long time, if ever, that you've had a conversation with one of your friends about which safe you should have at home.

Oftentimes, I'll hear from brands that they are in a low involvement category and there's no way a word of mouth campaign would work for them. More often than not, they're wrong. And here's a case in point.

A few years ago we received a call from a past client who had taken a new role at SentrySafe—an 80-year-old family-owned business that is the market leader in home and small business safes. SentrySafe manufactures more than 200 models of safes and sells through its own site as well as major retailers, including Target, Walmart, Costco, Lowe's, Staples, OfficeMax, Amazon, and others.

All good credentials. But why would someone think about, talk about, and most of all recommend a safe—even one such as SentrySafe, where 94 percent of all customers say they would recommend the brand and would buy another from the company?

Protecting the Important and Irreplaceable

SentrySafe had done some strong branding work and come up with the concept and tagline: "Protecting the Important and Irreplaceable."

When we conducted a Digital Footprint Analysis to understand where (i.e., blogs, forums, photo sites, YouTube, Facebook, Pinterest, Twitter, etc.) consumers and small businesses were talking about safes, we discovered, perhaps not surprisingly, that they really weren't. In fact, there was less than one mention (.89) per day during a 30-day period across all social channels of people talking about (much less, recommending) safes.

Now, this didn't mean SentrySafe products weren't recommended. They were. Over and over again. And it also didn't mean that "Protecting the Important and Irreplaceable" wasn't a great tagline. In fact, studies showed that people really got the sentiment and value once they put it into content.

What it did mean, however, is that people didn't seem to have much occasion or interest to talk about home safes or relate them to their lives without being asked. What people were talking about in droves, however, were things that were directly relevant to their lives at that particular moment: a pending wedding, an upcoming anniversary, planning for a baby, organizing their finances, taxes, retirement—you get the picture.

Our job was to figure out how to ensure that people connected these meaningful life events or situations to the need for and benefits of organizing and protecting items and information against fire, theft, or some other type of loss.

SentrySafe's Shareable Story

We wanted to create a "story" that would nurture and promote the SentrySafe brand but also sound the way that people talk—sharing their cares, concerns, and recommendations—all using real time keywords, of course.

Ultimately, what we created with SentrySafe was a Shareable Story that combined some of the brand's most important characteristics: fireproof, waterproof, secure, organizing, affordable, and so on with words that consumers use every day to talk about the needs that a SentrySafe addresses.

The *home base* (or key message, as you'll soon learn) of how we wanted to talk about SentrySafe is, "I count on SentrySafe to help me protect the important and irreplaceable things in my life."

Once the full map was completed, as you'll see below, we created partnerships with key bloggers and influencers to share the importance of what SentrySafe delivers, but within the context of the bigger topics people were already talking about, such as Disaster Preparedness Month and Spring cleaning:

> *If you've been a reader for very long, you know that I constantly remind my readers to keep their valuable documents all in one place. The Grab-n-Go Binder is a Survival Mom staple! However, what if that all-important binder becomes a casualty of a house fire, a hurricane, or a flood? Insurance policies, birth certificates, and all those documents that will help put your life back together will be ruined or scattered to the wind.*
>
> *This safe, the "SentrySafe" Fire-Safe HD4100, is built like a file organizer on steroids.*
>
> **—SURVIVAL MOM**[1]

> *This Combination Fire-Safe, in my opinion, is the best on the market. I wouldn't want anything different to protect my DVDs, hard drives of my family photos, important documents stored on the hard drives, and all of the paperwork such as passports, birth certificates, car titles, and everything else I need to keep completely secure and safe. This Combination Fire-Safe truly is a sentry that watches over my valuables!*
>
> **—A THRIFTY MOM**[2]

In addition to receiving positive recommendations from online influencers, SentrySafe also found a unique way to demonstrate the durability and quality of the safes through online "live burns," where products were filled with valuable items and cash and then set on fire to show how the safe would protect in the event of an actual fire. Consumers were able to interact with the brand during these events through Twitter.

The Vital Link: *The Critical Connection Between Search, Social, and Your Brand's Shareable Story*

The need for a Shareable Story seems obvious—the best way to get people to recommend your brand is to know what you want

consumers and customers to say and then help them to do it—
through your product and/or service offerings and your marketing
initiatives.

Increasingly, though, there's a whole new reason to make sure
you get your Shareable Story right. Five of the six top influences on
search ranking are directly linked to how people are talking about,
recommending, and sharing your brand in social channels.

Think, for a second, what a crucial role Google, Bing, Yahoo!,
or another search engine has on what you see, learn, buy, vote for,
and so on. The ability to become prominent, and relevant, in today's
modern search algorithms is critically important for any brand.

In a recent article on SocialMediaExaminer.com called "3 Tips to
Manage Your Social Media Reputation," author Sara Lokitis writes,
"According to a click-through rate study published by Slingshot,
**the number-one ranking on Google gets about an 18% click-
through rate and the number-two organic listing gets about 10%**.
Regardless of the actual percentage, the data proves that the first
search engine results page is the most important for your brand's
reputation."[3]

It should come as no surprise that Internet searches on sites like
Google and Yahoo! can play a vital role in where and how you are
recommended—and shouldn't be minimized as you begin to craft
your story and search for relevant keywords with which to write it.

The integration of Google's "Search plus Your World" and the
increasing number of Facebook and Twitter search results has made
search engine monitoring much more important for any brand eager
to target where, when, and how its story is shared.

According to the *Searchmetrics SEO* blog, "Social media signals
. . . from Facebook, Twitter, and Google+ are frequently associated
with good rankings in Google's index . . . while lower values (e.g.,
keyword position in title) have a negative correlation. Therefore, we
can say that the largest correlation occurs between Facebook Shares
and the lowest between the 'number of words in text' for the U.S.
and 'keyword position in title (words).'"[4]

Clearly, Facebook and other social media "shares" count more
toward Google search engine ranking results than keywords in
your website (see Figure 9.1). Therefore, don't fill your site with
marketing jargon in order to make it rise higher in the search engine
optimization (SEO) rankings. Instead, concentrate on what your
consumers are sharing and what your brand shares within social
media.

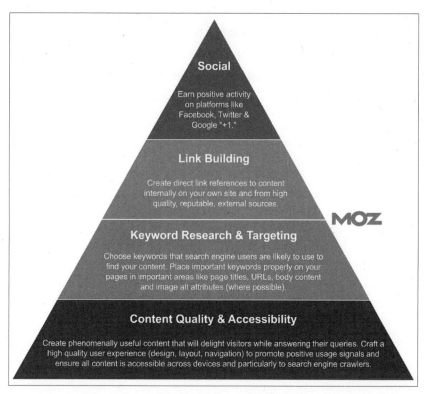

Figure 9.1 The SEO Pyramid. (Source: Scott Willoughby, "The SEO Fundamentals Pyramid," Whiteboard Friday, December 12, 2008, http:// www.seomoz.org/blog/whiteboard-friday-the-seo-fundamentals-pyramid.)

The Importance of Social Content Within Search Engines

Currently, there are over *3 billion Google searches every day.* To capitalize on consumers' habitual use of search engines, brands need a strong base of content that leads up to social sharing from consumers.

Discovering where your brand is unique is important in this process—unique keywords that have less search "competition" will allow a brand's Google rankings to rise.

You want your consumers to share your messaging, but your message has more long-term influence than just a few recommendations. According to Searchmetrics.com, "Social signals have an extremely high correlation to good rankings in Google's index . . ."

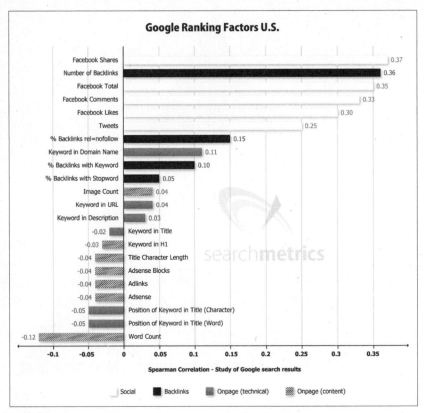

Figure 9.2 Search Engine Ranking Factors. (Source: Searchmetrics.com.)

while "Facebook sharing is now the number 1 contributor (even over the number of backlinks) to driving positive search rankings in Google." (See Figure 9.2.)

Now that you have a clear understanding of the importance of creating your brand's Shareable Story, the next question is how to do it.

Help People Recommend You in the Way You Want to Be Recommended

People don't talk, let alone recommend, in taglines. As additional proof, when was the last time you heard someone say, "I'm going to McDonald's because . . . I'm lovin' it"? Or reached for a Coke while saying, "I'm opening happiness"? Instead, what real people do, repeatedly, is recommend companies, products, services, and brands in ways that are **natural for them**.

What *is* natural for them? Believe it or not: stories. People talk in stories. They share with stories. They console in stories, and they absolutely recommend in stories.

In the last chapter we discussed the power and reach of "social listening" and how vital it is to know where messages are coming from, where people are talking, even the *what*, *why*, and *when* of people talking.

But now it's time to discuss the *how*: how people talk, how they share, and how powerful your message can be when you understand the basic ways in which consumers communicate.

Bottom line, it all starts with a message.

The Traditional PR Model

In the more traditional way of spreading a marketing story, PR professionals would share specific messages that they wanted the media to print in a news story. It might be the opening of a new bank, the announcement of a new CEO, the breaking of a new record, or something else. Mostly, press releases were seen as "announcements," one-way proclamations of events that had occurred and were expected to be significant.

The problem with making such one-way announcements and expecting them to get leverage, let alone coverage, is that this way of thinking is linear—the way consumers talk is *not* linear. Now more than ever, consumers tell one another stories.

Now, when I say "story," I don't mean *Anna Karenina* or *War and Peace*. I mean short tidbits, narratives, and strong messages that convey powerful meaning. It could be something as simple as, "I was late for a big job interview when I spilled coffee over my white blouse. I bought one of those 'Tide stain remover sticks' in the hotel lobby, used it in the bathroom, and by the time I got to my interview the blouse looked better than new."

Or it could be something as significant as, "I was stranded on the side of a dark and lonely road, in the middle of a snowstorm, radiator fluid gushing everywhere, miles from any service station, when I called State Farm Insurance. In less than an hour, I was rescued by a tow truck from the nearest service station."

These real-life, real-time, person-to-person stories are far more valuable, and universally more relatable, than any tagline dreamed up. Which is not to say that taglines and slogans aren't effective; they are. But when it comes to the power of Shareable Stories, they are more icing than cake.

The Power of a Shareable Story

Now that your brand has begun monitoring for your conversation and ascertained the *who, where, what,* and *why* does this matter for your consumer base (what they're already saying), the next most important step is to specifically and effectively craft the story that you want to have shared—including the keywords that you want to make sure you are owning when it comes to search behavior in your category.

Chances are, if we don't know how we want to be recommended, people will likely do it a different way.

To be truly effective, everyone inside your organization has to be in alignment in terms of how you want to be recommended. Once you have that clarity, everything you do will be focused on making sure you are delivering in a way that makes those recommendations a reality.

From the listening work, you already have a good idea of the following insights:

- What messages about your brand do you want your consumers to share with one another?
- What makes your brand unique in the marketplace?
- What do you have that your competitors don't?
- Why are consumers recommending you? What are the most positive, useful, and special things about your brand?
- What is your competitors' messaging? What are they saying about you, if anything?

What you have likely learned, very quickly, from all of this information is how you stand in recommendations among your competitors. Now you've got some choices to make:

- If you are happy with how you are being talked about and recommended, you simply need to formalize the story that's being presented and create ways to encourage more of the same responses.

- If you are less than happy with how you are being recommended, you need to figure out the disconnect and determine what it will take to become recommended in the ways you want.
- If a competitor "owns" the position you want, you need to determine if you can achieve that position—take it away from your competitor—or refine your position to take advantage of the "gap" in the marketplace.

Crafting Your Brand's Shareable Story

Ever heard people talk about having an "elevator pitch"? In essence, what they are saying is that they have been able to boil down the key takeaways about their brand in such a succinct way that they can effectively share it on a quick elevator ride.

But some elevator rides are longer than others. You may have just 1 floor to share something. Or 5 floors. Or if you work in a skyscraper as I do, you may have 80 floors or more to share your story.

The best Shareable Stories accommodate the shortest elevator rides to the longest ones—in other words, you can share a little information or a lot of information based on the person's interest.

The key is that you have thought out, in advance, what those messages are.

That's Not How I'd Describe What Makes Us Different

I love facilitating Shareable Story sessions with our clients. Sometimes, leadership teams are aligned on who they are and what makes them recommendable. More often, people in different departments—or even on the same team—have a different idea of the key reasons their brand should be recommended.

The fun part is helping brands realize—with the benefit of the information gathered from the listening work and studying their brand strategy—exactly what makes them recommendable and putting a story behind it.

Since you are telling a story—and expecting your consumers or customers to be telling a story about you—you've got to prioritize your keywords, points, and sentiments.

Our Goal: A Completed Shareable Story Map

It's always helpful when beginning a process to know where you want to end up.

To help illustrate this point, let's take a look at the Shareable Story map for SentrySafe (Figure 9.3).

The center of the story is the brand's ultimate takeaway—its "home base" message. This *must* be in "consumer speak" without any marketer jargon. The driving question of any home base message is: *What is the one takeaway I want to ensure someone recommends about my brand—the one-floor elevator statement?*

Once your **home base** is established (bubble 1), you are ready to start telling the story and the reasons why someone would recommend your brand.

Surrounding the home base are four to five key point bubbles (bubbles 2 through 6). These points elaborate on your central, home base message.

And as you work around the map, you'll see various touch points you can fill in for longer versions of your story. So, in our proverbial elevator, the home base story assumes you've only got one floor to share your message, the outer bubbles assume you may have five to six floors to elaborate on your brand "story," and filling in the entire map assumes you're going all the way up to the penthouse level.

The second level of the Shareable Story map can be up to five parts:

1. How your brand leads your industry
2. How your brand is positioned to succeed
3. How your brand addresses a specific market need
4. What the market expects from your brand and/or your industry
5. The market demand or customer need for your brand

The outermost level of the Shareable Story map is compiled of additional points and facts that "prove" your second-level descriptions. As mentioned, these expound on your story in ways that add richer detail for both you and the consumer to digest.

Ultimately, you are looking for brand advocates, influencers, and consumers to share that central message—this is why it's pivotal to really boil your brand down to its ultimate goal and vision. At your company's core, what exactly are you bringing to market, and why should the consumer care?

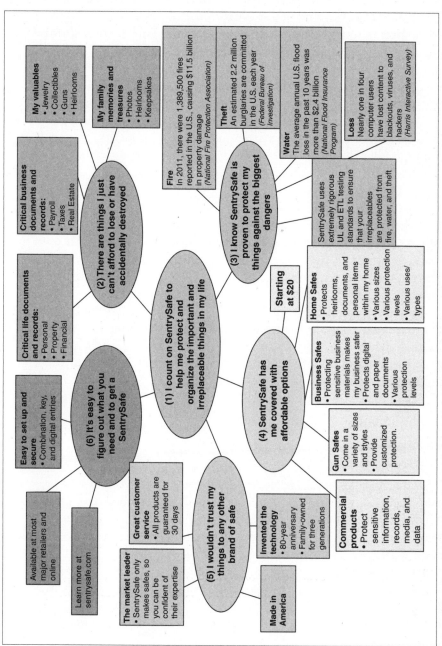

Figure 9.3 SentrySafe Shareable Story Map. (Source: Zócalo Group.)

Remember, also, that you're creating a story not just for external consumption but for internal digestion as well. This Shareable Story becomes *the* driving focus of all internal and external media touch points you'll engage with. And you'll know it's an effective one when you see it spread across these touch points, from copy to your website to your blog to social media to print and onward and outward.

What you'll see happen, if you've taken the time to fill out a story map and craft one that's realistic and also representative for your brand, is that the story will be given life. The sharing of that story will become habitual as you and the rest of your company embrace it and it begins to organically seep across your branding messages.

This is vital because it has to flow from you to the consumer, not the other way around. Without a story crafted by you to share, consumers will likely share one anyway, but it will be one of their own making. Generally speaking, the more you can guide the consumer chatter, the better, which is why having a strong message beginning with a Shareable Story is so vital to your WOM success.

Now that you have your messaging, your keywords, and search approach, what should you do with it all? In this next section, we will discuss the four quadrants of social media—paid, earned, owned, and shared—and how to use them most effectively with your own, personalized recommendation strategy.

The Integration of Paid, Owned, Earned, and Shared Brand Strategies

The Word of Mouth Marketing Association (WOMMA) was created in 2004, and it has since become widely recognized as the official trade association of the word of mouth and social media marketing industry. I have been fortunate enough to be involved with WOMMA from very early on, having served on its board for a number of years and serving as its president.

In less than 10 years, I'm amazed to see not only how WOMMA has grown and evolved but also how quickly and pervasively word of mouth, social media, and digital marketing have become such crucial components of the marketing and promotion industry.

As social media really began to take hold, say, about four or five years ago, I can vividly remember the lively debates that would occur in the WOMMA boardroom about the strict divide between "paid" and "earned" media.

It was almost as if, while few companies had any trouble paying for print ads or radio time, there was a kind of sanctity around WOM marketing and the belief that you simply couldn't pay people for their recommendations.

In fact, somewhere around 2008 or 2009, I can recall the WOMMA board was considering kicking a member out of the organization because the member had been so aggressive on the paid side (paying individuals to tweet or blog on behalf of a brand) of generating WOM recommendations.

My, how times have changed.

Since those early, almost "frontier" days of social media, what most brands that utilize WOM marketing have come to value is the integration of paid, owned, earned, and shared media in driving recommendations.

Early on, paid, owned, and earned media looked and felt very different. Agencies and vendors often specialized in one or the other—and the marketing world was seemingly safe, secure, and predictable.

Each of these media streams—paid, owned, earned, and shared—has become an essential pillar of marketing. Each enhances and amplifies the other. Increasingly, consumers don't even bother to differentiate among them.

In developing a formal "recommendation driven" strategy, paid, owned, earned, and shared media must blend together seamlessly. To begin the discussion of how to marry that ultimate blend for your own brand, here are some thoughts on each of these forms of media.

Paid Media

Paid media used to be, of course, advertising—and was usually identifiable in print, broadcast, or online. Paid media *is still* advertising, and examples include display ads, pay-per-click search ads, and sponsorships.

In the earliest days of social media, you didn't see a lot of paid promo because, quite frankly, there just weren't a lot of business models in place to take advantage of. But as social media has exploded and sites like Facebook, Twitter, YouTube, and the rest have worked to find ways to make money from their services, the opportunities for paid media have evolved as well.

Now, of course, every time you see a "promoted" tweet, that is a form of paid media. Every time you see "sponsored" around a blog post or Facebook ad, that is a form of paid media.

The plus for paid media is near on-demand implementation, some degree of control, and scale. The growing popularity of social advertising on social media sites like Facebook, Twitter, LinkedIn, and YouTube adds another option for marketers to gain presence in channels where consumers and buyers are spending a lot of their time.

Another plus for paid media is the ability to target a specific audience and address it directly. Since so much of media, particularly on sites like Facebook, for instance, have to do with likes, shares, and similar interests, there is a host of focus information available to help guide your paid media in the right, versus the wrong, or scattershot, direction.

What's also interesting is that it's getting harder and harder to tell paid from earned media. Now that blogs are so respectable and prevalent, it was inevitable I suppose that they would also look for ways to monetize their content. While banner ads and such are still popular, there is a new form of paid media where some bloggers, for a fee, will discuss or promote your product in transparent and credible ways.

It's interesting to watch mainstream sites like Gawker.com and Jezebel.com run a series of "regular" blog posts and then to run across one marked "sponsored" that looks, reads, and feels just like the rest.

As with all things social media, transparency is key. The Federal Trade Commission (FTC), in fact, has quite strict guidelines about transparency in paid media, which is why a site like Gawker clearly labels its "sponsored" posts to distinguish them from its regular, workaday posts, or why when you suddenly see a tweet from Nathan Fillion or Neil Patrick Harris on your thread, it says "sponsored" so you know why it's coming and where it's coming from.

Owned Media

Owned media is content created and controlled by a brand, whether it's a website, blog, or the brand's own social media channels. Owned media is about brand control, and it includes digital media, content, and assets such as websites, blogs, newsletters, white papers, and social media accounts.

Brands are increasingly behaving like publishers with editorial staff managing content creation teams. "Content marketing" is the hot topic when it comes to owned media, and it can facilitate brand information discovery through search and social channels.

Earned Media

Earned media is otherwise known as *consumer-generated media* (CGM). In short, it's how consumers react to and discuss the brand, either with the brand directly or with their peers.

It can take on many forms, from posts on social media sites and tweets to user reviews on e-commerce sites or in targeted forums. Earned media can also be the result of public and media relations efforts to "earn" coverage in industry publications, both online and offline.

Shared Media

Shared media is about the co-creation of content and media between brands and community. Brand social web participation and interaction with consumers on sites like Facebook, Twitter, and YouTube that results in content is "shared media" because it's a result of a shared interaction.

Integrating Your Paid, Owned, Earned, and Shared Recommendation Strategies

As you begin to build your recommendation strategy or social plan, the questions you ask yourself and your team should be these:

- How do we establish and maintain regular engagement with our target audiences?
- How do we foster this relationship with a steady stream of back-and-forth, updates, information, and the occasional special or spicy event promotion?
- How do we keep this steady drumbeat of information, updates, and awareness going all week, all month, all year, every year?

While articulating their Shareable Story and a recommendable brand strategy, companies must decide what they want their consumers to do while investing in each of the above types of media—paid, owned, earned, and shared.

Do they want consumers to be aware? Do they want to engage with the consumers? Do they want their consumers to act? And when is it appropriate for the consumers to recommend?

Clearly, what we want is a combination of all four—paid, owned, earned, and shared—and, yet, many brands simply skip over some of the integral brand building steps like awareness and engagement to rush to a recommendation. But as you can see in the four strategies below, each is an integral part of the recommendation process as each layer builds toward the next:

- **Awareness.** Ensuring that as many people as possible within a target audience, or general market, know about a brand, product, service, or benefit
- **Engagement.** Ensuring that the right people and/or as many people as possible interact with the company or brand
- **Action.** Driving trial and sales and/or specific product experiences
- **Recommendation.** Turning consumers into active advocates for the company or brand

Today, every brand and every recommendation, no matter how big or how small, no matter how reserved or vocal, online or offline, begins with a relationship.

And relationships have to be tended. It's like any marriage that is working toward a long-lasting future; you can't just have a nice ceremony, move in together, and expect it to just randomly "happen." You have to tend it, nurture it, pay attention to it, and put the work in if you want marital success, let alone bliss.

So you make sure to connect and check in with your spouse every day. You talk about your work, the kids, family and friends, neighbors, and random tidbits. Every week you try to do something fun together, as a family or as a couple.

There are the regular casual Friday or Saturday night dinners, but also maybe every month you make a reservation, get dressed up, hire a babysitter, and go someplace fancy for a special evening together.

And perhaps every few months you take a romantic weekend away together, be it to the beach or the mountains or a resort or simply a "stay-cation" for just the two of you. In this way you keep the focus on each other, and the relationship grows, organically, but not randomly.

In much the same way, you need a recommendation strategy, not just a story that gets told randomly and by happenstance. This strategy can get framed out for the entire year, month by month, week by week, even day by day, if that's how tightly you want to reach your bull's-eye. At Zócalo Group we actually have a calendar where we highlight, on each day of the week or month, and so on, what type of strategy we'll be using. Is today about awareness, engagement, action, or recommendation?

The fact is, you can drive this behavior within a fairly reasonable degree of expectation if you follow this strategy closely and follow a realistic, effective recommendation strategy along the course of a carefully plotted time frame, be that by the month, season, quarter, or year.

Ultimately, companies who closely monitor their company's real Shareable Story versus their perceived advertising slogans generally come out ahead in the recommendation age.

Identify

Discovering Those People Whose Recommendations Influence Your Brand's Purchase Decisions

I magine if one of the world's biggest corporations, a company with more brand-name subsidiaries than most companies have product descriptions, were to make the radical decision to shift focus away—to the tune of billions of marketing dollars—from traditional paid TV, radio, and magazine print advertising and drive its marketing focus instead toward WOM or, in their words, "one-to-one marketing."

That's just what Procter & Gamble did when in early 2012 it announced its intention to slash $10 billion in costs over the next five years by switching to more digital marketing strategies and progressing toward what the company's CEO calls "one-to-one marketing."

P&G, home to some of today's mightiest brands (26 of which have sales of $1 billion or more) including Cascade, Bounty, Charmin, Nyquil, Tide, Bounce, and IAMS pet food, will be using digital tools to build a closer, more personal relationship with shoppers, capitalizing on a wider effort to enhance its marketing and innovation capabilities.

Robert McDonald, P&G's previous CEO, told the *McKinsey Quarterly*, "With digital technology, it's now possible to have a one-on-one relationship with every consumer in the world. The more intimate the relationship, the more indispensable it becomes."

One would think that creating such personal, one-on-one relationships would cost more money, not less, but in fact P&G plans on saving those billions of dollars in a variety of cost-cutting measures,

113

including restructuring its marketing department to have fewer high-paid executives and more staff members who can actively monitor online chatter and respond faster, leaner, and more personally.

In advance of the cost-cutting, consumer-reaching measures, P&G has launched what it calls its "Consumer Pulse System," its term for analyzing online chatter across a variety of mediums. Discussing the revolutionary new system, P&G's McDonald explains, "Comments are grouped by brand and delivered to a relevant individual staff member. We have operations in around 80 countries, our products are sold in almost every country, and we touch more than 4 billion consumers every day. Imagine all those data points."

Data points indeed. Clearly, reaching all 4.5 billion total consumers is a challenging, if not impossible, goal. No doubt the company is planning to increase its spending in technologies that allow its brands to form more personal relationships with its consumers and influencers, allowing the P&G advertising team to work more efficiently and create messaging that resonates with the company's target consumers.

But *every* target consumer? With a company like P&G, with brands like Tide and Bounce, success—at least in the short to midterm—will come not in reaching all of its consumers but in identifying and reaching those who matter the most: the brand fans, industry eminents, and everyday influencers.

It's a little like round robin. If a hole opens up in my schedule toward late afternoon and I want to play a game of pickup ball at the gym, I don't have time to call enough guys to make it worth my while. But if I call one friend and tell him to call one friend, by the time I'm at the gym there can be a dozen guys standing around waiting for me, no problem.

Likewise, as we'll discover later in this chapter, you can save a lot of time, effort, money, and resources—obviously what P&G is planning on doing—not by focusing on everybody but identifying and reaching your influencers and letting them spread the word for you.

Identifying Your Brand Fans

Earlier, we discussed the importance of *brand fans*. Talk about getting one-on-one and personal; these folks are your intimate and voluntary cheerleaders, the ones who vocally and frequently support you in ways it would seem inauthentic and physically impossible to do on your own.

You likely have brand fans; nearly every brand does. The problem is finding them so you can reward or at least monitor them, perhaps even "guide" them into using your shareable story so their brand fandom isn't quite so . . . random. But beyond simple monitoring tactics, how else can brands find these people?

The answers range from the most basic and simple to the seriously advanced and complex.

If you are running and managing your own social platforms—particularly Facebook, Twitter, Pinterest, YouTube, and Google+—you've probably already noticed individuals who regularly give you positive feedback, Likes, Pins, or Shares. Despite some brands' boasting millions and millions of fans, research has shown that only 1 to 3 percent of them are truly engaged and are your likely brand fans.

Many brands have their own customer relationship management (CRM) systems in place to collect consumer data—these systems are full of opportunities to pull brand fan names and information. The key is to focus in on what your definition of a brand fan is so that you can use the CRM data to help you drill down, locate, pinpoint, isolate, and identify those who qualify as brand fans, according to your definition.

Being in possession of so much data is a good problem to have, but a problem nonetheless. What do you do with it all? How to sort it all, and where to start? Clearly, to avoid data fatigue, you'll want various filters in place to assist you.

Filtering that data through a company like Fliptop or Full Contact allows brands to see how social media–connected and influential their community already is and to narrow down from there:

- Which brand fans use Twitter the most?
- Facebook? Pinterest? Tumblr?
- How do they use them?
- How often?
- For what?
- Retweeting?
- Original content?
- Blogger or nonblogger?
- Forum fan or frequent reviewer?

Knowing the fans' social accounts, along with their preferences and presets, then allows you to figure out who your most influential fans are within those parameters and where, and even how, to target them. Just imagine P&G trying to get a grasp on which of its 4.5 billion consumers are the most vocal, positive, regular, loyal, and so on. You can bet filtering is at the top of P&G's list, and that's just the beginning of the kind of background work the company will need to do to achieve its goals of spending more one-on-one time with digital brand fans.

Identifying Brand Fans Beyond Your CRM Data and Social Channels

We've all heard how pervasive "big data" has become—nearly every transaction, engagement, or web search is recorded in some form or another.

Once you've got a clear model of what your brand fans likely look like, data brokers like Rapleaf and Acxiom can further help you identify new brand fans—on an international, national, regional, or local level. Whether it is sorting by income, children, marital status, or other premium data fields, many of these data providers can also measure social impact and influence.

There are also a few brand advocacy platforms on the market that promise to help brands identify and engage with their biggest fans. Some of these allow you to "rent" fans from a pool of people who have signed up to receive new products and share their impressions. Others make it easy to send promotions and referral offers to your CRM or e-mail lists—asking them to Like you, post a review, or refer a friend.

In early 2013, Zócalo Group launched the next-generation brand advocacy platform, Fan Rally, that helps brands identify their biggest advocates and then engage them either for a new product launch or on an ongoing basis with information, experiences, and feedback opportunities—all supported by an advanced reward and recognition game platform.

Given the growing and recognized importance of brand advocates, it is likely other advanced programs and platforms will be coming to market.

Identifying Your Industry Eminents

How does someone become an industry expert? In many cases, these individuals become recognized as being regular writers, speakers, bloggers, promoters, or leaders on a certain topic. They gather and share information—often getting quoted by the media or other experts. Previous chapters discussed the importance of engaging the entire influencer ecosystem that, as we covered, is composed of not just brand fans but also a category known as *industry eminents*.

While each group in your own company's influencer ecosystem is of equal value to a brand, in this section we'll concentrate on how to identify those industry eminents with expertise in your target industry and high reach as well.

Who would go to bat for you in your industry? Who respects you, your organization, and your products and services enough to bring them to the attention of those in the know? To reporters and journalists and bloggers and others of influence, who could catapult your success from fan centric to industry respected?

How and Where to Find Industry Eminents

Oftentimes, you'll want to look beyond the obvious to identify those who might be industry eminents for your brand.

For example, we worked with Unilever to introduce a new Dove deodorant for women a few years ago. Working to drive sales, we worked with the brand to focus our strategy on reaching "beauty enthusiasts" through online and offline engagement via the leading experts who impact them.

In addition to targeting "beauty experts," we expanded our expert list across a full range of industry eminents, including these:

- Image consultants and coaches
- Stylists and style experts
- Spa leaders
- Dermatologists
- Estheticians
- Active females
- Time-saving experts
- Dating coaches
- Travel experts
- Celebrities
- Business leaders and executives
- Wedding consultants
- Adult beauty pageant personnel

In total, more than 500 eminents were identified and reached, with active participation by 89 percent of them—eager to learn about and share news about a breakthrough product.

When gauging whether an industry eminent is right for your company or brand, it's best to consider the following criteria:

- **Overall reach.** This includes on the national and local levels. We assume that only the "big dogs" count, but the fact is that local experts can do wonders in more specific, hands-on ways than a national brand advocate can do halfway around the country, or the world.
- **Visibility.** How "visible" are the influencers? Do they publish often in respected industry journals? Or blog repeatedly? If so, how popular is the blog? What is its traffic like?
- **Reputation.** How credible are they? Would their names pull weight in your industry, or would they tarnish your own reputation by association?
- **Knowledge.** Are they recognized as being knowledgeable in your space? Professional knowledge around a certain topic, skill set, expertise, or industry is often what sets eminents apart from fans.
- **Accessibility.** If the eminents are locked away in an ivory tower or behind "handlers," they're likely not worth the energy and resources needed to engage them. True eminents have a hunger and willingness to share with other experts and those who are able to help educate them.
- **Relevance.** Industry eminents tend to specialize in one industry, making them more relevant than nonspecialists. For instance, if you're in the food industry, you may find eminents who specialize in sweet treats, pastries, desserts, and the like. This relevance could work significantly in your favor if they were to get behind your new gluten-free prepackaged brownies, for instance.
- **Tonality.** What is the tone of the potential eminents' online and offline presence? Do they embrace or are they at least open to brands, new ideas, and other opinions? Or are they very clearly opinionated or critical in a way that could be damaging to your brand?

Christine Cea, senior director of marketing communications at Unilever, making such iconic brands as Dove, Lipton, Suave,

Hellmann's, and AXE, has been a longtime proponent of influencer and word of mouth marketing.

"How people talk about and recommend our products has always played an important part in selling, dating back to Lord Lever, who started making brands in the era that ushered in advertising," said Cea. "With the emergence of social media, a valued peer-to-peer recommendation from 'someone I know' has grown exponentially to also encompass 'someone like me' where that 'someone' may actually be a total-yet-trusted 'stranger.' At its core, our mission remains the same as it was in Lord Lever's time: to create best-in-class products that help people look good, feel good, and get more out of life. However, marketing today has an added imperative driven by the proliferation of screens: to communicate with breakthrough content that clamors for attention, compels talkability and sharing, as well as creates a two-way engagement to foster brand advocacy, which is essentially a recommendation on steroids."[1]

The Everyday, or Peer, Influencers

In 2003, Ed Keller and Jon Berry of Roper ASW released a book titled *The Influentials: One American in Ten Tells the Other Nine How to Vote, Where to Eat and What to Buy* (Free Press).

These individuals are not necessarily the people you'd expect, the authors point out—not America's most affluent 10 percent, best educated, or even the "early adopters." They are the 10 percent of Americans who are most engaged in their communities—and they wield a huge amount of influence in those communities.

You can probably think of the type: the PTA leader, the school board chair, the head of the neighborhood parks board. Or maybe it's the head of the local Porsche club, runner's club, or state orchid grower's organization.

Back in 2003, Keller and Berry noted that significant advances in communications had occurred since the founder of the Roper Opinion Research Company, Elmo Burns Roper Jr., was hired by the Standard Oil Company of New Jersey (now Exxon) to develop a model for identifying opinion leaders.

Today, the "influentials" still exist—but thanks to social media, many of them have a significantly larger and more far reaching platform than they did just a few years ago.

Fortunately, there are a variety of tools (both in the "paid" and "free" categories) available to help you find peer influencers on a local, national, or international level. None of these tools are without limitations or detractors, but each can play a meaningful role in helping focus your efforts:

- **Klout (klout.com)** measures an individual's influence based on his or her ability to drive action on social networks.
- **Kred (kred.com)** allows users to view anyone's "most influential content and see his or her social profile as a 1,200-day visual stream."
- **Appinions (appinions.com) and Little Bird (getlittlebird.com)** are both designed to help brands identify, analyze, and monitor influencers.

These online tools allow users to search by topic to find influential online personalities for outreach. Imagine you're launching beauty products aimed at vampire wannabes. (These exist, by the way—both the products and the audience.) Now imagine going onto Klout, for instance, and discovering that not only is there a category for "vampires," but simply by clicking on it you can discover both the "top influencers" in that category and also the latest "buzz" in the topic.

By the same token, a liquor company looking to position its new flavored tequila might search "tequila" to find out who has been most recently (and passionately) talking about high-quality tequila and might choose to reach out to them based on their online posts. While the goal is to automate as much of this process as possible, obviously the more hands on and human centric your research, the more accurate and applicable it will be.

Case in point: a second way to find influencers is simple yet complicated all at once. It takes legwork, attention to detail, and dedication, but you'll be able to find those influencers that might not have a Twitter account or public Facebook page—and, before you ask, "Yes, those people *do* exist!"

It's called Google.

Yes, it's becoming rarer and rarer for anyone to not have at least a basic Facebook page—but just opening a Facebook account doesn't mean that's where someone is going to do the most of her influencing. Just as critically, not everyone blogs, not everyone tweets, and not everyone has her own personal website from which to preach or cheerlead about your product.

In some areas and industries—like academia, agriculture, and healthcare, just to name a few—there may be quite influential consumers, yet their online presence is quite small. This doesn't make them any less valuable—just a bit harder to find.

Make sure to expand your view beyond just the industry you're in to ensure that you're seeking eminents who may have "crossover" appeal. For instance, if you look for eminents only in the "prepackaged healthy snack cakes" industry, you may miss out on eminents who could still extol your product's virtues to a vast and powerful collateral audience.

Perhaps there's a really zealous blogger who covers the travel industry but runs a weekly column about fast, healthy treats on the go. His influence and recommendation could boost your sales in airport gift shops, snack bars, convenience stores, and so on.

Now let's take a look at another case study that will show how P&G is on the right track in looking to shift toward a more one-on-one, personalized relationship with its 4.5 billion customers.

The Nissan LEAF

As the first fully electric car, the Nissan LEAF represented a breakthrough new product in the automotive world—a zero-emissions vehicle. To help Nissan build awareness, educate consumers, drive interest, and stimulate trials, we created an online and offline word of mouth campaign with a big idea—give test drives to anyone who connected with Nissan LEAF via social media and talked about the vehicle.

For their influencer program, we of course made sure to identify automobile influencers as one main category of influencers, but we also know full well if you're too myopic, you'll miss out on a whole new audience.

So we also made sure to identify those eminents who were experts in environmental sustainability and those influential consumers who have chosen to live "green" lives. While cars might not be the first thing on their list, their interest in the environment fits perfectly with the messaging and goals of the LEAF team.

This led to the creation of a 23-city test drive tour executed jointly with a sister agency Omnicom Agency. Our word of mouth campaign solicited "hand raisers" and attracted influencers, including a variety of high profile celebrities, to help talk about and recommend the Nissan LEAF.

By listening to conversation, we found key celebrities who were talking about green issues. We invited them to try the LEAF—without paying them—and they quickly became advocates for the brand. By creating talkable and shareable experiences—both online and offline—for bloggers, brand fans, industry eminents, and high profile celebrities, Nissan was able to reach more than 45,000 consumers via the test drive tour. Additionally, the conversation generated over 100 million online impressions and grew the Nissan share-of-voice from 10 to 25 percent—surpassing key competitors Chevy Volt and Toyota Prius.

One thing every company looks for, particularly in the earned numbers categories of things like social media and WOM marketing, is return on investment (ROI). Most important then, the campaign drove order reservations for the Nissan LEAF. In fact, the program generated 20,000 orders three months ahead of schedule.

Let's see how the campaign broke down by the numbers:

By the Numbers

- It generated more than 100 million online impressions.
- It reached more than 45,000 consumers via the test drive tour.
- In August 2010, there were 175,000 registered users without Nissan **ever having run a single television spot for the vehicle.**
- It generated more than 100 million media impressions including 400 broadcast hits and more than 200 online media and blog placements.
- It improved its Twitter following by 56 percent from 1,667 followers in October 2009 (typically reaching 15,000 followers per month) to 8,854 in January 2011 (typically reaching 2,479,965 followers per month).
- A Nielsen BuzzMetrics study in June 2010 found that marketing campaigns and overall awareness toward the LEAF campaign were viewed more favorably than the Chevrolet Volt campaign.

"We know how important recommendations are among today's buyers," notes Erich Marx, director of interactive and social media marketing at Nissan North America. "We put great energy into not only producing best-in-class vehicles, but also ensuring we take care of Nissan owners before, during, and after the sale. Social media and word of mouth are key to helping us do it right."

Parting Words: *Finding—and Minding—Your Influentials*

As you can see, there is real ROI, hard target success to be found in identifying, targeting, and reaching your key influencers. Whether they're brand fans or industry eminents, finding key support and WOM recommendations in your targeted categories propels your one-on-one marketing efforts to new heights when discipline and detail-oriented listening and recording work are applied.

The power of influencers lies mainly in their ability to go where you can't go, reach where you can't reach, and tap into the power of their networks; big or small, male or female, young or old, and so on.

Regardless of your company, product, brand, or key demographics industry or scale, there are influencers out there who can take your WOM and recommendation marketing to the next level; but not if you never identify them.

CHAPTER 11

Activate

Creating Compelling Content and Experiences That Engage—The 90/10 Rule

At the start of Oprah's 2004 season premiere, the talk show host gave free cars to 11 needy families. This would have been touching enough, and generous enough, indeed. But then Oprah dropped an even bigger surprise on her live studio audience. She told them that there were gift boxes under their seats and that "one of them" included the keys to a twelfth free car.

As the audience rummaged through their boxes, an electrifying commotion ensued—revealing Oprah's second, even better surprise: EVERY box under EVERY seat included keys to a new car.

"EVERYBODY GETS A CAR!" Oprah screamed to her stunned audience. "EVERYBODY GETS A CAR! EVERYBODY GETS A CAR!" And we all watched, either live or on follow-up news reports, wondering why we didn't have enough sense to have been on Oprah's show that day.

What kind of car did Oprah give away that day? It was a 2005 Pontiac G6, a middle-of-the-road sedan retailing for around $28,000, donated by General Motors in the hopes that the buzz of Oprah's live TV antics would revitalize the long-stagnant Pontiac brand.

There was great buzz surrounding the event, but not necessarily in a way that helped Pontiac achieve its goals. As the spectacle played out on national television, the car became part of the background. And Oprah seemed to be far more enamored at her ability to give away the cars than giving the G6 its paid-for spot in the sun.

So when the dust settled and the buzz died down, how did the promotion work for the ailing car company? After five more years of increasingly dismal sales, General Motors eventually relegated Pontiac to the land of lost and forgotten auto brands.

It turns out that Oprah really had something to shout about that day after all. Her highly watched, highly touted act of generosity ultimately marked the pinnacle of the Buzz Marketing Period.

It was all downhill after that . . .

So, Whatever Happened to Buzz?

We founded Zócalo Group in 2007, right as marketers were beginning to realize that this revolutionary new thing called "buzz marketing" wasn't all that it was cracked up to be.

Sure, there were a variety of books out there, ranging from *The Anatomy of Buzz: How to Create Word of Mouth Marketing* (Crown Business, 2002) to *Buzzmarketing: Get People to Talk About Your Stuff* (Portfolio, 2005), that promised they could get anyone talking about any product, event, or service. And once *The Tipping Point* by Malcolm Gladwell took off, forget about it; it was all buzz, all the time.

In many cases, these books and their authors were right. But what were they *really* talking about when they used the word *buzz*—and did it *really* build the brand or move sales in any real or measurable way that could justify the time and resources spent on achieving it?

These were the questions that we at Zócalo Group asked ourselves and that, once burned on this "business of buzz," many of our clients began asking *us*. In fact, most of our new business calls began coming in from brands that had launched buzz campaigns. They had often received a respectable amount of noise and often gave away lots of samples. But things quickly quieted down. Now they wanted to know what came next. How could they monopolize on, even monetize, this positive buzz? And just as important, how could they keep people engaged, talking, and recommending once the flash of a buzz campaign had worn off, the dust had settled, and they had to determine the ROI of the campaign?

What many found was that building buzz, as Oprah had so deftly showed us all, is the (relatively) easy part. The challenge is in monetizing the buzz and turning it into something more than simply being "the party bore."

The Party Bore

I bet you've all had the following experience: you go to a party and strike up a conversation with someone who seems to be a perfectly agreeable guest. You exchange the usual party pleasantries. You determine whom you know in common and maybe even share a laugh or two, and a quip about the weather or your favorite sports team or TV show.

Then, being the engaging conversationalist you know yourself to be, you instinctively ask a question about the person's work, hobby, or special interest. Suddenly, a spark catches, the momentum shifts, and the mutual exchange that had been so pleasant one minute earlier turns, abruptly and unexpectedly, into an exhaustive monologue from your new "friend."

You nod instinctively, merely being polite, and the speaker takes that as a sign that you find him as interesting as he obviously finds himself. So he continues. And continues. All the while you desperately work to catch the eye of your friend, spouse, or even the host's dog—anyone or anything that can interrupt the flow and give you an excuse to beat a hasty retreat.

Turns out, you've just met . . . the party bore. And when that man goes home later that night, he tells his wife about meeting you—one of the most interesting and engaging people he's ever come across. And you tell your spouse that you were trapped for what felt like "hours" and wonder why she didn't notice and come earlier to save you.

So, what happens the next time you see the party bore? You wave from across the room and do everything possible to keep your distance, including making small talk with the house plant or sprinting into the nearest broom closet for the duration of the party.

"No way," you say to yourself. "I'll never get trapped like that again."

In many ways, buzz is a less intimate way of being the party bore. It proves that not all conversation is good and that simply talking isn't always the same as communicating, and it is certainly a far cry from engaging.

And, just like the party bore, buzz creates a lot of noise with little results. It can mask or cloud the real issues at work in the general public, who are on the receiving end of all your "buzz speak." Are they generally interested, engaged, and enthused about what you're saying, or are you the brand equivalent of the party bore?

To note the distinction, you have to understand the fundamental difference between buzz and engagement.

The Age of Engagement

As the era of buzz quickly came and went, just like buzz itself, you could watch the learning curve play out. Every brand, it seemed, was rushing to fill up its social media quota, grabbing friends and followers as fast as they could double-click, driving up the metrics and stacking the deck. Then, after a certain threshold or deadline or quota was reached, it would sit back, wind up, and ask these questions:

- How do I put these numbers to work?
- What does all this data mean?
- Who are all these people, and why are they following, Friending, or Liking us?
- How do I get these people—I mean, I *assume* they're people—to act?
- What do I do with them now?

What you do, in a nutshell, is **engage them.**

If 2009 through 2012 was the age of accumulation for brands— feverishly working to build up their number of fans, Likes, and followers without really understanding what they would do with them later—then 2013 going forward is certainly the age of engagement.

Through special offers, freebies, contests, and the like, brands have accumulated throngs of people, who now will either choose to actively or passively engage—or simply drop—brands that they've somehow connected with in the past.

And you, as the brand, have a choice as well: you can become the brand equivalent of the party bore—holding one-sided conversations and building buzz that lands on deaf ears because it is so generic, repetitive, and impersonal—or you can find ways to truly listen to and engage with your consumers, customers, employees, and prospects in ways that really matter to them.

And, ultimately, to you as well.

The 90/10 Rule

When it comes to engagement—getting people invested in your message, forming authentic relationships, building credibility and trust, and so on—I'd like to suggest using the *90/10 Rule*.

The 90/10 Rule states that you spend 90 percent of your time engaging with people across your social networks. Informing them, entertaining them, educating them, sharing with them, asking for their input, and listening to them.

You share things that are relevant to people who are interested in your category—or what it represents, that is, health and wellness—and engage in a true, mutually beneficial, and interesting exchange.

And then, you spend the remaining 10 percent of the time actively sharing your brand messages—or encouraging people into action of some kind.

Unfortunately, many brands follow the 10/90 Rule. Instead of engaging, interacting, educating, informing, entertaining, conversing, and listening for 90 percent of the time, they spend only 10 percent of their time doing any of that.

The rest of the time, 90 percent of it (or more), they are actively blitzing their connections, friends, fans, followers, constituents, network, and so on, with constant requests, calls to action, repeated referrals, and so on.

How It Works

Engagement is the slow burn, like any relationship, that takes its time to build to momentum, which, as we'll see, is anything from awareness to action to a full-fledged recommendation.

People who worry more about buzz than engagement tend to expect something for nothing. They tend to still be doing traditional advertising—after all, what is buzz if not simply "broadcasting"?—in an exponentially more modern, sophisticated, and social world that respects and rewards relationship building rather than "advertising."

What the 90/10 Rule does is put relationships over expectations. It is not just an event, like giving away a car, but a habit—a lifestyle that permeates not just the marketing and promotion teams but the entire organization.

It becomes habitual in how you plan to roll out a new product, not just days or weeks in advance but months ahead of the event itself. It's about committing time and resources to the care, feeding, and maintenance of your core group of brand fans and influencers so that they can further spread that relationship by sharing your engagement with others.

We will learn shortly the value of content marketing—podcasts, webinars, white papers, articles, e-books, personalized promotions, and so on—and how you can leverage works you create or even collect yourself to entertain, inform, and engage with your target audience in ways that far surpass blitz or buzz marketing.

But over and above how you engage, you must value the act, the spirit, of engagement in and of itself. Take the same party scenario and now flip it. Suppose, instead of asking you about yourself for the first 5 minutes of the conversation and then launching into a 55-minute diatribe, your fellow party guest did the opposite: spent a few minutes introducing himself and establishing a connection before beginning a back-and-forth conversation in which neither of you dominated but both participated. Suppose he asked and answered, related and regaled, pushed and pulled, and generally connected with you in a way that was personal, personalized, and full of personality?

Engagement is the same as a really good conversation, and like any good conversation, it's addictive. When you have a great conversation with someone at a cocktail party, it's energizing.

Time flies by and you look around to find the party breaking up before you even knew it got started. Then, the next time you see that person, be it at a party, coffee shop, restaurant, or friend's house, rather than hiding in the broom closet until he's gone, you flock to that person, eager to go back to that well of sincere and generous, personalized interaction.

When we see a company doing well in social media, customer service, and in personal interaction, we know why: its employees are engaging with people. They're not relying on marketing or promotional blitzes or the false high of buzz, but instead they're participating in true conversations online and off.

Why It Matters

Engagement is about building, not buzzing. When you spend 90 percent of your time engaging your audience, you're not just giving your time away. You are spending it wisely by closely following your interactions. It's not all charity. That 90 percent of engagement is also spent collecting data—listening to online chatter about you and your products and/or services and brand. (See the sidebar "The 2013 Super Bowl.")

The 2013 Super Bowl

The 2013 Super Bowl, a veritable Academy Awards of what many in advertising consider to be the epitome of buzz-worthy branding, offered a variety of instantly catchy "moments." Were they effective? Were they worth the money? Time will tell, I suppose, as to whether or not any of the year's most talked about ads truly engaged the audience:

- A supermodel kissing a nerd
- A horse trainer being reunited with his Clydesdale
- Some snazzy movie clips from *Iron Man 3*, *World War Z*, and *Fast and Furious 6*
- Taco Bell giving a shout-out to senior citizens who love the nightlife
- Amy Poehler shopping at Best Buy

There is a time and a place for buzz, and clearly advertisers feel like the Super Bowl is it. But . . . were any of these commercials engaging to the point of earning new customers, building brand loyalty, or inspiring any further discussion beyond, "Yeah, that was pretty cool" around Monday's watercooler? Again, time will tell.

For me, the only true moment of immediate, instant, and connective engagement to truly emerge from the 2013 Super Bowl ads was the brilliant Oreo "twitpic" that went out shortly—and I mean *very* shortly—after the lights went out in the Superdome.

As millions of Americans turned to social media to fill the time while both teams cooled their heels in a powerless stadium—according to ComputerWord.com, "the Super Bowl drove more than 24 million tweets about the game and halftime show." Meanwhile the folks at Oreo tweeted the brilliant ad, "You can still dunk in the dark!"

Now *that's* engagement: personalized, immediate, and reactive.

Witness the way Hasbro, makers of the Easy Bake Oven that has been traditionally reserved for girls—in design, advertising, taste, color, and so on—responded to the online petition of a teenage girl who wondered if the company could make a gender-neutral Easy Bake Oven for her four-year-old brother. McKenna Pope was encouraged when her little brother, Gavin, told her he was going to ask Santa Claus for a "dinosaur Easy Bake Oven" for Christmas during the holiday season of 2012.

But McKenna was soon discouraged to find that the famous ovens came only in pink and a floral print purple, neither of which would appeal to her little brother. She started a petition on Change.org, and she eventually got 40,000 signatures of other would-be pastry aficionados who agreed with her that the ovens should appeal to both boys and girls. Recently Hasbro invited McKenna and her family to its company headquarters to reveal some new gender-neutral designs, predominantly in black and silver.

While Hasbro says the new designs have been in the works for some time, that was no reason why the company couldn't engage with a young girl and her brother to help reveal the new designs in a way that would both respect McKenna and her brother and other potential consumers who might not have become aware of the design changes otherwise.

This type of "instant engagement" doesn't happen often, but it wouldn't have happened at all if Hasbro had been more invested in building buzz than in listening to its actual target audience.

Attaching Yourself to Something Bigger Than Yourself

One of the building blocks of true engagement is put in place when a brand attaches to something larger than itself. In other words, true engagement occurs when people begin to look to a certain brand for more than just the product it sells or the service it provides.

Case in point: Does Nike sell just running shoes and tank tops, or does it sell the active fitness lifestyle that makes it the "Apple of active sportswear"? Does Whole Foods sell just organic soy butter and gluten-free almond granola, or does it sell a lifestyle of responsible shopping, spending, and eating?

What gold standard brands like Nike and Whole Foods (and a host of others) provide that makes them so recognizable—and their brand fans so loyal—is the "something extra" that helps consumers attach themselves to something bigger than themselves.

To wear Nike running shoes is to be part of a "tribe" that worships at the altar of fitness and the active lifestyle. It is code, part of a secret language that true Nike enthusiasts speak merely by aligning themselves with a brand that's become synonymous with a just-do-it mentality that seeps into every facet of their daily life. Others who aren't quite part of that tribe yet desperately want to speak that language can do so merely by purchasing a part of the lifestyle brand.

Likewise, to shop at Whole Foods is to pledge allegiance to "responsible" shopping, trusting that the food you're buying—at a premium, no less—is nutritious, healthy, fresh, organic, and more.

You are spending your money in the hope, trust, and belief that the purveyors of Whole Foods are supporting local farmers, bakers, recycling plants, communities, and the like.

It's nice to feel that every dollar you spend at the grocery store is going not just to feed your family but to build a community in a way that is both responsible and sustainable. That is engagement on a higher level—the fostering of "attachment" that turns consumers into brand advocates and products into lifestyles.

Starbucks is a company that has perfected the art of helping its consumers attach themselves to something bigger than themselves. Just perusing the Starbucks website is a rich and engaging experience. Almost every facet is designed to draw you into not just an experience but a world unique unto itself.

Starbucks devotees look forward each year to the "red holiday cups" signaling that a new season of fresh, seasonal flavors is upon them. They can read blog posts with headlines like "Helping Sumatran Farmers Respond to Climate Change" and "America's Future Depends on Jobs."

The company website's "Responsibility" tab is a plethora of feel-good, earth-friendly, global-positive resources that help you drink its coffee with the confidence that, like shopping in Whole Foods, you're not just consuming but investing in the planet's future.

Its brick-and-mortar cafes are designed to be both exclusive and accessible. Once you speak the code of how to place your order and find your favorite beverage, size, toppings, combinations, and seat, it's an invitation to come back again and again and again. The funky music, the new artists, the book recommendations, and hip staff all contribute to this "exclusive but accessible" atmosphere that promotes not just the act of buying a cup of coffee but of investing in a lifestyle.

Engagement is about connection. What connects you to coffee? Very little, but companies like Starbucks are very invested in engagement and offer a variety of ways to connect with what start out as coffee drinkers and turn into brand fans because of that "something bigger" Starbucks gives them.

The New Definition of Content and Content Marketing

New strategies for engagement require new forms of marketing, like **content marketing**. Traditional, one-way marketing of old relied on static, unchanging, one-way images and copy that broadcasted, but rarely engaged. Today's philosophy of engagement first and requests for action second requires a new form of marketing, and content marketing is a great way to fit that bill. (See also the sidebar "The Path to Recommendation.")

The Path to Recommendation: *Mastering the Four Phases of Involvement*

As I mentioned earlier, engagement isn't an event. It's a way of doing business. It's also a process that follows a clear path.

As a brand, you should plan out—on an calendar—where, how, when, and why you are going to involve, share, question, play, and simply engage with your consumers, customers, prospects, or fans.

At Zócalo Group, we call this trail the "Path to Recommendation," and it involves mastering the four phases of involvement:

1. **Awareness.** The first phase of involvement is simple awareness. This is the easiest way for consumers to interact with you because it requires so little of them. Maybe you've got a new brand, and you just want to keep your name out there. You want to be visible. You want people to see something, share it, and simply be aware of it. Maybe you're just attaching yourself to positive things, events, or organizations, doing things that drive activity that leads to awareness.

2. **Engagement.** As we've seen throughout this chapter, engagement is a more active form of involvement between you and your vast connections across social media. Maybe you want to engage them with some content, like a video tutorial, white paper, new blog post, or song download. Maybe you run a giveaway or contest on your blog, or you simply ask them to comment on a timely or relevant blog post. Maybe you want them to share something on Facebook or retweet something you've posted on Twitter. The important part to remember about engagement is that it's not simply "code" for selling. It's different. At this stage you are building relationships, not interrupting them with calls to action. That comes next.

3. **Action.** In the action phase, I actually want you to click on something and check it out. Sign up for this. Pass on this coupon to someone else. Write something specific on this. I can't ask you too many times to take an action. I have to be deliberate about it. Is there a sense of reciprocity involved? Are you on overload? How much can I ask, how often, when, and where? These are all challenges to overcome in the action phase.

4. Recommendation. Finally, the recommendation phase is the culmination of this process, the final destination on our Path to Recommendation. Here is where all of the goodwill, content marketing, reciprocity, and relationship building (hopefully) come to fruition. Here is where, if you've followed the process, believed in it, and participated in it fully, you can feel comfortable asking for recommendations, suggesting they pass along a link or a five-star rating, a comment or a coupon, or something else.

The great thing about this Path to Recommendation is that it's transferable along all types of social media. It works on Facebook and Twitter, Pinterest and LinkedIn. It works on your website, your blog, on YouTube, and anywhere else your brand fans and influencers congregate, gather, and recommend.

According to *Wikipedia*, "Content marketing is an umbrella term encompassing all marketing formats that involve the creation and sharing of content in order to attract, acquire, and engage clearly defined and understood current and potential consumer bases with the objective of driving profitable customer action. Content marketing subscribes to the notion that delivering information to prospects and customers drives profitable consumer action."

Basically, content marketing is about using information to move products and services. For our uses, "content" can be anything from blog posts to online newsletters, podcasts and webinars, interactive online events, daily quotes, tips or statistics, white papers, e-books, audio or video downloads, and so on.

So, for instance:

- A company that sells cleaning products might also provide an online portal that offers video tutorials on how to safely remove stains, clean a carpet, and accomplish other cleaning projects. The company might provide downloadable white papers, manuals, or printable safety posters in conjunction with its products.
- Starbucks might offer a free Christmas album full of holiday favorites anyone can download from its website during December. The company might populate its blog with articles from some of today's top experts in sustainability, recycling,

climate change, or other ecological topics to help brand and establish itself as a company leading the charge in corporate ethics and responsibility.

- A publisher might offer a free chapter from a dozen of their upcoming "chick lit" releases in a downloadable e-book available for Kindle or Nook, on iTunes and Smashwords, or some other reading platform.
- A clothing line might hire several of today's top fashion bloggers to post weekly video blogs, or v-logs, featuring their products or simply makeup, fashion, and accessorizing tips.

Brands have the ability to either create and/or curate content. In other words, Starbucks doesn't necessarily have to be originating everything on its site about sustainability in-house with a team of writers, artists, researchers, academics, and the like for the content to be effective.

Merely by gathering some of the Internet's finest articles and experts on these matters and "curating" them on its site, the company is offering and branding that content as its own, regardless of who may have originally authored it. This still offers the full engagement experience without the full creative experience.

Or a company like Amazon.com might offer one free Halloween download of spooky songs or scary stories for each of the 31 Days of Halloween.

Not only does this offer promote the individual artists who sell their wares on Amazon (engendering goodwill among those artists toward the content provider), but it also provides content, free of charge, to both loyal users and would-be loyal users who may stop in once or twice to download a few songs, find the process easy, enjoyable, and addictive, and come back to pay for their song downloads next time.

An Example of Sustainable Engagement: *Harley-Davidson*

One of the challenges facing any brand is that of sustainable engagement. One company that has mastered the art of sustainable engagement is Harley-Davidson.

The Harley-Davidson brand is extremely well known, whether you're a biker or not. And when you've got customers that are willing to tattoo your logo on their body—you've got brand loyalty.

Founded in 1903, the Harley brand actually went through a rough patch in the 1960s, even declaring bankruptcy. Through a concentration on quality and some innovative marketing techniques, company cofounder Arthur Davidson was able to bring the brand back to its former glory.

The importance of community has flowed through Harley-Davidson since it reemerged from bankruptcy. According to Ceptara.com, "Harley-Davidson has been a consistent sponsor of the 'Harley Owners' Group,' which has grown from 73,000 members in 1987 to 450,000 in 2005 to over 1 million members today."

Harley-Davidson has a strong sense of tradition. Annual and popular rallies in Sturgis, South Dakota, and mini-events throughout the year and group rides at dealerships throughout the country enforce the history of the brand, as well as its concentration on quality. These continuous events also act as "invitations" to a growing family, one that's welcoming and full of folks just like you.

Branded merchandise makes it easy for consumers to implicitly recommend the brand. After all, when was the last time you wore a brand name you didn't like? It doesn't hurt that the merchandise is as cool and reminiscent of the lifestyle as the motorcycles themselves.

Harley does buy advertising—but it focuses on the *brand*, not specific products. It's selling a lifestyle—not just a motorcycle—and it does it through sustained, aggressive, personal, and interactive engagement.

Parting Words About Engagement

As social media has grown in popularity in the last eight years (believe it or not, Facebook was launched only in 2004), the need for engaging content has grown exponentially. While the need for creative advertising has always existed, now it's up to brands to actually correspond with their consumers on a more personal level.

With the increasing comfort levels of online sharing (the modern blog even evolved from the online diary), consumers are more willing than ever before to share exactly what they're thinking, and brands, with the right strategy, can naturally fit into those conversations.

CHAPTER 12

Protect

Identifying and Neutralizing Determined Detractors: Hear Me's, Reputation Terrorists, and Competitive Destroyers

I n January 2012, the marketing team at McDonald's thought they had the perfect social media campaign to kick off the New Year: they launched a Twitter campaign using the hashtag #McDStories.

The idea seemed innocent enough. The team would launch the campaign, and legions of inspired McDonald's customers would start sharing heart-warming stories about having their first dates over French fries, celebrating baseball game wins with hamburgers, and recalling their kids' delight at their first Happy Meal.

To make sure the campaign got launched with a bang, they paid to have #McDStories featured on Twitter's home page. However, a mere two hours after launching the program (which must be a record somewhere), McDonald's was forced to shut down the campaign.

Instead of gushing love notes, #McDStories was filled with snarky quips and McDonald's detractors who turned it into a #bashtag to share their #McDHorrorStories.

Forbes magazine reporter Kashmir Hill quickly reported on the story with "McDStories: When a Hashtag Becomes a Bashtag." And to his credit, McDonald's very capable social media leader Rick Wion was one of the first to respond.

"Part of being in social media is knowing that you can't control the message 100 percent of the time," Wion noted. "As Twitter continues to evolve its platform and engagement opportunities, we're learning from our experiences."

What Just Happened?

So, what went wrong? How did a company that gets so much of its paid advertising right take this wrong turn?

Jeff Wilson, partner and chief customer experience designer at Sensei Marketing, posted a blog titled "Social Media Is Creating Bad Customers" to explain the situation.

"Why? It's simple. . . . Because people deep down are bullies or at the very least indifferent to bullying. Add to this how easily the social media public is influenced by a mob mentality and you get recipes for McDStory after McDStory."

His explanation just goes to underscore the dark side of social media marketing and the power of negative WOM. Wilson went on to explain that, in his view, social media gives the average person four factors empowering bad behavior, particularly against brands that are naively unaware of the disparity between their real and perceived online perceptions:

1. **No guilt.** There is no remorse about bullying a brand. It's much easier to do because no one "gets hurt."
2. **The mob.** Lots of other people are doing it. Whether they are the instigators with a real story or trolls making them up, it's easy to find others who will join you.
3. **Relative anonymity.** Anonymity strips many people of fear. "No one will know if I say this" is the common feeling and easily overwhelms any feelings of restraint a person might normally have.
4. **No accountability.** Probably the most significant factor is the sheer lack of accountability in anything said in social media. Without accountability as a "natural check" on actions, you get an environment devoid of any punishment.

It's easy to see how a company as proficient in traditional, one-way advertising—with its catchy radio jingles, touching TV commercials, glossy print ads, and Happy Meal movie tie-ins—as McDonald's could underestimate the dark side of two-way, fully interactive, ultimately transparent social media marketing.

But what's to prevent mere mortal companies like yours and mine from making these same mistakes? How can we avoid the online bullying, mob mentality, and generally ugly behavior of Internet trolls and anonymous haters?

Well, we may not be able to avoid it, but we can certainly do everything in our power to protect our brand image regardless of it, and that's just what this chapter is all about.

The Power of Protection

The power, and peril, of social media is the ease with which merely dissatisfied consumers can quickly find their voice and turn into Determined Detractors. With a few mouse clicks, they can easily voice their displeasure with you or your brand.

For many, this experience of finding their voice, often for the first time, can be addictive. But even when it's not, in general, the impact of consumer reviews is growing, and with that, the importance of monitoring negative reviews.

Let's consider the scope of negative reviews, as well as the damage they can do, by this sampling of what should be disturbing statistics for all of us:

- "67 percent of consumers say they would not buy a product if it had as few as 3 negative reviews." (Source: Lightspeed Research)
- "A high product rating increases the likelihood of purchase for 55 percent of consumers." (Source: DigitalVisitor.com)
- "Over 75 percent of review users reported that reviews have a significant influence on their purchase, and depending on the category, that number can be as large as 87 percent." (Source: comScore)
- "80 percent of those surveyed say that negative information they've read online has made them change their mind about purchasing a product or service someone recommended to them." (Source: Cone Communications)

More and more often, reviews and ratings are becoming a significant factor in how, what, when, and even why consumers buy what they buy or, just as significantly, don't buy what they go without.

While the casual consumer may write a review or two, tweet about a product, service, or experience or give a thumbs-up or thumbs-down on something they feel strongly about, there is a new breed of focused, purposeful, and increasingly powerful reviewers out there known as Determined Detractors.

These Determined Detractors come in three flavors: Hear Me's, Reputation Terrorists, and Competitive Destroyers.

Hear Me's

This particular group of Determined Detractors will deal mainly with customer service representatives. The fact that this sort of detractor group exists cements the need for customer service reps to be taught how to handle negative social media posts.

For whatever reason—poor customer service, a bad shopping experience, slow delivery time, whatever—these consumers are angry with a brand and simply want someone, *anyone* to know about it. Would it be great if the person they express their unhappiness to was one of your own customer service representatives? Ideally, yes, but barring that, it could be anybody, anywhere, offline or on.

To that end they typically *do* try to reach out to the brand through traditional channels (e-mail, phone, "contact us" form), but for whatever reason, their issue is not resolved to their satisfaction. As a result, they choose to go public with their frustration and need to be acknowledged.

Not every Hear Me plea will go viral, but if or when one does, look out. Here is one case in which a Hear Me probably got a much larger audience than he intended, and the company in question had to do a lot more PR spin as a result: In September 2009, a popular blogger from *TechnoBuffalo* named "Jon" posted a video to YouTube about a terrible experience he had with Dell's customer service. He detailed his treatment, and to date the video has been viewed over 48,000 times and still exists on YouTube.

As a result, the brand reached out to Jon and allowed him to join its Consumer Advisory Panel in 2010. Jon followed up his initial "Dear Dell" video with an update to let his viewers know how Dell had improved its service. This was a good outcome. Had it not been resolved as carefully, the incident could have been disastrous, and this Hear Me plea could have proven to be a lose-lose situation for Dell. Instead, the company heard about it, responded to it, and acted responsibly to resolve the situation, creating instead a win-win.

So how can *you* avoid gaining more Hear Me's, or barring that, how can you deal with the ones you already have? There are three distinct ways you can move a Hear Me out of the Determined Detractor column and straight into the Satisfied Customer column instead:

1. **Identify.** First, have a constant monitoring "station" or team in place so that you can stay abreast of online chatter to help nip any problems in the bud. As you'll see throughout this chapter, Determined Detractors increase in severity the longer their needs go unmet. Therefore, the best way to stop such detractors at the relatively harmless Hear Me level is to respond promptly and positively to try and solve their problem.
2. **Isolate.** Next, once you've identified a Hear Me, the next step is to remove the person's messages from mainstream channels so that the discussion is no longer public. We call this "isolation" because we're putting the detractor in a bracket where we are listening but the rest of the world isn't necessarily privy to that conversation. Remember, the Hear Me's just want to be heard, so once you identify them, the next step is to isolate them so that the conversation becomes much more personal, but far less public.
3. **Solve.** Finally, the conversation should become a one-on-one discussion of both the Hear Me's problem, his or her needs, and ultimately, the solution to that problem.

You can see the progression of these three steps writ large in Jon's story from above. First he was identified, likely after posting his "Dear Dell" video on YouTube. Next, he was isolated by being invited to participate with Dell on its Consumer Advisory Panel.

Finally, Jon's problem was solved to the point where he felt compelled to go online and post another video updating the company's solution. In short, he was "converted" from a decidedly Determined Detractor into a brand advocate.

What's unique about folks in the Hear Me column is that, once their vocalizations have stopped and they've actually been listened to, they often become valuable fonts of wisdom as to how not to conduct customer service in the future.

The best thing you can do is turn a Hear Me into a They Satisfied Me Advocate. The worst you can do is consider the case closed without doing at least some type of "exit" interview to see how the problem could have been avoided in the first place.

Reputation Terrorists

Our second "branch" of Determined Detractors, Reputation Terrorists, fundamentally do not agree with a particular company or brand—its mission, products, or something else. This may be because they've had a bad experience with a brand or simply, irrationally, because they resent its existence.

Unlike Hear Me's, who are basically out to resolve a personal problem with the company, Reputation Terrorists are personally out to defame, detract, or even destroy a company's reputation, both online and off.

They are active, verbal, even purposeful, and like real terrorists, they wage "campaigns" designed to actively achieve their goals. These campaigns can be quite focused, intense, and effective.

As the name implies, Reputation Terrorists are far more purposeful about their "cause" than Hear Me's, for whom the situation is far more personal. Reputation Terrorists don't go away quite as easily as Hear Me's, nor are they quite as easily satisfied.

Still, you can't just throw your hands up in defeat, and there are ways to defend against Reputation Terrorists. In fact, the first line of offense against these Determined Detractors is frequently a strong defense:

1. **Monitoring matters.** To that end, find a way to constantly monitor online chatter to identify Reputation Terrorists before they take up arms. The longer the Reputation Terrorists fester over real or perceived slights, the stronger their resolve grows. By the time they become active campaigners, Reputation Terrorists become harder and harder to please. By addressing their concerns early through strong online awareness and chatter analysis, you can hopefully cut potential Reputation Terrorists off at the pass.

2. **Apply preventive maintenance.** If you do not, if you are truly "tardy to the party," you will be made aware of the Reputation Terrorists through their actions, words, or constant complaints, and then hopefully a little counterprogramming can help. We've talked at length about how your advocates can help build and promote a brand, but here is a case in which they can often rush in to defend the brand as well. Reputation Terrorists don't happen in a vacuum, and for every zealot who is out to hurt you, there are often several more who will rise to defend you.

That is, *if* you have nurtured them carefully and created a brand worth defending. This is when the term "preventive maintenance" really comes into play because, honestly, you can't ask brand advocates to defend you; it simply rings hollow. But they will defend you if you do all those things we've talked about in this book beforehand so that your "goodwill bank" has enough deposits to cover the solid work your brand defenders may do on your behalf.

3. **Fight fire with facts.** One of the primary weaknesses of Reputation Terrorists is that they often base their arguments on feelings versus facts. That is, they feel slighted and passionately and proactively slander you based on those hurt feelings. True, the longer they wage war against your reputation, the more organized they become, but regardless their battles are often fought on the emotional versus the rational battlefield. Therefore, when you've identified the Reputation Terrorists and homed in on what, exactly, their beef is with you, you can begin controlling the damage in the opposite direction: with facts over feelings. Do your homework, and get out in front of the damage control by responding with level heads and plenty of facts. For every piece of false information the Reputation Terrorists might post about your company, you must counter with sending two or more positive, factual pieces of information into the marketplace.

4. **Clarity is critical.** Finally, be proactive about clearly stating your position and making it known in the marketplace. The fact is, people will be people. They like to "take sides," and the only way to come out a winner in the fight with Reputation Terrorists is simply to believe in your case and state it clearly. Remember, Reputation Terrorists are on a "mission" because they believe they are right, and they set about telling the world, or at least "their" world, how right they are. You must be just as right—in fact, you must be more right. You must stand above the fray and combat feelings with facts and confusion with clarity.

Competitive Destroyers

One of the most insidious and well-funded types of Determined Detractors are those known as "Competitive Destroyers." As the name implies, these aren't your average citizens or disgruntled consumers, but instead, they are active competitors who "act" like average citizens or disgruntled citizens with the express interest in tarnishing or all out destroying your brand image.

Rival brands often take small digs at one another through social media (or more often in advertising), but there are some "battles" that take that competition one step further.

Take Microsoft, for instance. You wouldn't think that a power player, industry leader, and overall global titan would have to stoop to anything as low as competitive destruction, but that's exactly what the company did in a botched campaign that went awry and lives in infamy as one of the more notable rivalry failures of all time.

Obviously, for top players in the technology game to stay on the top, they must keep an eye out on the competition. But actively sabotaging the competition is a tricky game that when, done wrong, can prove disastrous.

Everyone knows the stakes in smartphone technology, to say nothing of sales, are the highest of high. So when trying to find converts for the Windows Phone 8, Microsoft approached Twitter with the express intention of showing up one of its rivals, the Android, by asking for horror stories about its malware features.

Microsoft attempted to convince Droid users to switch to the new Windows phone by encouraging them to use the hashtag #DroidRage. Unfortunately, the campaign went terribly awry.

Almost instantly the plan backfired when Microsoft made the innocuous enough sounding request on Twitter: "Do you have an Android malware horror story? Reply with #DroidRage with your best/worst story, and we may have a get-well present for you."[1]

Android fans proved to be both a loyal and vocal bunch, almost immediately taking over the hashtag and using it against the Windows phone and its problems with the smartphone, which sparked another hashtag, #WindowsRage.[2]

The drama was vocal, brutal, and blindingly swift. It is also a textbook case in how *not* to be a Competitive Destroyer.

Are you making the same mistake by failing to monitor online social chatter or, just as bad, ignoring it? In this next section, we will discuss ways to counteract all three of these Determined Detractors and protect your precious brand image in this most transparent and vocal of times.

Protect: *Getting Proactive in the Media Age*

As we've seen in this chapter, the damage of negative perception on your brand can be increasingly severe. With so much going on online, the longer a negative perception exists without a strong offense or defense, the more likely people are to (a) see it and (b) believe it.

Here are some tips to help you protect your brand image by getting proactive in the media age.

Know When, and When Not, to Get Excited

Not every tweet is the end of the world, and not every blog post is going to go viral. Not all Determined Detractors are created equal. Some have a big audience and cast a wide net, so when they speak, thousands, maybe hundreds of thousands, of people will listen. Others have a compelling message that gets picked up by those who choose to believe it.

Others are simply tempests in teapots. In other words, they may tweet once or twice about a lousy experience in your store, and a few people may read or pay attention to their tweets, but they will then quickly move on with their lives. So it's critical that you not send out your brand's equivalent of the National Guard every time the chatter grows dark. Take the following variables into account first:

- **How much traction is the message getting?** If a negative tweet never gets retweeted, if a negative Facebook posting gets only one or two Likes, if a negative blog post doesn't get any comments, it's likely to not have very much traction. If, on the other hand, the reaction is too overwhelming to be ignored, be grateful that you found it in enough time to control the damage.
- **How big is the Determined Detractor's reach?** Again, not all Determined Detractors are created equal. Some are just dabbling in the art of reputation terrorism, while others are quite serious and have amassed quite a reach. Before going into spin mode, it's important to determine if a simple e-mail response from the customer service department can quell a coming storm, or if it will take calling in the "big guns" and taking your case directly to the marketplace.
- **How sustained is the attack?** A random tweet, a frustrated Facebook post, even a rambling blog post can all be the start, or the end, of a prolonged attack. It's important to determine

if the online chatter is a one- or even two-time event or if it's a more sustained voicing of frustration likely to go on until the matter is resolved.

Have an Escalation Plan

You can't reinvent the wheel every time customers take to Yelp to complain about slow room service or the proverbial—or literal!—fly in their soup. In this completely transparent age of social media that has given all consumers a voice, it is nearly inevitable that some negative chatter will occur to varying degrees for every company at some point.

If you have an "Escalation Plan" in place, you can categorically face each challenge in a clear, measured, and proactive way. For instance, with such a plan you can respond to X amount of tweets or Facebook Likes or blog post, and so on, with a specific chain of actions that is an appropriate response. So, for example, if it's a fairly minor complaint in your user forum, or a scathing product review on Amazon.com, you know that you can do A, B, and C to resolve the situation because it's worked before and it will work again. Also, if the attack escalates to a personal blog full of venting about your product or if there are multiple bashings in multiple forums, you can do D, E, and F to resolve the situation.

Know What Category You're Dealing With

It's critical to understand which category you're dealing with as well: Hear Me's, Reputation Terrorists, or Competitive Destroyers. Why? Aren't they all bad? Well, true, none of them are good, but some are worse than others, and all require a different strategy to overcome. For instance, you don't need to bring out the heavy artillery when dealing with a simple Hear Me, so why bother?

By the same token, if you don't bother working consistently and persistently to counteract the deleterious effects done by a Reputation Terrorist, you'll never get the job done. So knowing what you're up against is one of the first steps in knowing how to combat him or her.

The Best Offense Is a Good Defense

Remember these three letters: ABM. They stand for **Always Be Monitoring**—monitoring your online chatter, being aware of your "real" versus your "perceived" position in the marketplace, is always going to be your best line of defense, and offense, against all of these Determined Detractors.

After all, if you can move fast enough to resolve situations or, better yet, prevent certain situations from occurring in the first place, you will steal the thunder from all of these Determined Detractors and leave them with nothing else to do but praise your name. Or at least not smear it all over social media.

Believe in the Power of the Marketplace

Finally, as a wise man once said, "The truth will out." The marketplace is, for the most part, self-policing. In other words, if you are a good company with a solid brand, stellar performance, great service, and a congenial online disposition, consumers will generally "shout down" those detractors who are way off base in trying to tear you down.

Even the most unreasonable consumers know that not every retailer, restaurant, hotel, or car dealership is going to be firing on all cylinders every minute of every hour of every day. Shipments do go missing, soup does get cold, the ice machine breaks in the middle of the night, and service trucks break down. For some Determined Detractors, these occurrences are enough for a company to be forever smeared. But for most, it's the cost of doing business in the real world. If you do enough of the right things often enough, the marketplace will generally absorb, even ignore, and occasionally even shout down those Determined Detractors who, for whatever reason, turn a bad consumer experience into all-out warfare. While it's not enough simply to let the marketplace even itself out, it *is* a factor that is generally working in your favor around the clock.

■ ■ ■

In summary, the best power of protection is often merely in good policing. I can't imagine any company in this day and age NOT being aware of their real versus perceived online image, but the fact is many companies are hesitant about dipping their toes into those waters simply for fear of discovery.

But you must know what you're dealing with in order to either (a) capitalize on the good chatter and/or (b) minimize or neutralize the bad. Doing anything less is simply irresponsible when there are so many free or near-free tools to help you monitor your brand awareness night and day.

The fact is, in a backhanded way, Determined Detractors can do most companies a solid favor. How? By making them aware of very real problems that exist in the quality chain of their organizations. Where there is smoke, there is generally fire. You can't merely discount all Determined Detractors as crackpots, crazies, or shut-ins with nothing better to do.

If you are putting out repeated brush fires that often come down to the same sources—bad services, inferior quality, lack of consistency, mismanagement, and so on—don't just consider the source but consider the problem as well.

As we'll see in Chapter 13 on customer service solutions, there is no greater satisfaction than turning Determined Detractors into Brand Advocates. And the lessons you learn in turning a (highly) dissatisfied customer into not only a satisfied one but one who is willing to **voluntarily** go to bat for you online and off will make it even easier to recruit new advocates out of satisfied customers!

No one wants to deal with an irate, verbal, and persistent detractor, but whether learning to avoid these types altogether or doing damage control to counteract their presence once they've got you in their sights, you and your brand will grow stronger as a result.

PART 3

Beyond Marketing: Operationalizing Recommendations

CHAPTER 13

Customer Service That Gets You Recommended

Sometimes, it all comes down to the cookies.

For more than 25 years, Hilton Worldwide Inc.'s DoubleTree by Hilton hotel brand has delighted weary guests with warm chocolate chip cookies at check-in. From the moment those first cookies came out of the oven, DoubleTree began receiving positive feedback—first in suggestion boxes on site and later, as technology emerged, through hotel review websites. Then social media happened, and travelers worldwide started posting reviews on TripAdvisor, Yelp, Booking.com, Google, Kwikchex, and countless other sites, mostly about, you guessed it, the cookies.

In an article titled "Checking In? Hidden Ways Hotels Court Guests Faster," the *Wall Street Journal* reported in early 2012 that just as the hotel industry began getting its collective arms around managing post-stay reviews, travelers started commenting and reviewing hotels minutes after they stepped into a hotel's lobby.

"A guest's first impression is even more critical these days because of social media," noted WSJ reporter Andrea Peterson. "In the past, guests usually waited until after they checked out before posting a review on TripAdvisor or Expedia, so hotels would have time to recover from an initial service snafu. Now, with guests tweeting and posting Facebook updates about their vacations almost in real time, a bungled first impression can be immediately broadcast to hundreds—even thousands."

Of course, the often miserable, delayed, and expensive state of air travel almost ensured that guests walked into hotel lobbies frustrated and looking for an outlet.

"Guests show up totally stressed with their shoulders up to their ears. They've gone through travel hell," says Niki Leondakis,

president and chief operating officer of Kimpton Hotels &
Restaurants, a chain of 54 U.S. properties. We've all been there.
Cramped quarters, lost baggage, slow shuttles—by the time we're
finally in the hotel lobby, we're almost preprogrammed to go in with
two strikes already loaded.

So, what did DoubleTree do with its fabled cookies in order to
counteract this "lobby tweeting" phenomenon? They began "cho-
reographing" the presentation to "get as much mileage out of the
cookie" as possible, says Jim Holthouser, Hilton Worldwide's global
head of full-service brands.

Now, all associates are trained to hand guests the cookies first
thing. Forget checking in, forget two forms of ID, forget parking
passes; the cookies are the thing. "Doing that before money changes
hands has a bigger impact on guest perception," says Holthouser.
Indeed, customer satisfaction scores on the "overall arrival experience" have improved, Hilton Worldwide says.

Scores are one thing, but as we've learned throughout this book,
chatter is quite another. Guests around the world now talk about the
cookies at check-in, setting the stage for a great visit:

- John P @CRJRP tweets: "Best part of staying at the
  #DoubleTree hotel is the fresh, still warm cookies they give
  you when you check in. #Classy."
- Doaa Awaysheh @awayshehd tweets: "Still believe that the
  best cookies in #Jordan are by @doubletree #Aqaba."
- farah md isa @farahanjuna writes: "Cookies are delish!
  Omnomnom. @DoubleTree by Hilton Hotel Kuala Lumpur."[1]
- Raymond Tjandra @Mondrayish tweets, "Props to
  @DoubleTree for being the first hotel ever to give me an
  awesome cookie just for checking in. Thank you."[2]

And just to make sure guests stay enamored with the cookies,
DoubleTree highlights them on their own Twitter page: DoubleTree
by Hilton @doubletree. "Sharing deals, travel tips, customer service,
our CARE culture, and of course cookies!" says the DoubleTree
listing, with a cookie as its profile picture. "It's all about the
#LittleThings that make travel more enjoyable."[3]

Could it be that simple? Could a simple cookie turn the tide
on a bad hotel stay? Or make a good one seem, somehow, better?
Well, yes and no, but as we'll see in this critical chapter on customer
service, clearly . . . every little bit helps.

Customer Service, Social Media, and Recommendations

Remember the last time you had a problem with a brand, company, or service? Maybe your delivery was late, the product was inferior, or you were treated rudely or perhaps not as kindly as you preferred or thought the situation warranted.

What, if anything, did you do about it? Chances are, if you're like most consumers, you either suffered in silence, wrote to the company via e-mail or letter, or possibly you gave the company's 800 number a call. But that's changing fast. In fact, an increasing number of consumers are turning to social media—or *social care*, as it's increasingly being called—that is, "customer care" via social media—to get satisfaction.

According to a 2012 study released by NM Incite, what had been a joint venture between Nielsen and McKinsey, nearly half of all U.S. social media users—47 percent—seek customer service through social media channels. The study also found that 18- to 24-year-olds are the highest users of social care, with 60 percent of women and 57 percent of men seeking service through social media.

Some 51 percent of social media users engage in social care more than once a month, and almost 1 in 10 of those individuals use social media for customer service **on a daily basis.** And just as you start thinking this doesn't apply to your customers, the study notes that social care use is consistently high across gender and income and education levels. It also translates to positive WOM, as 71 percent of those who have positive social care eventually go on to actively recommend the brand.

Even if a phone number is easily accessible, a full 30 percent of social media users now prefer to contact a brand for customer service through a social channel compared with the phone. Increasingly, customers are taking a pass on using all the previously standard methods of complaints or praise—letters, faxes, telephones, e-mail, and contact forms—in favor of Twitter and Facebook.

Why? Because it's faster. It's also more convenient for them, it's anonymous, and it falls in line with so much of how and why we use social media in the first place: convenience, speed, ease of use, habitual behavior, and so on.

Of course, it's not just how consumers are contacting companies that is rapidly shifting due to the advent of social media. It is also the lengths they're willing to go when they feel neglected or ignored.

When customers don't feel like they're being heard, one of two things will happen: they'll go to a competitor or they'll find a bigger, more public megaphone to get your attention. An innocuous tweet might evolve into a scathing blog post—or even an entire blog—about your business incompetence.

The "New Marketing"?

The volume, speed, and public nature of social media is forcing an inevitable convergence of customer service and marketing. When customer complaints and your responses (or lack thereof) are publicly visible in your social marketing, every service interaction becomes another data point in the overall perception of your brand.

The world actually *is* watching, and every step you take is now available for public consumption. Perhaps it was inevitable, then, that the rise of social media has made customer service the new marketing. Think of it: everyone who approaches your company via, and for, social care is a personalized, targeted, and viable prospect eager to be invited back into the fold:

- Your pizza was late? You tweeted about it? Let us make that right for you.
- Your cashier forgot to ask you to use your rewards card at the register? You shared that on Facebook? Here, let us show you how to apply those points, plus 500 bonus points, with this simple code.
- Your shipment arrived damaged and you posted pictures of the packaging material on your blog? Here is a free Amazon.com Prime membership for one year. Now go tweet about that!
- The theater was sold out and you had to sit in the front row for all four hours of *Les Miserables*? We're sorry; here is a picture of the entire theater staff having our (very uncomfortable) morning team meeting in the front row—and a couple of free passes for the inconvenience.

Regardless of customer care or social media, responsiveness has always been half of the marketing equation, and personalization the other. Thanks to social media, it is now possible for companies to be (more) responsive by creating a fully personalized experience to deeply understand your customers' wants and needs, to meet them where they are, and to incorporate social media listening, response, and engagement into your contact center methodologies.

With the growing regularity, omnipresence, and direct impact of social care, it seems natural that consumer brands, in particular, would be fully embracing the shift. After all, here is an opportunity to answer personalized issues with expediency and TLC on an immediate, individual, and case-by-case basis. Basically, here is an open invitation to respond with vigor and practicality and to make converts of (nearly) every complainer.

But that's not quite the case—yet.

Another recent study, this one by STELLAService, points out how big of a gap still exists between social care and marketing. Only 2 of the top 25 online retailers—Zappos.com and LLBean.com—said they replied to 100 percent of daily customer service questions posted to Twitter. According to STELLAService analysts, in a recent 45-day study, the average for replies within 24 hours was just 44 percent across the top 25 online retailers. What's more, 6 of the 25 retailers didn't reply to service inquiries over the same period **at all**.

For someone like me, who has watched social marketing campaigns succeed by inches instead of feet, who knows that even the smallest details—like a warm cookie at check-in or a personal tweet back from a company customer service representative—make all the difference, such results are even more troubling.

Outside of the retailer study, a general study of consumers using social media for service found that only 36 percent reported that their issue was solved quickly and efficiently (and, I would add, probably personally as well). Furthermore, 14 percent reported that the company engaged quickly but did not solve their issue, and 10 percent reported that they never received a response at all.

Clearly, customer care is an issue for every company, and if you've been answering 1-800 numbers and answering the mail since your company started, force of habit can be equally hard to change. But change it must if you are to find the "sweet spot" between marketing and social care.

Redefining a Business Model by Becoming Highly Recommended

In 2000, Victor Ciardelli launched Guaranteed Rate, Inc. (www .guaranteedrate.com) to be a different kind of mortgage company. He'd been a leading traditional lender and just knew there had to be a better way.

Sure, he offered low rates and fees. But he also added features and services that allowed his clients to easily understand the mortgage process and transparently evaluate the total cost of a home loan. All with "we're in this together" customer service.

Guaranteed Rate knew that obtaining a new mortgage or refinancing a home is stressful and filled with complexities that can be overwhelming and confusing. The company focused on being recommended—knowing that if it got that right, all the rest would follow.

It did. Within three years, Guaranteed Rate became Chicago's largest independent mortgage lender. Today, Guaranteed Rate is the largest independent retail mortgage company in the United States, employing more than 2,800 people in 161 offices and doing business in all 50 states and Washington D.C.

Even more impressive—and indicative of its highly recommended philosophy—Guaranteed Rate has a 77 percent Net Promoter Score, much higher than the 18 percent banking industry average and one of the highest of any company in any industry (in the vicinity of Apple, Costco, Trader Joe's, and USAA). And the company's customers give it a 96 percent satisfaction rating with comments like:

- "I received an excellent rate and was able to refinance my condo in 30 days. The process was smooth and did not encounter any snags."
- "I just bought my first home and could not be happier. Any questions or concerns I had were immediately addressed, and I was kept up to date on every step of the loan process."
- "Thanks to the recommendation I received from my brother in Chicago, my experience with Guaranteed Rate was great! I heard repeatedly from my listing agent and broker how highly they thought of Joe (mortgage broker)."

The Proper Care and Feeding of Social Media

So, how *do* you respond to customers who are eager, even desperate, for a little social care? How do you turn customer service complaints into recommendation gold mines? And finally, how do you join the ranks of such elite folks as Zappos.com and LLBean.com by handling social care in the right way? You can start by finding out where customers are lurking, reporting, chattering, praising, questioning, critiquing, and complaining.

A recent article on TechJournal.com, "Getting Customer Service Right on Social Media Boosts a Brand," points out that there is a wide variety of social media platforms that consumers turn to for social care, but Facebook and Twitter are clear standouts.

"Among social media users," the article states, "consumers are most likely to comment on or ask a question about a company's product or service on Facebook, both on the company's page (29 percent) and on their personal page (28 percent), followed by the company's blog (15 percent) and then by Twitter, both on a personal handle (14 percent) and a brand handle (13 percent)."

A recent American Express Global Customer Service Barometer reported that people who have used social media for customer service "at least once in the last year" are willing to spend "21 percent more with companies they believe provide great service"—in contrast with the general population, which is willing to spend 13 percent more.

The American Express Global Customer Service Barometer also found that more than three in five Americans feel companies have not increased their focus on providing better service, and of this group, 32 percent felt businesses are paying less attention to providing good customer service. More than 80 percent of these consumers say they have abandoned a purchase because of a poor service experience.

But there are companies who are doing this right, and one of them is Zappos.com. The company started experimenting with social care on Twitter in 2008. "We weren't perfect when we got off the ground," said Rob Siefker, director of customer loyalty at Zappos.com, "but we've clearly gotten better at it."

Have they ever. Of the 500 employees that are part of Zappos .com's customer loyalty team—which handles e-mail, phone, live chat, and Twitter correspondence—about five full-time members handle all of the tweets. The company built out its own system to alert team members by e-mail when the company is mentioned on Twitter, even going as far as to "crawl" the service for possible misspellings of "Zappos."

"What we're seeing is that customers are turning to social media channels for customer service, regardless of whether and where a particular brand is actually equipped to handle customer service over social media," said Gadi BenMark, senior vice president of NM Incite's advisory division, in an article on Parature.com.

"Today's customers choose when and where they voice their questions, issues and complaints. They don't care if a company is set up to answer customer questions on Facebook, or if it has an actual Twitter handle for customer service. The implications," BenMark warns, "are enormous for brands that are not implementing effective social care. There is also great upside for those that understand that the lines between marketing and customer service are blurring, and take action to organize, operate and manage performance in this new merged world."[4]

So, let's break down what we now know about social care and put it all together before moving forward:

- Very few of today's top companies respond to every daily customer service question posed using social media.
- Many retailers never respond to customer service questions at all.
- Companies aren't responding quickly or efficiently enough for those who do complain.
- Or they're responding quickly but not efficiently; or efficiently but not quickly.
- Companies may be waiting for consumers to complain in the carefully designed channels created for them—phone systems, online complaint forms, e-mail addresses—while ignoring when their customers use social media to lodge a complaint, comment, question, or suggestion.
- Many consumers feel businesses are paying less attention to providing good customer service.
- More than 80 percent of these consumers say they have abandoned a purchase because of a poor service experience.
- Over 70 percent of those who experience positive social care (that is, a quick and effective brand response) are likely to recommend that brand to others versus 19 percent of customers who do not receive any response.
- The majority of Twitter and Facebook users expect a response from a brand within the same day of posting.
- More than 50 percent of Twitter social care users expect a response within two hours of posting.

Obviously, switching from traditional customer care to social care can seem a little like turning the *Titanic* for many companies, especially larger ones or those particularly resistant to change.

But the stakes are high, and the social care trend is only gaining momentum, not slowing down.

How high are the stakes, exactly? It is often said that for every single consumer complaint you do hear about, there are one to two dozen that you don't. The magnitude of that guesstimate can be staggering when you take into account what you are hearing versus what you're not. This means that every consumer complaint, no matter where it's coming in—your 1-800 number, e-mail, website, Facebook, or Twitter—is a vital piece of information you can neither do without nor ignore.

I know this can sound challenging. You've gone to all that hard work to set up the proper channels for complaints and service calls to get resolved, and now everybody is using Facebook and Twitter! But as described in the sidebar "Listening to and Acting on What Consumers Are Telling You," you can use this information to learn how to respond to what consumers are saying in both timely and personal ways.

Listening to and Acting on What Consumers Are Telling You: *Seven Strategies for Success*

Clearly, consumers are greedy for feedback, whatever the form. But responding willy-nilly, without a program or protocol, can do more harm than good. The following seven strategies can help to ensure that your responses are both timely and focused to provide the maximum benefit for you and the consumer:

1. **Provide as many opportunities for feedback as possible.** To ensure that all countries are heard from, keep whatever corporate feedback opportunities exist, but also be aware of how your consumers are seeking social care on Facebook and Twitter as well.
2. **Monitor all feedback avenues regularly.** Be sure to make "sweeps" of these comment areas regularly, and have systems in place (see next steps) to respond when "complaint chatter" arises.
3. **Respond in a timely manner.** Have a strategy in place for response times at each point of contact to ensure that you are always responding in a timely manner.
4. **Respond with an open mind.** Many companies have made a bad problem worse by taking the defensive when they're

supposed to be providing solutions. Oftentimes complaints can seem petty and trivial when it's you who's being complained about, but respond with an open mind to ensure that you never come off as defensive or negative.

5. **Make the appropriate apologies and explanations.** Part and parcel of handling customers' complaints, regardless of which portal they come in from, is apologizing and offering explanations.

6. **Solve the problem promptly.** Regardless of why it occurred, or when, or how loudly the customer complained, offer a timely and effective solution to the problem.

7. **Show the consumer that you've solved the problem promptly.** To close out the complaint, remind the customer of how, and even when and how promptly, you solved the problem with a follow-up contact.

Having a specific strategy in place can help you manage customer complaints no matter how high the frequency or drastic the severity. While no two cases are alike, you can gain predictability and efficiency around your social care solution by planning for it ahead of time—and rectifying it quickly.

Success in Motion: *The Eurail Story*

A recent photograph featured on Eurail's Facebook page says it all about this 50-year-old travel company and how it has managed to thrive in an industry more associated with the past than the future: Several khaki-and-sweater clad travelers are preparing for a scenic Eurail trip through Romania and Bulgaria circa 1970. Knee socks are prevalent, briefcases are everywhere, and there's not a cell phone or tablet in sight.

One can imagine that only the train tracks themselves have stayed the same in all that time. Certainly how tourists travel, book their trips, and even complain when things go wrong have evolved light-years beyond when this slice-of-life snapshot was taken.

And yet the company who owns the train in the picture, and on whose Facebook page the candid picture was posted, Eurail, has managed to evolve along with its customers. One can imagine that there are few businesses more "brick and mortar" than train travel.

And yet, perusing its social media presence, one can see why such an old-fashioned company has managed to not just survive but thrive in modern times.

Everywhere on its Facebook page you can see the signs of constant chatter monitoring, questions, answers, and above all, service. Nearly every post elicits a random question or two, many unrelated to the original post, but someone from Eurail always responds just the same—with confidence, patience, and vigor!

Their FB page, Liked by 111,000 thousand fans, features travel photos, educational videos, and thousands of Likes and comments for nearly every post. Although the company has been active on FB only since 2006, it has won two prestigious awards for its social care and service: Mashable's coveted "Best Social Media Customer Service Award" and the "Interactive Media Award" in the travel category from Rail Adventure Itineraries.

You may never have heard of Eurail before and have no desire to visit Europe by rail. And yet few can dispute that this company has managed to embrace the younger generation where they are: online, on Facebook, and in real time. While the company still has the traditional means of handling reservations, booking travel, and answering questions, it's plainly evident from its social media presence that it is not only quick to respond to consumer questions, concerns, and even complaints but it is also positive and determined to find a solution as well.

Meeting the Customers Where They Are:
Creating the Customer-Centric Company

It's easy to be inspired by the proactive nature of a company like Eurail or our earlier examples of DoubleTree, Zappos.com, and LLBean.com. But it can be challenging to refocus your energies when you're doing your best just to get customers, let alone serve them.

But in these rapidly evolving times, it's critical that you not only address the topic of social care but also have protocols and procedures in place to ensure that the entire company is consumer focused. It's no longer a luxury to think this way. It is a necessity if you are to thrive in modern times.

If you think I'm overstating the case or even overreacting to the importance of social media as customer service because I'm simply hypervigilant about it in my career, consider this startling statistic from SocialMediaToday.com: "It is estimated by the end of 2012, 80 percent of companies plan to use social media for customer service purposes. When given positive customer service through social media, around 71 percent of consumers will recommend the brand. Not only will customers recommend the brand, those who engage with companies via social media are likely to spend between 20 percent and 40 percent more money on those companies."

The evolution of social media is not only blinding but rapidly leaving those who don't understand or value its power in the dust. The number of Americans who claimed that social media influenced their buying decisions has doubled in the past year alone, and with this emerging trend toward social care, that number is expected to increase exponentially until nearly all of us are influenced, in some way or another, by what we hear, see, and experience online through social media.

Listen First; Act Second

We've talked a lot in this book about chatter because that is what social media conversations most often sound like to the uninitiated: random chatter that is almost impossible to pinpoint, let alone decipher.

But there is meaning in that chatter. Chatter begins as one individual making one comment, and it spreads as other interested parties respond to that statement with comments of their own. If you see these online conversations as gold mines instead of gossip or claptrap, you will begin to understand their value and importance to your organization.

I admit, the chatter can be overwhelming, even intimidating, at first. But just like any challenge, little things can make a big difference. Here are some simple but effective ways to start turning that chatter into content and applying sound principles today so that you'll know just what to do with all that chatter tomorrow:

- **Just wade in.** You have to start sometime. Why not now? Why not with your Facebook page? Your Twitter account? Your corporate blog or website forum or even e-mail complaint address? Focus on one portal at a time, and simply wade in. You might be surprised by how clearly the picture

of your online brand reputation comes into focus once you
start listening to it more effectively—or at all.

- **Begin to categorize the chatter.** As we've seen throughout
  this book, not all chatter is created equal, nor are all
  customer complaints. Don't get me wrong: all are critically
  important, but not every tweet requires a rush to Defcon
  4. Some are merely suggestions, while others are specific
  responses to isolated incidents or outright dissatisfaction.
  Some are irrational; some are all too rational. It's important to
  categorize the chatter so that you can (a) begin to see problem
  patterns but also (b) begin to develop a personalized but
  relatively repeatable response for each category.

- **Prioritize your responses.** Every complaint should get
  a response, every time. That's the ideal. But on the path
  to that ultimate destination there should be a system for
  prioritization so that, at the very least, those complaints
  marked "medium" to "high" priority are responded to and
  resolved quickly. For every company, the system might be
  different, depending on, for instance, how much staff you
  have devoted to the social business cause, what metrics or
  measurements you're using, how big a role technology plays,
  and so on. But what would be the same across the board is a
  way of alerting those in authority of when a message, thread,
  trend, or topic crosses the line from low to medium priority,
  and particularly when something trends from medium to
  high priority. What sends something from a medium to high
  priority? If there's recognition that this perception of reality
  might go viral or damage the brand, it should be given a
  higher priority of response. Inside every organization, the
  best thing to do is to start a ranking system of extremes.
  Know what to look out for, what language indicates a danger
  level, or how many comments indicates a topic is trending.

- **Be prepared.** Finally, know how you want to respond before
  you respond. I can't stress this last one enough. Avoid knee-
  jerk responses, defensiveness, or any kind of "circle the wagon"
  protectiveness. Listen with an open mind, and respond in kind.

At some point, of course, you will want to do more than just listen; you will want to engage with the consumer as well. Knowing
what's being said first is important to knowing how to engage
second.

Active Engagement

Marketing has always been about brand reputation, and customer service was always about helping people. For both, step one was to listen to what customers were saying, and eventually I think somebody said, "Hey, why don't we try and help this guy rather than just note that he's unhappy?"
—**LARRY ROBINSON**, Vice President, Product Management,
Radian6 Salesforce Marketing Cloud

Naturally, listening and monitoring activities are valuable for information gathering but they are also a prelude to the more active form of engagement. In other words, once you've listened and learned what the problem is, it's time to engage one-on-one with a consumer to respond to and rectify the situation.

The more you listen to online chatter, the more you familiarize yourself with what's being said about you on blogs and forums, on Facebook and Twitter, you'll come to understand that social media isn't about broadcasting. Instead, it's about connecting.

All of this monitoring behavior is leading up to this: active engagement. And engagement is when you meet customers where they are and interact with them as they are. Look at the folks at Eurail—hopping onto Facebook posts and answering questions, offering suggestions, all with helpful language and useful links.

It's not about another random come-on or coupon. It's a distinct and personal response designed to solve a problem, answer a question, or offer a solution before it becomes a problem.

Someone in a thread is asking about the best type of pass to get for a European trip, and someone from Eurail steps in to provide a solution. It's personal, it's prompt, and it's specific. It's also detail oriented and time-consuming; I get that. It also works, and when you can find a strategy that works, particularly in something as rapidly evolving and constantly demanding as social media, you stick with it!

Customers can be engaged in a variety of ways. For instance, you can respond to a conversation already in progress, such as a discussion of travel itineraries or spaghetti recipes or solutions for athlete's foot. You can weigh in with a response, you can offer a solution, point them in the right direction, even ask to direct message (DM) them to respond more personally to the discussion and take it off site.

Or you can begin the discussion by doing one of the following:

- Asking a question
- Posting a poll
- Posting a picture
- Starting a contest
- Trying some other interactive content

Or you can do both: begin a discussion on your Facebook or Twitter pages and follow the thread in a meaningful manner while also offering hints, suggestions, humor, answers, and so on.

Or you can use a discussion someone else started to merge or leap off into a topic you already know people are interested in and discussing. The point in any of the above cases is to be genuine and avoid selling. This is not a broadcast but a conversation. Be specific about your purpose for being there, and leave your marketing and promotional agendas at home.

One thing we should all recognize by this point is how sophisticated and super-aware your social media audience can be. They can smell a bait and switch, come-on, or advertisement a mile away, and randomly inserting some inane marketing speak into a genuine and engaging thread or discussion is one great way to destroy any goodwill your previous engagement efforts might have garnered on your behalf.

Above all, engage with sincerity. It's okay to thank a customer for a compliment or even constructive criticism. It's all right to sincerely ask a question or offer a solution. No one can get this right all the time, and if you're wondering about what to say, pretend you actually are having a conversation. Listening carefully, monitoring closely, and engaging actively are ongoing behaviors, not events.

Let the conversations evolve naturally, and learn as you go. If you're sincere in your efforts and you have an effective strategy in place, the behavior will not only be appreciated by your customers but it will also become habitual throughout your organization as well.

Parting Words: *If You're Online, You're in the Game (So Why Not Play to Win?)*

The bottom line when it comes to social care is that it's a necessary part of the modern social media landscape. You can't run from it, hide from it, or even avoid it. And if you have a social media presence at all—and why wouldn't you?—you must be prepared, and well prepared, to deal with customer complaints via social media.

The sooner you deal with it, strategically, sympathetically, and sincerely, the sooner you will see how social care is far from a chore and more of an opportunity to learn about, meet, identify, and interact with your core audience. For most companies, it's an untapped resource—a pool of prospects waiting to be approached, consoled, cajoled, interested, invested, and, above all, engaged.

I talk a lot about engagement in this book. That's because it's the *how* to all of this *why*. It's the physical representation of all we know and can possibly do about social media. It's getting one-on-one time with people, actual people, despite the fact that you're engaging primarily through technology and the Internet.

Engaging is about making connections, and making connections is about finding customers. What better place to find a customer than those places you already know they're talking about you? What better way to convert skeptics than to contact them directly, suggest something, answer a direct question, or better yet, offer a solution?

Such is the power, and the opportunity, of social care.

CHAPTER 14

Attracting and Keeping the Best

Becoming the Most Recommended Place to Work

magine you are an executive for a gaming company—working for a behemoth like Activision, Nintendo, Microsoft, EA Games, LucasArts, or even one of the small boutique studios with a ravenous audience.

It's a big, big business. In fact, a market report by Transparency Market Research—*Gaming Market: Global Industry Analysis, Size, Growth, Share and Forecast 2011 to 2015*—states that the global gaming market is expected to reach $117.9 billion in 2015, growing at a compound annual growth rate (CAGR) of 13.7 percent from 2011 to 2015.

And it's as competitive as all get out. A hit new system, like Microsoft's Xbox One or Sony's latest PlayStation console, or an addictive, stay-up-all-night new game, such as *Call of Duty: Black Ops II* or *Just Dance 4*, almost ensures that your company—and you, as an executive of that company—get a record-setting payday.

While there are, of course, many factors that lead to creating a hit new game, one of the most critical is attracting and keeping the most talented developers, designers, programmers, artists, producers, and testers—in fact, doing so will make or break your success.

Given the importance of this talent—and their likely youth and social connectivity—a recent story in Kotaku.com (which bills itself as the "definitive digital hub for video game news, reviews, cheats, design, and entertainment") likely sent a wave of terror through each of these high-powered game company executives. A writer going by the user name "Superannuation" authored a scathing blog post titled "Pissed Off Employees Bash Pretty Much Every Major Video Game Company."[1]

While gaming executives may have been quick to dismiss Superannuation as a disgruntled, bitter, and disenfranchised ex-employee, a deeper read quickly showed a different story. It turned out the posting wasn't just one long rant from Superannuation himself. Instead, he was merely cataloging a long list of industry complaints that actually originated from another website: Glassdoor.com.

What sets GlassDoor.com apart, according to its website, is its "'employee generated content'—anonymous salaries, company reviews, interview questions, and more—all posted by employees, job seekers, and sometimes the companies themselves."

It's a little like Yelp and TripAdvisor.com for the corporate side. And it's not just EA Games or Nintendo we're talking about here. From Disney to Wells Fargo to Facebook to In-N-Out Burger, employees and other insiders "rate" companies just like users rate movies on Netflix or books on Goodreads.com.

So now prospective employees of nearly any company can simply search for it on GlassDoor.com and discover the inside scoop. Reviewers leave one- to five-star ratings on everything from career opportunities to work/life balance, from compensation and benefits to culture and values. There is even a special category where users can rate the CEO.

Like every other ratings system, ratings should always be taken with a grain of salt. For instance, not just some but *all* of the user-generated reviews are anonymous, therefore giving users a "free pass" to be completely open. Those who are already leaning toward bitterness and disenfranchisement might go even further since they know there will never be any repercussions.

Also, for larger companies with feeder offices, franchisees, and so on, it's not always clear whether the review is for corporate or field opportunities, further muddying the waters.

Even so, the Kotaku.com post by Superannuation quoted liberally from former employees of all the major video game players. For instance, a current employee at Activision's Santa Monica HQ wrote, "Milking the margins comes first. So, if you love games, be prepared to leave that love at the door."

A former employee at Activision Publishing opined, "Due to the fact that my off-site developers and vendors were everywhere from East Europe to China, I was constantly working off hours to set up conference calls at any time of the day or night."

Finally, this withering denouncement from a former employee at Blizzard's Irvine HQ: "Blizzard is a sweat-shop, I feel sorry for anyone that has to work there."

Even when taken with a grain of salt, those are some bitter pills to swallow for the gaming industry's upper echelon. So it would seem that just as social media and the Internet have made a company's products and services transparent, it has also made the companies themselves transparent.

Imagine, as little as five or six years ago, how challenging it might have been to track down insider information on a company before applying there. You would have basically had to hire, or become, a private investigator to track down former employees, locating where they lived or finding their phone number, ask them questions, and so on.

Today a simple website lays bare the entire company's dirty laundry. One can imagine how damaging a low rating on GlassDoor .com or other company reviewing sites might be to prospective employees and how it can hurt an organization's chances at hiring the best and the brightest, particularly those savvy enough to "check the company's references" before applying.

The Value of Employee Recommendations

Consumers trust products and services that have been recommended to them by their friends. Likewise, when companies look for new hires who are going to move seamlessly into the organization, are already aware of its culture and values, and are clearly interested in the position, they have more success when those applicants are referred by the company's employees themselves.

Therefore, much as a person-to-person referral can fuel a company's product or service line to unmitigated success, so can the value of employee referrals help your company become among the "most recommended" places to work. According to Jobvite.com, one of the Internet's first social media recruiting companies, employee referrals now lead the charge in new hires (see Figure 14.1).

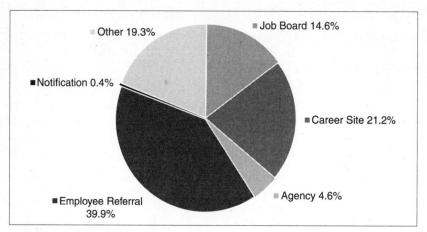

Figure 14.1 Hires by Source Type. (Source: Jobvite.)

Jobvite also claims that "out of every 100 referral applicants, about **seven of these will get hired**; while job boards will produce one hire for every 246 applicants." What's important to companies when looking for quality employees who will actually still be there by the time their benefits kick in is (a) how quickly they can hire on and get to work and (b) how long they'll stick around.

Jobvite is quick to point out that not only are employee referrals "faster to hire" but they also stick around much longer as well. Claims the recruiting site, "Employee referral candidates move through the hiring process 55 percent faster than those who came through the career site, taking only 29 days from application to hire."

"Referral hires also stay at a company for much longer," the recruiting site says. "About 46 percent of referrals and 29 percent of those hired through career sites stay for three years or more, while only 14 percent of those hired from job boards stayed" (see Figure 14.2).

What's important to remember about employee referrals is that you, as a company, are filtering through applications and interviews based on "linkages" that already exist within your company.

Using your existing employees' social media networks and some leverage in the form of referral program incentives, you too can find your next employee closer and faster and have them stick around longer through the magic of employee referrals.

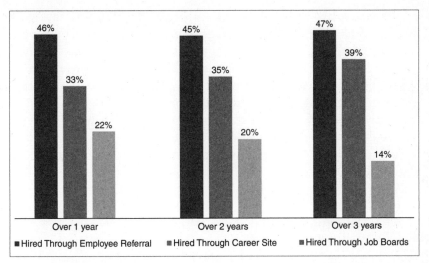

Figure 14.2 Average Length of Employment. (Source: Jobvite.)

Employee Fans: *Five Ways Social Media Has Changed HR Forever*

For much of this book we've talked about how to find brand fans—those consumers loyal enough to your company to recommend you to their family, friends, and online network. But now we're shifting our approach (though only slightly) to talk about how to find "employee fans."

As the name implies, employee fans are those workers who love you enough to recommend working for you to their social network. Although it's hard to put a dollar sign on such employee fans, anyone who knows the worth of good HR knows just how valuable employee referrals can be when it comes to both recruiting *and* retention.

While satisfied workers may be nothing new, employee fans as a phenomenon is only one of the many ways in which social media has changed human resources forever. Here are five others.

It Has Helped Employees Find Their Voice

For better or worse, social media has given us all a voice; your employees aren't immune. As the GlassDoor.com story reveals, no longer are employees content leaving nasty notes in the company suggestion box. Today, the whole of the Internet is their suggestion box, and they're not afraid to use it.

However, by recognizing and accepting this fact, you can work harder to listen to your employees' voices just as you would your customers' voices, and you should take their voices no less lightly.

Monitor how employees are talking about you, and where, why, when, how often, and about what. Not to punish them but to capture the insights as to what's working and not working—just as you would with your customers or consumers. Likewise, listen for what you're doing right, and do more of that as well.

It's important not just to monitor employee chatter but, as you do consumer chatter, also address it. Here are some simple ways to do just that:

- **Make responding a priority.** Much as we prioritize consumer chatter, there are low to medium to high employee concerns. Should the guy who complains about wanting a healthier lunch in the cafeteria every week get the same level of response as someone who's politely bashing the company in forums? Well, it depends. Regular, ongoing concerns should be addressed quickly so that they are no longer recurring. But, realistically, an employee mutiny will probably take precedence. But you'll never know if you don't have some kind of system in place for prioritizing such chatter in the first place.

- **Have steps in place.** Part of making responses a priority is putting steps in place for someone to respond. This could be through e-mail, text, a quick phone call, or even a personal visit, but you can't just plan to plan. Make a plan and stick to it so that monitoring employee chatter isn't all you're doing. You're also responding to it as well.

- **Make it personal.** Depending on the size of your company, you may or may not be able to approach every employee on a case-by-case basis to address every concern. That's what prioritization is for. But if you can't make the response personal, give it to someone who can—a team or department leader, a direct supervisor or division head, or someone else.

- **Go to them.** Have you ever made a reservation at a nice restaurant and then been told you have to call the day of your reservation to confirm or lose your table? While this makes life for the restaurant easier, it's one more hoop for you to jump through. Don't make your employees jump through hoops to get a response. Instead, go to them. Physically, if possible, but if not, make it as convenient as possible for them to talk further about the issue with you. This could mean, for example, scheduling a call when it's right for them, joining them for lunch, or taking them to lunch.

It Has Created True Transparency

As we saw in the cautionary tale about the gaming industry at the beginning of this chapter, you no longer have to just worry about what customers are saying about your products and services. Today you have to consider how your employees, or former employees, are talking about you on social media channels as well.

When you find yourself confronted with an irate and anonymous employee who is not shy about voicing his or her opinions about the inner workings of your company, your first reaction might be to call your lawyer, but your second reaction should be to parse what is being said, then address any real and rational concerns, and hopefully, eliminate them.

The only way to combat transparency is to have a company with glass walls. In other words, be proud of everything you do so that anything that is broadcast online is only ever positive. While it can be a challenge to make every employee happy, here are some simple ways that you can reach out to disgruntled employees to help resolve issues quickly and definitively:

- **Create an outlet for open discussion.** It's important to steer the discussion offline and face-to-face. We want our employees to come to us first, not go to the Internet. Many times, perhaps, they've tried that and failed, and so they resort to kvetching online. In that case, creating an outlet for open discussion is one way to prevent future employees from doing the same.
- **Tell them where to go to get help with their issues.** Have a chain of command in place that makes it easy for employees to voice their concerns. If their concern is with their supervisor, give them options for discussing their supervisor in a nonjudgmental way for which they won't get punished. When employees feel there is an outlet for them to be heard within the organization, they rarely look without for support instead.

■ **Provide mediation.** Oftentimes employees who find themselves complaining about work online aren't ticked off necessarily with the entire organization but with only one aspect of the company or, more specifically, one person within the organization. In that case, talk to both employees, and work to resolve the conflict before it gets out of hand—or any worse.

It Has Changed the Recruiting Process

As we've just seen in the previous section, social media has made an internal employee referral program not only more effective but longer lasting as well. Today current employees can help you find future employees by mining their social networks or helping you mine them in some kind of joint organizational effort.

What's more, the transparency of social media is a two-way street. When screening for potential new hires, don't forget to do your due diligence and scout for any online irregularities in your applicants' social media presence.

Racy photos, racist tweets, ugly rants, questionable affiliations, or other online evidence is hard to hide and easy to spot, if you use social media as a filter as much as a magnet. Not only will this help you filter out undesirable applicants but it will also help you avoid "blowback" to your company's brand if your competitors spot them after you've hired the person.

Here are some typical things to look for when scouring social media for your next new hire:

■ **Do they present themselves professionally?** Modern hires aren't just employees but brand representatives. Will new hires, based on their social media activity, positively or negatively reflect on your company?

■ **Are they a good fit for the organization?** It's amazing what people will post online and how much of themselves they reveal on Facebook, Twitter, Tumblr, and the like. It can be particularly exhilarating when you come across a job candidate who not only presents himself or herself professionally but appropriately as well. For instance, if you're a funky, fun, fresh company, does the employee seem . . . funky, fun, and fresh? If the position is creative, does the candidate seem creative and insightful?

- **Can they communicate?** If you are hiring people in communications—editorial, creative, marketing, promotion, and so on—do their social media activities reflect on them as competent communicators? We can all "cheat" on Twitter by getting creative with abbreviations and such to make it under the 140 characters or less maximum, but . . . does the candidates' poor spelling, limited vocabulary, and atrocious grammar continue even when character count is not an issue? That could be a problem for those seeking communication jobs or even hoping to advance in the company.

- **Do they have a history of trashing former employers?** It's easy to spot racy nightclub pictures littered all over the prospects' Facebook pages, but dig a little deeper. Do these people have a history of trashing former employers or spilling company secrets or otherwise disparaging the workplace? If so, what makes you think they won't do that to you as well?

One caveat: companies who use social media to rule out candidates based on things like sex, religion, disability, sexual orientation, race, and other line items are obviously at risk for legal ramifications when it comes to discrimination lawsuits. Be sure that legal is aware of HR's social media activity and that both departments work together to ensure that you are, in fact, screening and not discriminating.

It Has Helped Companies Retain Employees

Social media has helped HR improve on its retention by ensuring that the majority of new hires are now found through employee referral programs, particularly those heavily invested in social media.

However, by treating employees as "customers" and approaching social media monitoring and online chatter in the same vein, you can also increase employee retention by alternately increasing employee satisfaction on and off the job.

Here's how it might look if you encouraged your employees to use social media to their, and the company's, advantage:

- **You could hire and recruit online.** The times they are a changing, and no longer is LinkedIn the only social media site worth posting jobs to. Dig deeper and spread wider your social media wings as you begin to use the Internet to aid in your next recruiting drive. Many industries have specialized websites and forums where job hunting is a natural growth of visiting, such as MediaBistro.com for the news, publishing, and journalism industries. Many companies have also started using online applications on Facebook to help filter résumés coming in through their social media network. Did you know that HootSuite.com tweets every new job opening via a dedicated HR Twitter account? Says HootSuite CEO Ryan Holmes, "The entire process is public, transparent, and out there for everyone to see. This fosters community among job hunters and staff right from the start, and we get to know candidates on a more personal level."

- **You could brand constantly—to future employees and future customers.** Good people want to work for progressive companies just as consumers want to buy from organizations that get them, and reach them, where they spend the most time. Allowing employees to use social media for work and social purposes gives you an edge on those who don't as well as the opportunity to brand yourself as an organization that welcomes transparency and isn't afraid to show its more personal—even social—side.

- **You could make the company personal.** People love getting the behind-the-scenes scoop on companies. Pictures of employee Christmas parties, seeing how different departments work, and live tweeting a seminar or a CEO's town hall meeting are all ways to make the company open, transparent, and personal to both potential employees and customers.

- **You could reach employees where they are.** Your employees are using social media, whether you approve it or not. When you not only accept this fact but embrace it, you open yourself up to a new world of opportunities for reaching employees where they are.

It Has Helped Companies Become Branded as Good Places to Work

One of the biggest takeaways from this chapter in general and this section in particular should be that social media affects every aspect of the organization, even, particularly, human resources.

What's apparent now is that branding is also an organization-wide effort, and it doesn't stop with marketing and promotion. Through concerted and valuable HR efforts, the company's brand can spread as not just one that offers quality products and services but as one that represents a quality employee experience as well.

Being known as a great place to work will make your brand more attractive to employees, but in the new world of social media, it will not go unnoticed by the consumer market as well.

Here are some simple ways to enlist your employees to help showcase your organization to their world and the world at large:

- **Encourage employees to photograph and share internal events.** A staff birthday party, a celebration in honor of a special achievement, a charitable event, even a "team meeting" at the local coffee shop can all help to personalize— and brand—your company to potential employees, business partners, and customers. We are used to showing a unified face in our corporate advertising, our outreach or broadcast materials, even our building's facade. But inviting people inside, be they potential employees or customers, invites them to get to know us better as well. And we shouldn't be afraid of that.

- **Be as personal as possible.** People like to work for—and with—people, not just organizations. The more you allow your employees to use social media, the more you personalize the organization. I know a respected social media expert who regularly tweets "dispatches" from business meetings, catering tables, coffee stations, coffee shops, airports on the way to client meetings, lavish spreads at client dinners, and her employees hunched over a conference call. Nothing, and no one, it would seem is out of bounds. And yet I feel as if I know her, and if I were going to apply for a job at her organization, I would feel well prepared in knowing the kind of culture and work ethic she espouses. And if I were a client looking to hire her, I would have no doubt about her abilities or skills to market herself, let alone me!

- **Have HR regularly profile employees.** A great way for the company to get to know your employees and to give employees fuel to share with their own online networks is to profile different people from different departments regularly.

Take their picture, interview them, be irreverent and fun—why so serious???—and then post it far and wide. This not only invites people inside the company to get to know each other well but people outside the company too.

■ **Hold more events that are easily shared.** When you awaken to the fact that you can no longer really be a "closed-door company," you can reenergize employee events by having more of them. It's easy to fall into the routine of the usual Christmas party in the winter, employee picnic in the summer, showcase of employee "events," but when you also see them as branding opportunities you can become far more creative and compelling.

Case Study: SAS

One company that has embraced its role as a social and highly recommended business is software giant SAS. Named the number one company to work for on *Fortune* magazine's "100 Best Companies to Work for in the United States" list—and appearing elsewhere on the list 14 years in a row—SAS takes being a social business seriously:

■ Reading the "Employees" section of the company's *2011 Corporate Social Responsibility* (CSR) *Report* is like peeking in at their playbook for creating the optimal social business. One of the first standouts is what SAS calls "the Hub," a kind of internal social media platform for which 5,800 of the company's 6,105 full-time employees had signed up in the site's first 60 days.

■ SAS polled the Hub users, and it found that nearly all of the company's employees, or 95 percent, agreed with the statement that they were "adequately informed about the company from direct internal sources (e.g., webcasts, podcasts, SAS Wide Web articles, blogs, etc.)."

■ Much like its inspiration, Facebook, the Hub has "like it" and "thank you" features, and it regularly features live webcasts from leadership. Communication is clearly part of SAS's MO, as witnessed by the company's virtual communications summit to "share ideas and best practices in global communications strategies," as well as an employee video contest to "share ideas for talking about the SAS story externally."

How to Become a Social Recruiter: *The Importance of Leveraging Social Media in HR*

One trend that is emerging in the Digital Age is that of social media affecting every branch of the company. Look at what happened when Dan Cathy, CEO of Chick-Fil-A, let loose his thoughts on gay marriage: the viral impact of his comments across social media made the fast food chain a lightning rod for public opinions, moving the entity from business titan to political hot potato in less than 24 hours.

Has the chain's business improved since then? Time will tell, I suppose, but this much is clear: there should be no question about who is *not* applying for jobs at Chick-Fil-A from now on.

Is that the kind of reputation the company wanted? Perhaps. Is it the kind of company perception *you* want? Doubtful. In good times and bad, most of us want to work with the best people, regardless of race, sex, or sexual orientation.

But such are the times we live in. Look at how John Schnatter, founder and CEO of Papa John's, has made such a big deal about his feelings on Obamacare. While his well-publicized and frequently quoted sound bites taking on the politics of healthcare in the modern age might have garnered the company millions of free impressions, what will the fallout be when it comes time to hiring quality mid- to high-level employees? Again, time will tell, but in this Digital Age it's critical that companies mind not just their external brand but their internal brand as well.

In other words, what will current and future employees make of your brand? The stunning transparency of social media has made every company an open book, and it has made every potential employee a sophisticated and avid consumer of any and all online chatter about prospective employers. Even those companies who don't lead the daily news cycle on *Huffington Post* or Mashable.com are still vulnerable to the whims of social media.

While HR reps may feel like social media is best left to the front-of-the-house employees in the marketing or other creative departments, the fact is, social media cuts a wide swath, and there are far more reasons why HR departments should embrace social media rather than shy away from it.

In fact, new data from ComplianceAndSafety.com sheds interesting light on this phenomenon. According to the site, "91 percent of recruiters use social networks."

This staggering figure merely indicates how prevalent social media is in how employers find employees, and vice versa. And yet, from the same study, ComplianceAndSafety.com found that "almost half of U.S. companies block their employees from accessing social networks."

While productivity is important to every company, the fact is that social media is a gold mine for HR departments, and not just in terms of employee referrals. Here are some other distinct ways to leverage social media for HR.

Broadcast Your Corporate Culture

Even when not posting specific jobs to popular online forums and blogs, you can still capitalize on social media to help broadcast your corporate culture and increase the perception of your organization as a desirable place to work.

While LinkedIn seems to be the default, and for many companies the only, social media site where they'll post jobs, the "pin board" site Pinterest can be an attractive alternative.

Here you can post candid photos from the workplace, the corporate picnic, humorous cartoons that encapsulate your workplace philosophy, famous quotes, or even customers enjoying your products and/or services. Anything that helps put the spotlight on your company as a progressive, pleasant, and even fun place to work can help publicize your corporate brand as highly recommendable.

Don't Overlook the Obvious

While devoting time to social media, don't neglect to post open positions on your own company's website and/or blog. This allows you to control the information about your own company, the job description, necessary minimum requirements, and so on.

Many job listings are cold and generic, but if, as you do in the rest of your social media efforts, you take this opportunity to brand yourself and your organization, you can make the job description more inviting as well.

Make It Personal

Finally, don't be afraid to let your HR department get a little creative, and a lot personal, with your corporate web space. Post photos of your current employees, and have mini-interviews with them, paying particular attention to how those interviews might sound to potential recruits.

Have leaders from each division, or those in frequent need of new hires, blog regularly to express how "a day in the life" might feel working for your company. Such personal insights help prospects understand the ins and outs of your company in a more personal, individual way. This helps put "like with like." In other words, those prospective employees who don't particularly "get" your corporate culture likely won't apply, while those who do probably won't be able to wait!

Now It's Your Turn: *Why a Happy Workplace Is a Recommendable Workplace*

This is not a chapter about hiring and firing, recruiting and retention, or even happiness on the job. It *is* a chapter about making your company a recommendable one. Because recommendable companies are:

- More likely to attract top talent
- More likely to recruit top talent
- More likely to retain top talent
- Places employees want to come to work at, talk about, and spread the word about
- Places employees feel comfortable recommending to others
- Places where new employees can't wait to start
- Places other companies fear losing their top workers to
- Places employees at other companies have "heard good things" about
- Places quality workers are naturally drawn to

The fact is, it's just as important for people to recommend your company as a great place to work as it is for customers to recommend your products and services as great things to buy and/or use.

That's because without quality employees who truly enjoy working for you, it can be hard to nearly impossible to deliver quality products and services in a way that meets consumer demand.

So how do you keep employees satisfied so that they will recommend working for you to only the first and brightest? Here are some ideas that will help your company be as recommendable by employees as it is by consumers.

Out with the Old, In with the New

Well, first, throw out those old, traditional notions that only money and vacation time mean anything to your employees. A recent study by CareerBliss.com found that "the happiest employees in the U.S. credit their bliss to first-rate employee incentives, ample benefits, career advancement programs, and great work-life balance. The companies that have been the most dedicated to cultivating and advancing these things in the past year have seen employee happiness soar."

Understand what your employees want and need, and give it to them, within reason. Then stand back and let them do their jobs. Employees who feel creative in their work, who have ownership of their projects and tasks, and who actually enjoy coming to work will be front and center and the first to recommend their place of work to others.

Make Recommendation Easy

Don't put obstacles in front of those employees who want to rave about you all over the Internet. Walls have two sides, and if you block employees from using social media to talk about your company for fear they may say something bad, you are also—by proxy—keeping them from saying anything good as well.

Give Them Opportunities to Learn

Nearly every company I work with—make that, nearly every company I work with where the employees are consistently "happy" to be there—offers opportunities for learning.

Some help pay for employees to go to school or attend workshops or otherwise gain critical skill outside of the workplace, while others provide learning opportunities on the job in the forms of, for example, additional responsibilities, project ownership, and opportunities to be creative. And some do both.

Either way, it's important to enrich the lives of your employees so that they feel that their time with you, no matter how long it lasts, was worthwhile. The key is, the more worthwhile you make your employees' time, the longer they'll want to stick around.

Parting Words: *Becoming the Most Recommended Place to Work*

In this recommendation age, it is critical that we update every facet of our organizations to run at peak efficiency and in complete transparency; HR is no different. While there are many pros and cons that come part and parcel with using social media, the fact is we can no longer avoid living a connected life.

As millennials, who came into this world, it would seem, with technology attached at the hip—or, in this case, attached at their fingers—become more and more prevalent in our workforce, we can no longer deny how, when, and where they seek jobs.

And with social media so readily affordable and available to our current employees, we can only hope to tap into their vast networks to find valuable employee referrals who attach themselves to us faster, stay longer, and are happy enough in their current positions to recommend us to future employees as well.

CHAPTER 15

Creating Products and Offerings Your Customers Tell You They Will Buy

Product Innovation and R&D

O n March 6, 2012, a consumer going by the profile name of "RedHeadGrandma6" began offering creative and innovative tips to the Clorox Company—a global powerhouse that markets brands including Clorox bleach, GreenWorks, Pine-Sol, Burt's Bees, Glade, and others—in more than 100 countries.

In less than a year, she shared 12 meaningful product ideas and provided thoughtful commentary on 12 other concepts proposed by others. Before you dismiss RedHeadGrandma6 as a bored retiree, take a look at her suggestion for premeasured Clorox pods:

My idea is to have pre-measured Clorox. Enough to do a pail full of cleaning with hot water. I would package the premeasured Clorox in one and two units. Priced less than a gallon of regular Clorox. A lot of us consumers are watching our pennies, especially senior citizens. We want to purchase Clorox to get the job done. Smaller containers make it easier for those of us with arthritis to handle, they are not as bulky. Some of us our [sic] too lazy and it is more convenient to use pre-measured items while also cautious that it doesn't splatter, easier to control & handle.

Other consumers liked her idea, giving it five stars in their online forum voting system. And, as a company, Clorox thought enough of her contributions to feature her on its website. Another consumer, "Laura," shared her concept for Clorox Foam, complete with an illustration:

> *My idea is Clorox Foam! I love Clorox products. I use bleach on a lot of stuff when I am cleaning, the most thing I use it on is my kitchen sponges, but I hate that I am always fearing the bleach splashing. SO, I was thinking how nice it would be if bleach came in some kind of foam or even a gel. It would be nice to have a dispenser on the wall with a can of this foam or gel and be able to just put the sponge underneath it and it dispense either by me or by itself. That way I never worry of it splashing on my clothes or me having to keep a bottle of bleach under my sink. A nice dispenser of Clorox bleach made especially for the kitchen and for use on sponges to keep bacteria at a bay!! I think this would help consumers a lot to get rid of all the hidden bacteria we have around, keep us healthier. And I also think a lot of consumers would buy this type of product if advertised correctly.☺[1]*

As one might imagine, none of these suggestions happened by accident. To increase Clorox's virtual R&D capabilities, the social media team created CLOROXCONNECTS® (www.cloroxconnects.com)—a site that enables the massive cleaner brand to brainstorm with customers and suppliers, in real time.

Through the online platform, Clorox employees are able to connect with inventors, suppliers, and consumers for innovation, incubation, and sourcing ideas. In that vein, users can log on as "consumers," "inventors," or "partners." The users can then submit ideas, in text or with pictures, and other users can rate or even review them in the comments section.

What's the payoff for users, other than seeing their ideas online, that is? To encourage participation, Clorox uses incentives that are perfected in gaming. People who post answers or add rating comments are awarded points. There are different levels of difficulty, and contributors who demonstrate expertise can advance to problems requiring greater creativity, knowledge, and participation. There are also periodic contests and prizes, like a recent one featuring a $1,000 grand prize and four $250 runners-up.

CLOROXCONNECTS is a registered trademark of The Clorox Company and is used with permission.

Greg Piche, the innovation sourcing lead at Clorox and the founder of CLOROXCONNECTS®, says the effort has been a huge success. "CLOROXCONNECTS® helps feed our trend and needs analysis," he explains. "Consumers talk about ideas for new products, and through the analysis of those unaided conversations, we're able to supplement our trends and insights. Secondly, CLOROXCONNECTS® gives us a large group of consumers who are readily available to review concepts that we generate. This rapid feedback helps us find our way through the very iterative and non-linear innovation process."

One early success, Piche notes, came after Clorox posted a question about a specific compound for its Hidden Valley salad dressings. Five responses quickly came in. The company decided on a solution within a day and actually brought the contributor into the product development process.

By targeting its different audiences, CLOROXCONNECTS® has been able to segment what it gets out of each group. "If we need to get a quick read on the concept, we go to the consumer community and post a survey or host a virtual focus group," explains Piche.

"If we need a tactical solution to a pressing technical question, we can tap into our supplier base and find answers. If we want fully baked solutions, we can post a challenge to our inventor network. We're also able to identify prolific super users and then bring those folks into private co-creation communities."

The concept is already bearing fruit, as Clorox notes: "We've opened the door to innovation," the site claims. "Because the next big idea can come from anyone, anywhere."

Tapping into Open Innovation for Instant R&D

OUR MISSION:
We're all about innovation!

Our purpose is to facilitate consumer brainstorming, exploring, and sharing ideas to help The Clorox Company develop and improve products you love!

clorox connects

© 2014 The Clorox Company. Reprinted with permission.

Witness the CLOROXCONNECTS® mission statement (above), which is telling about how other companies can tap into innovation for instant, real-time research and development. After all, "innovation" is right up there in its mission statement. The company also makes it clear that this is no charity event. The site is designed, as the mission statement says, "to help The Clorox Company develop and improve products you love!"

Clearly, the effort is weighted on the company's side, so beyond the occasional contest or "feel good" ratings, why are consumers, suppliers, and partners participating in this community? And what has the company learned so far?

In a presentation to a group at a social media event named "BlogWell," Piche explained: "People love to do this. When asked, people love to share ideas, and they feel valued when they're encouraged to do so. They're eager to talk about features that frustrate them, things they like and how something could be made better."

While it is still early in the process, results are encouraging. And outsiders are noticing. When making a "buy" recommendation on The Clorox Company, the Motley Fool, a multimedia financial service company, noted: "What impresses me most about Clorox is its ability to innovate and find new product ideas . . . new initiatives, or just great Clorox facts such as this note posted . . . through its crowdsourcing initiative called CLOROXCONNECTS®."

So, you're not Clorox. I get that. But how can you benefit from innovation the way companies like Clorox do? The fact is, innovation is not a technology. It's a mindset—and it's free.

In his introduction to a report called *Social Media for Corporate Innovators and Entrepreneurs,* author Stefan Lindegaard writes a great summary of the power and potential of what he refers to as "open innovation." "Open innovation is about bridging internal and external resources and acting on those opportunities to bring better innovations to market faster," says Lindegaard.

He goes on to include how social media has not only revolutionized the business world but innovation as well. "With social media," he explains, "your ability to extend your network of contacts who may be able to assist you in your innovation process widens dramatically."

The fact is, according to Lindegaard, we are going to see more and more open innovation on the open market in the near future: "Recently, the power of integrating social media into innovation has taken hold. It's still in its early phases, but make no mistake, this trend is gaining momentum every day, and there is no turning back."

Co-creation: *The Future of R&D*

Open innovation, it turns out, is the gateway to something we now refer to as *co-creation*. Remember when Red Robin opened its Facebook fan page to followers and friends so they could suggest and ultimately design the restaurant chain's new hamburger combination?

Or how about when Frito-Lay offered a million dollars to the winner of its "Do Us a Flavor" contest, in which all varieties of new potato chip flavors, from "sesame chicken" to "curry onion," from "pulled pork" to "chili dog and onion," poured in via social media channels?

Welcome to the world of co-creation. Here social media exists to connect consumers to companies (and vice versa) in a mutually beneficial union. Here is where ideas are fully and freely expressed in a way that encourages consumer interactivity and puts companies in direct contact with potential customers from a wide variety of demographics, many of whom they might never be able to tap into without open innovation.

While McDonald's will not be "outing" its secret sauce any time soon, nor will the Colonel be revealing KFC's "secret" recipe, what company in good conscience could ignore the power and potential of nearly real time, virtual focus groups in a variety of forms and formats?

The fact is, co-creation has a variety of benefits to offer companies of all sizes as they use social media and the Internet to elicit consumer responses, suggestions, questions, comments, and ideas about a variety of new or improved products and services.

Here are some of the main advantages of co-creation.

Frequent Customer Engagement

Imagine being able to engage with your customers in a virtually endless loop of feedback and solicitation. Such is the online nature not just of social media itself but of open innovation and co-creation as well. For users of the CLOROXCONNECTS® site, inspiration may strike at any time.

Fortunately, the Internet is open 24/7/365, allowing consumers to upload pictures, sketches, and descriptions of their new product ideas or improvements at any time of day or night. With comment boxes and other forum features, your company can have someone readily available to capture, compliment, and respond to such suggestions, directly engaging the consumers in a way that is both rewarding for them and advantageous for you.

Much like monitoring online chatter about your corporate brand or new product launch, you can have an individual or team who frequently monitors your online page, forum, or virtual suggestion box to ensure that the site doesn't grow stale and that folks are being regularly and individually recognized.

Fresher Ideas

You know how your on-site brainstorming sessions occasionally grow familiar, cold, and stale? Oftentimes that's because it's the same creative group sitting in the same conference room playing the same politics and batting about the same tired old ideas they couldn't get passed through in the last pitch session.

Imagine inviting the world to "pitch" ideas via your Facebook fan page, a special Twitter promotion, a Pinterest board or Tumblr page, a blog, dedicated forum, or devoted suggestion site, which is basically what CLOROXCONNECTS® is.

While there are bound to be more than a few "clunkers" suggested, you never know where the next iPod idea will come from. RedHeadGrandma6, are you listening?

More Loyal Customers

There is no doubt that we form "bonds" with particular companies over shared experiences. We all have that "special" restaurant we go to for family occasions—birthdays, holidays, graduations, promotions, and the like. Is it the best restaurant in town? Not usually, but it's the "warmest" in the sense of familiarity and fond remembrances.

Just as we associate certain songs with the pleasant moments we experienced while listening to them, we can form "attachments" to certain companies that have provided above average consumer experiences. How likely do you think RedHeadGrandma6 is to buy off-brand cleaning products when she has interacted so closely, and successfully, with Clorox employees while on their online forum? Not very likely.

And how likely is she to recommend Clorox products to her family, friends, neighbors, and just about anybody else who will listen? Very likely. Which leads to our next and final benefit of co-creation.

Greater WOM Momentum

Imagine enlisting a "trusted team" of citizen creatives—everyday consumers who, through their brand loyalty and co-creation interaction, have earned coveted, and of course honorary, "consumer ambassador" spots on your R&D squad.

Now imagine them as committed brand fans, loyalists, and cheerleaders eager to spread the word as the "product" they've suggested or tested or merely commented on nears its inevitable launch. Can you imagine the WOM momentum that can build and build as the launch date grows closer?

It was interesting to watch the Frito-Lay "Do Us a Flavor" contest gather steam on the Frito-Lay Facebook fan page. There was a clear timeline for the contest, and as the judging portion neared, you could almost feel the momentum swell as people rushed to get their last-minute ideas in and become a part of this social media "experiment."

I must admit to checking in on the progress of the contest as I researched this chapter, only to find the judging process in session, and quite frankly, the suspense was palpable. I can only imagine how it must feel, not just for finalists but for those who followed the contest from day one, hoping their flavor combination might win.

And once the final winner is announced, imagine how many participants—and this contest garnered millions of comments, Likes, responses, suggestions, questions, comments, and interactions—will rush out as soon as the product hits the shelves to give it a try? That is WOM momentum in action, and it should be something to behold.

Will it be well worth the $1 million Frito-Lay is offering to the contest winner? I imagine the company has recouped that money in advertising dozens of times over by now.

Why Didn't We Think of That? *Kraft Foods and the Story of the 100-Calorie Packs*

We believe Nabisco 100 Calorie Packs is a great example of a product success that was really driven by great consumer input. It delivers on the need for consumers to have great tasting snacks that help them stay true to their personal health and wellness goals.

—**JEFF SIGEL**, Brand Manager, 100 Calorie Packs

Not every case of co-creation is as public as the Red Robin, Frito-Lay, and CLOROXCONNECTS® examples we've been studying so far in this chapter, proving that in open innovation as with everything else, variety is key and open-mindedness is king.

Take Kraft Foods, for instance. Long before Facebook and Twitter made co-creation a breeze, the snack food giant was already ahead of the curve in working with another forward thinking company, Communispace, to set up various "pilot groups" of 250 to 300 women in order to get their candid and fresh input on a variety of new products the company was developing.

What came out of one such pilot group was not their views on current Kraft Nabisco products (now part of Mondelez International) but what they'd like to see. The women in one such group claimed they weren't into diet foods and were tired of starving themselves.

Portion control was a big issue for them—knowing when to say when. They also wanted to "treat" themselves and were looking for healthy snack choices that would be filling, tasty, not "fake" and yet not make them feel guilty for the rest of the day.

What's more, Nabisco found, the pilot participants tended to think in terms of calories, so a lot of discussion was spent around how many calories were "enough" but not "too much" for, say, an afternoon snack. After much discussion, the consensus was that 100 calories was that "just enough" amount. And with that, Nabisco's ubiquitous, highly successful (the product line hit $100 million in sales in under one year), and frequently imitated 100-calorie snack packs were born.

Courtesy of Communispace, here is a sampling of the comments straight from their communities:

- "I always viewed 'dieting' as having negative connotations. I've always concentrated on making 'healthy' decisions."
- "I don't deprive myself of anything. When I want something that I really shouldn't have, I have a very small serving (like candy bars—I get the snack size). I find that I am more satisfied with watching what I eat when I know that I can have anything. When I felt there were things that were off limits, that is what I wanted most."
- "To stay satisfied while losing weight, I don't deprive myself of anything. For me, it's all about portion control. If I want sweets, I just have a small amount. If I deprive myself, I'll binge on the item I miss."
- "The only time I really look at calories is in snacks. I know I can only go up to 100 calories. . . . If it is more than that, I usually won't buy it."

It's interesting to note how powerfully the pilot program influenced one of the nation's biggest companies in what surely must have constituted a significant investment in R&D, testing, product redesign, and launch. One can only imagine the folks at Kraft Nabisco wondering, at some point during the process, if co-creation was actually the way to go.

Charting Your Own Course for Co-creation: *A Blueprint for Success*

While this is not necessarily a book about research and development, clearly, listening to one's customers and making them as big a part of the product development phase as possible is one sure way to indoctrinate them to your culture, see them become loyal brand fans, and get them to recommend you to others. Which, incidentally, is what this book is about.

So, how do we do this? How do we reach beyond our own conference rooms and pitch sessions, laboratories, or bull sessions to actively engage the customers in helping us to help them by creating products and services they actually *want* to use?

You can start by following the five simple steps I've listed below, personalizing them for your industry, size of company, culture, vision, and brand so that you interact with the right consumers to get the right results of your own co-creation efforts.

Design Your Blueprint

Plan to plan; that's first, foremost, and always. While clearly open innovation and co-creation have decided upsides when it comes to R&D, rushing in without a clear blueprint for how you are going to proceed is a disaster waiting to happen.

Having a plan that is dictated by your goals and objectives will keep you moving forward toward bringing out products and services that your customers will actually want and that will fit their needs.

So, first, before you rush into open innovation, ask yourself a few probing questions such as these:

- What do we hope to accomplish with this venture?
- What, specifically, are we trying to achieve?
- Is it to come up with our company's next big thing?

- Is it to improve on an already existing product, service, or system within the company?
- Is it to spot check a current system our customers have had problems with in the past, such as the 1-800 number or product packaging?
- Are we simply "fishing" for new product or service ideas that might be of use in the future?
- Or, last, are we just eager to open up the lines of communication in a more regular and reoccurring way?

Regardless of your goals, big or small, local or national or even international, it's important that you create a crisp, clear, and definitive blueprint before you launch any co-creation or open innovation initiatives.

As for any project, a blueprint will create "guardrails" around how much and how fast you proceed, and it will help you with tracking and measuring the project and your progress throughout the process.

Pick Your Outlet Carefully

Maybe your company doesn't have the resources to create a CLOROXCONNECTS® forum that is closely monitored and rigorously maintained. Maybe you don't have an intense need to interact and engage with your customers on a daily, or even weekly, basis. If so, planning is critical to your success: when you know your goals, you'll also know what outlet to use to achieve those goals.

The great thing about social media is that it provides you a variety of avenues to explore so that you can find just the right fit for your co-creation possibilities:

- Using Pinterest, you might ask users to form a different pin board to post their product ideas, "dream" products, and so on. This could be a low-impact way of getting user-generated ideas without the full forum capabilities of, say, CLOROXCONNECTS® or something quite that intense.
- You might turn to YouTube as your social media venue of choice if, for instance, you wanted to post a series of new product demonstrations. Conversely, you could use YouTube to invite customers to post testimonials, queries, complaints, suggestions, or something else. People love the sudden impact of video, and filming themselves is a great ego stroke.

- If you need to reach a larger audience and tap into the "viral" factor of social media, you might find Twitter to be your venue of choice. Using Twitter, you can quickly and cheaply reach hundreds, thousands, even hundreds of thousands of people and get their feedback. For instance, you could use Twitter in any of these ways:
  - Run a contest to name your next menu item, pizza, burger, or something else.
  - Ask for new greeting card messages, taglines, movie teasers, or product name suggestions in messages to your company that are fewer than 140 characters.
  - Get input on which book cover, packaging, or logo people prefer.
  - Use hashtags in a creative way to easily categorize any of the above, such as #pizzaparty, #tagline, or #coveroff.
- In earlier chapters, we've seen how Red Robin and Frito-Lay used their Facebook fan pages to engage and enlist current and potential customers with various contests and "build-a-burger" promotions. In a similar vein, Vitamin Water also used Facebook to run a contest in which contestants could combine their favorite flavors and design the company's next drink.

Make It Easy to Enlist

Regardless of how ambitious or casual your co-creation activities are, you want to make it easy for everyone to participate. Sites like Cloroxconnects.com as well as the various social media sites—to which most of your consumers will already belong—make it easy for average citizens to become honorary company ambassadors.

If you've ever logged onto a new site, say, Pinterest.com or Tumblr.com, and you've been asked to "create an account" or "sign in with your existing Facebook or Twitter account," which one did you choose? If you're like most people, you simply clicked the Facebook or Twitter icon and registered with as little effort as a mouse click or two.

If you can adopt and adapt this technology for your own co-creation landing page, great. If not, then do the next best thing by making it as easy to enlist as possible. One username, one password, one confirmation, and that's it. Making folks jump through endless hoops to prove they're not a robot or they are who they say they are simply puts up a barrier between you and co-creation. You want them to come to the site, register quickly and easily, if at all, and begin co-creating.

Be Clear About Your Intentions

Fair warning about co-creation and legality, or at least ethics: check with legal to make sure that anyone entering a contest, contributing to a forum, offering a suggestion or product idea, contributing to an online focus group or quorum, or engaging with your company in some other way knows that they are doing so. In addition, make sure that they are not employees of the company and they are not entitled to future earnings.

All of this should be made clear in web copy, fine print, e-mails, texts, whatever the case may be, to ensure that all participants know their roles in the process and do not have skewed expectations at a later date when a product, service, or idea they may have helped contribute to, like a Red Robin burger, Frito-Lay chip flavor, Clorox cleaner, bottle of vitamin water, or a 100-calorie snack pack, starts showing up on their local grocery store shelves.

Remember the Focus

In all the trappings of Facebook contests and Twitter hashtags and forum participation and page hits and grand ideas, remember that this is all about R&D. And, while it should be an eye-opening and pleasant experience for both you and the consumers you enlist, it should principally be about gathering information:

- Ideas
- E-mail addresses
- Metrics
- Demographics
- Spending habits
- Income
- Favorites
- Least favorites
- Preferences
- Buying habits
- Expectations
- Experiences

Consider the Power of (Powerful) Feedback

In keeping with good record keeping, measurement, and data parsing, the power of feedback comes mostly from its authenticity. More is not always more, and in the case of co-creation, quality will usually win out over quantity. Surely you will get a lot of feedback when you directly ask for it, but how meaningful will it all be?

If you've ever bothered to visit the Frito-Lay Facebook fan page for its "Do Us a Flavor" contest, you'll see that while many of the commenters are sincerely earnest about their flavor recommendations, just as many are certainly jokes and hardly worth considering. (Butterscotch, anyone?!?)

To ensure that your feedback is both purposeful and powerful, consider posing the right questions and making them relevant to real life. AirTran Airways conducted an online survey back in 2009 that posed the question, "What do you think should be on every AirTran flight?" Much like the "Do Us a Flavor" contest, no doubt the responses were wildly creative, but reading between the lines, the company was able to see a running theme: customers, by a predominant vote, wanted one thing on every AirTran flight: Wi-Fi. Well, they got what they wanted; Wi-Fi is now available on every flight.

Monitor for Management

The "co" in co-creation implies that you will be collaborating with consumers in an active, authentic, and real way. Social media is designed for two-way conversations, and you would be doing your efforts in this area a real disservice if you were simply to listen and not respond, or if you asked and never answered.

Dig in and root around and pay attention and monitor and focus, and find out who's really participating. Like any online venture, the cream usually rises to the top. Find your own RedHeadGrandma6 and court her, and others like her, to form a collective of folks you can trust—consumers you can go to who continually provide quality feedback.

Reward and covet them, and recognize them for the gold mines of open innovation that they represent. Engage them as if they were on site. Heck, invite them on site if that's an option. There are no rules for how you co-create, and the more innovative you get around online R&D, the better!

Use It or Lose It

Finally, there's no sense going to all this trouble if you're not committed to using this information in some form or fashion. Admittedly, not every idea is going to end up on your menu, your factory floor, in your greeting cards, or in your store front windows.

There will be as many duds as there are doozies, and the power is in recognizing the difference. But even then, if all you do is sit on it or let it gather dust, what's the use of all this valuable information? How can you capitalize on all the time, effort, and resources you put into the initiative?

When there is a blueprint in place, when you have clear goals, aspirations, and outcomes for what you're doing, you can then involve the entire organization in implementing whatever bright ideas you manage to co-create, now or in the future.

If the feedback you get leads to a new product, get on it. If it reveals that a current product merely needs to be improved, consider yourself lucky. If it uncovers a broken link in your service chain, delivery time, leadership, sales, or something else, then take steps to make whatever changes are required to eliminate or rectify that damage.

You can honor the "co" in co-create, but not if you and the consumers you engage with during the discovery process don't actually "create" anything.

Going Forward

Co-creation is still in its infancy for many companies. Perhaps, not surprisingly, your own. You may still be struggling with mastering social media, let alone using it to solicit feedback and research on how to create products and offerings your customers tell you they will buy. But this chapter should hopefully provide an introduction not only to the concept of co-creation but also to how it can be implemented—in your industry, in any industry, in your company, in any company.

The fact is, even dipping your toe in this pool can do your company good. Engagement with your customers is always a plus. Above all, open innovation and co-creation are two additional ways to engage with potential brand fans in meaningful and repeated ways. Even if it never results in your company's version of a 100-calorie snack pack, isn't it worth getting your feet wet to find out?

CHAPTER 16

Tying It All Together

Becoming a Highly Recommended Business

As we begin the last chapter of this book, I'd like you to take a moment and picture the following scenario: a leading consumer products company, let's call it "OmniClean," believes there is room in the market for a new hand sanitizer.

OmniClean has been monitoring online conversations throughout the world—and noticing some interesting trends. Due to a very active flu season, consumers have a heightened awareness of the importance of regularly cleaning their hands—whether through routine hand washing with whatever soap is available or using some type of gel or spray hand sanitizer.

However, with the increased amount of washing and sanitizing going on, people's hands are really beginning to dry out—and the "solution" to avoiding the flu is now creating new problems. In particular, customers are not responding favorably to the alcohol and antiseptic smell of the hand sanitizers on the market (OmniClean currently produces both hand soaps *and* sanitizers), which lead to dry and "medicine smelling" hands the more often they use the products.

Fortunately, the social media and digital, marketing, and consumer relations teams at OmniClean have been completely integrated—sharing and comparing feedback, gathering insights, monitoring competitive products and sentiment.

In addition, the product innovations team has been engaging current customers through a private online community—getting a sense of what retailers are hearing in their stores about the products and competitors.

It's very clear what aspects consumers like about the current hand sanitizers (and why they positively recommend them) and what they think is wrong or missing—and why they negatively "recommend" them far and wide via social media.

While there is consistency in the feedback, there are also a number of nuances—particularly globally. Some markets like a certain scent; others don't. Some like the handy pocket-sized version; others think it's wasted packaging and costs too much for what you get. Some markets actually like the "medicinal" smell of the product—as it indicates product efficacy and users "know" that it works—while others find it offensive and want something more subtle. All agree that using the product more than four or five times a day causes noticeable hand dryness, which is at odds with what they're reading about how often they need to keep using it to stave off the flu.

A New Product Is Born

Over a five-month period of time, the team formulates a new product line called "Hands Free" with different scents, package sizes, and formulations—all of which are not only less harsh on sensitive skin but also include hand moisturizers and softeners for frequent users.

Through a secure online portal, employees, consumers, customers, and partners give feedback on Hands Free throughout the process— weighing in on all aspects, including manufacturing, brand name, packaging, and marketing strategies.

Feedback is carefully cultivated and shared—with all parties seeing and hearing the impact and influence their recommendations are having.

Prior to the launch of the new line, the brand identifies key influencers in targeted markets across a variety of categories—health and beauty, medicine, lifestyle, education, parenting, aging, institutional management, and so on. The influencers are given product samples from the entire Hands Free line and information on why and how product innovations were made.

As the product officially launches, the marketplace swells in approval and eagerly embraces Hands Free. The product is highly recommended across consumer groups, retailers, and experts, and the buzz grows exponentially with each recommendation.

It's a hit. And the feedback chain continues, giving those charged with monitoring chatter an endless loop to follow and engage.

Now, rewind all that and do over: if you look closely at the case study above, you'll find that our fictional company OmniClean follows everything you've learned in this book up to this point. It's no accident that it's a highly recommended company, nor should it come as any surprise that their Hands Free product line is an online and offline success story.

In fact, you could call it a science.

The Science of Becoming Highly Recommended.

The Highly Recommended Brand Is Well on Its Way to Becoming a Reality

Cleary, the next wave coming across small, large, and multinational businesses is moving from engaging in social media to becoming true social businesses.

Here is just a sampling of what some of the world's biggest consulting and technology companies have to say about social business and why they're spending so much time, energy, and valuable resources on it:

- **Accenture, on why the company wrote a book about social media.** "Through social media, massive numbers of customers are engaging in new ways with companies and each other. This is having a significant impact on businesses everywhere—whether companies know it or not. While it's not hard to start engaging in social media, it's challenging to effectively integrate it throughout an organization and to determine if it's having a positive economic impact on the business."
- **IBM, on why social business works.** "When you integrate your business processes with the right social tools, you secure a competitive advantage and pioneer new ways of doing business."
- **Oracle, on why it created a social relationship management suite, Oracle OpenWorld.** "By fundamentally changing the way organizations connect with their different stakeholders, social is changing the rules of business. . . . With the Oracle Social Relationship Management Suite, we are empowering our customers to embrace this change by integrating the tools required to listen, engage, create, market, and analyze social interactions into existing applications and services."

- **Salesforce, on why it established its Salesforce Marketing Cloud.** "The Radian6 Social Marketing Cloud will transform how companies listen, analyze, and engage with customers and prospects on the social web. Turn millions of social conversations into dynamic engagements that strengthen customer relationships."

Each of these organizations represents a sea change in the way Fortune 500 companies—indeed, every company—must respond to today's evolving and sophisticated online marketplace. Throughout this book you've become steeped in the power of recommendations and, what's more, the different ways to go about becoming highly recommended. Now it's time to tie it all together, much as OmniClean did with its Hands Free sanitizer line.

While there is a growing dialogue about the importance of becoming a social business, it's not enough—there is still too much ambiguity. There needs to be an agreed-upon focus and outcome for every department, team, stakeholder group, customer, and consumer.

That outcome is to become highly recommended.

Inclusion, Not Isolation: *The Highly Recommended Business Is a Total Business*

The important thing to note about not just our fictional OmniClean company but very real, very successful companies is that they don't just "do" social business; they *are highly recommended businesses*, top to bottom, inside and out.

In other words, for highly recommended businesses, social media has gone way beyond the realm of marketing and communications to impact all aspects of the organization:

- **HR.** Highly recommended businesses aren't just recommended for their products and services but for their business structure, values, mission, and driving philosophies as well. When you are a company that people both want to buy from *and* work for, then you are truly a highly recommended business in name and deed.
- **Marketing.** The marketing department for a highly recommended business, while daily challenged and charged

with near constant evolution, nonetheless finds itself no longer isolated from the average consumer but, instead, embraced by, or at least in league with, today's sophisticated and vocal consumer.

- **Sales.** The sales department is often one of the first to benefit from being a part of a highly recommended business. Teams know what customers want and need, and they find ways to give it to them—often before it's even asked for.
- **Customer service.** Companies who are highly recommended enjoy more satisfied customers and more feedback on why those customers who are dissatisfied chose to reach out—or speak out—in the first place.
- **Product and service innovation.** Becoming highly recommended helps give R&D not only more grist for the mill in the form of recommendations, ideas, feedback, and the like but also more targeted, realistic, valuable, and trusted feedback from a vetted and loyal network.
- **Packaging and design.** When P&D has only itself to work with, its options are limited but internal. When they have a vast network of internal and external, loyal and random social volunteers to draw from, not only is its job easier but it is also more successful each time out because it's getting real feedback from real consumers in real time.

While it's easy to talk about "multilevel integration" and "cross-silo expansion" in theoretical terms, we all know that evolution is hard on even the most willing companies, let alone those departments who are both adverse to change and reluctant to veer from the status quo. But evolve we must if we are to capitalize on the opportunities that social media presents for becoming highly recommended and ultimately adoptable.

The key is to focus on the benefits, both for each division or silo and the overall organization, as you evolve into a truly social business that is primed, ready, and ultimately recommendable. That should be easy to do as, across all areas (see bulleted list above), organizations become much more flexible as they actively listen and adapt to market opportunities in real time.

Even with the over-the-head obviousness of the importance of becoming social businesses, most companies today are still just scratching the surface when it comes to truly taking advantage of social media. Jumping in full force could easily become overwhelming, particularly given the specifics of your company, your individual leadership structures already in place, and the silos, divisions, and politics that currently exist.

According to Charlene Li, founding partner at Altimeter Group, "While social media is marketing focused, social business impacts all parts of the organization."

In fact, according to a recent Ketchum/FedEx Social Business Benchmarking Study, "Social businesses are looking beyond 'connecting with' people to building relationships with important stakeholders in a meaningful way."

We often forget that it's not just burger chains and hand sanitizers and potato chip companies that drive social business. Social media has changed the economic and commercial landscape so quickly, and so profoundly, that even electric companies(!) are making the switch from traditional to social business models.

"Traditionally," adds Ammanuel C. Moore of Baltimore Gas and Electric, "the relationship between utilities and customers has been limited to a monthly bill and sporadic phone calls. Today, however, that limited level of engagement is simply not enough. Our customers are looking for a robust, two-way dialogue, not only where it concerns storm-related power outages but to help them become more energy efficient and save money. . . . Social media allows us to interact with customers in ways that make them feel unique and important."

Defining Your Own Highly Recommended Business Model: *The Norm Versus the Exception*

As often happens after a tipping point has been reached and companies must rapidly adapt to a new, game-changing technology (remember the first few years of the Internet?), there is little existing framework in place when it comes to building a social business from the ground up.

At Zócalo Group, we naturally consider ourselves on the cutting edge of this new recommendation age—or is it the digital age? Or the social business age? See, we don't even know what to call it, it's so new. Yet every company we consult with seems to have a different and often drastic approach to how they will evolve into a social and highly recommended business.

What seems clear from both direct observation and reams of research is that while the direct and indirect return on investment on social media and recommendations might be difficult to measure, companies must evolve, and quickly.

While many companies make for many models, there are some distinct parallels among all highly recommended businesses:

1. **Philosophy.** Before you enlist a single department in your new highly recommended business model, you must consciously, and concretely, lay out your philosophy for doing so, and you must distribute it throughout the entire organization.

2. **Buy-in.** The entire organization, and all the departments and silos therein, need to be involved in all facets of becoming a highly recommended business.

3. **Flow.** Linking all the pieces and parts of your organization must occur organically. There must be a form of distribution, or a "flow," in place, so that what one silo does successfully, everyone else can adopt and what one department does unsuccessfully, everyone else can learn from and avoid.

4. **Feedback.** The most highly recommended businesses don't just monitor the online chatter about their products. They also monitor their own chatter about themselves as a company as well. Having ways to offer, provide, elicit, and absorb feedback is essential.

5. **Flexibility.** What every highly recommended business model must build in, and account for, is flexibility. There is simply no way to adapt to all the rapidly changing technology, platforms, mediums, and trends if you aren't flexible enough to adapt on a dime. While that can be challenging for businesses of any size, where I see it being the most successful is in organizations where there is flexibility not just at the top, with the leadership, but in every department as well.

6. **Freedom.** Finally, there must be freedom within each of those departments and silos to respond to their individual network "without a net." In other words, how being a highly recommended business will look and sound for, say, the sales representatives and their network will look and feel very different from how HR approaches being a social business. And that's okay as long as there is an approved framework in place for how to respond in real time.

One of the dangers of evolving into a highly recommended business is that, regardless of your philosophy, mission, or values, the rest of the organization will still merely see it as marketing.

Building your business model on the above six premises is putting one foot in the right direction, but the overarching theme must, again, be about how becoming recommended impacts, improves, and, yes, inspires every department.

From Theory to Reality: *What a Highly Recommended Business Looks Like*

The question companies ask me most frequently is, "How can I visualize all this once it's complete? What does a highly recommended business look like?" I think it's a really good question to ask, and answer, because for one, a highly recommended business is never truly done.

You can build a product, release it onto the world, watch its life cycle evolve, and halfway through that life cycle, begin to work on the next product, service, brand, whatever. You can staff a sales department or human resources division, put it in motion, and reap the benefits, almost from day one.

Getting your people to ever feel truly comfortable about being a business based on what other people are saying can be a challenge, but they'll soon get on board. The strongest companies, the *best* companies, are often those that are frequently tested and come out stronger as a result—not just as organizations but as is reflected in their products and services as well.

So here, at a glance, is what a social business can, and should, look like:

- **Focus on the fundamentals.** Highly recommended businesses know that the fundamentals of their businesses are based on the social. In other words, people—and what they say—come first, last, and always. No matter how many departments or divisions you involve, or how inherently the social business methodology gets ingrained in the organization, don't ignore the fundamentals of what makes a highly recommended business social. Continue to monitor—and then monitor some more—the daily and continual chatter that constitutes the facts and figures of what becoming recommended is all about.

- **Less is more.** Every relationship counts, which is why highly recommended businesses stay in the social media business and deal in the business of one-on-one relationships. The larger the company, the more successful social monitoring gets, the more you need to drill down to each individual relationship to make it matter, make it count, and make it work. Many companies that initially foray into becoming social businesses are really just swapping out traditional marketing with social media and using the same one-way, print advertising, billboard-not-conversation mentality but doing all of it within a two-way, conversational medium.

- **Participation is required.** Highly recommended businesses embrace participation. And yet, another big danger with setting up a highly recommended business model is to do what often happens with most new initiatives, be they mission or value statements, new corporate logos, or production manuals—that is, the companies "set it and forget it." That would be a mistake. As you continually monitor online chatter, you can't just record it and file it away. You must remain actively and consistently engaged in a real, meaningful, and regular way. Don't just do good work and pat yourself on the back for it. Rather, keep up the good work, week in, week out. That's the only way to be a social business in more than just name only.

- **Allow for adaptation.** A highly recommended business is continually adapting, evolving, and responding to not only its growth but to the growth of the medium and the growing sophistication of its network. Within a highly recommended business, you will hear and see the signs of it everywhere: in sales meetings and when hiring new trainees and in board meetings and on conference calls. This is adaptation, happening in real time and with the complicit cooperation of your customers and consumers.

- **Continuously improve.** Part of adaptation is growth, and part of growth is inevitably, continuously getting better. Having strategies in place to help you grow and learn from each interaction, and every iteration, will ensure that you look, and act, like a highly recommended business.

- **Much more than academic.** Highly recommended businesses are businesses first and social second. One of the biggest blowbacks I get from the rank and file in organizations is how this is just another "trend" that is going to eat into their production schedule and result in nothing more than a new trend next year, and the year after. Work still needs to get done, and the work of most companies—unless they are, in fact, advertising or marketing agencies—is not marketing and promotion. And yet, as we've seen not only throughout this chapter but through this entire book, becoming recommended impacts, improves, and inspires every division, team, department, silo, you name it. It's not just an academic exercise anymore than a taste test or a focus group or a 1-800 customer service line or a trade show or a recruiting program for college campuses. To that end, if you're going to become a social business, have the pipelines, the strategies, and the distribution in place to put great ideas culled from all of this activity into sincere and practical motion.

- **Call to action.** Highly recommended businesses act on the information they gather and continually integrate it into new product plans as functionality will allow. Not every idea is a bright one, but every exchange is valuable even if it results in knowing what *not* to do. It is not easy, or cheap, to continually monitor and interact with your online network, and it is less than effective if this is only an academic exercise (see above).

What will your own highly recommended business look like? Only time, adaptation, and evolution will tell. But here is what one social business looks like, and why.

What Can Being a Social Business Do for You? *Let Me Count the Ways*

Sometimes it's helpful to see a line-item list that proves the benefits of a costly initiative that will mean direct change and constant monitoring. So, in that vein, if you're still on the fence about what becoming a highly recommended business can do for you, let me provide such a list to count the many ways in which I've personally watched companies benefit from this revolutionary new business model.

To that end, becoming a social business will result in:

- More lively—and worthwhile—internal meetings
- More ownership for employees in each division
- Richer chances for employees to originate and nurture unique initiatives
- More frequent and stronger interactions with your customer base
- Easier, and longer-lasting, hiring as a result of becoming a recommendable workplace
- A richer, deeper understanding of your consumers, customers, and employees
- More personalized and targeted products, brands, and services originating in real-time responses to timely consumer needs
- Stronger and more consistent sales
- And much, much more

Parting Words: *Becoming a Highly Recommended Business*

By now, the evidence should be clear: the more connected you are to your customers, brand fans, cheerleaders, industry experts, and loyalists, even to your employees, the easier you are to recommend. Becoming a highly recommended company does not happen by accident; goodwill aside, this is about growing your business in demanding and rapidly evolving times.

Hopefully I've provided you with the proper road map to get you started on your journey to becoming highly recommended, but the most thorough blueprint would be able to flesh out only the bare bones of any specific action plan.

Every company, every culture, ever leader is unique, and to that end, your own evolution as a highly recommended business will be similarly unique. In the spirit of frequent updates in response to the latest social media platforms, trends, developments, technologies, philosophies, and practicums, I offer you an up-to-the-minute source for all things social business: www.highlyrecommendedbook.com.

As business trends emerge and new technologies appear, here is where I can update this book via blog posts, addendums, and special reports. I also welcome updates from readers as well, and I look forward to featuring many of your case studies as you share with me your progress from business to social business.

The future is here, and I pledged to do my utmost to prepare you for what's next. For now, though, your present is ready and waiting. You don't have to start big, but you must start. As you begin, remember to keep the focus where it belongs: on one customer, one commenter, one relationship at a time.

May you always keep this focus regardless of how successful your social business becomes and how often you are recommended and not just as a brand to follow, a rising star to look out for, a company to do business with, or simply just to work for.

Those companies that get recommended the most know the power of the individual consumers. Their customers are not just people to recommend them. They are people to design products for, devote services to, respond to, and sell to.

The companies I work with, have written about, or have even read about are not successful merely because they've become highly recommended businesses. They're successful because they were businesses who adapted to a social age much as they've done everything: one customer at a time. They learned, they observed, they adapted, and they evolved, and now social currency is a part of their entire organization, not just the marketing department.

If you don't appreciate employees on an individual basis, reward them, and give them ownership and opportunities to advance, you won't magically "adopt" an attitude of appreciation for your customers simply because of a few comments on your blog or negative reviews on Yelp.

At the end of the day, social media is like one big magnifying glass that cracks open your company and lays it bare for the whole world to see. Your faults, your flaws, your generosity, and your authenticity—all will be magnified to anyone interested enough to take notice. No company is perfect, and none of the businesses in the case studies we've read have embraced social media without a steep and often unforgiving learning curve.

The most highly recommended businesses know how to act while under the microscope because it's not an act. They work hard, make mistakes, apologize, learn from them, and make things right with the customers, the employees, the retailers, the journalists, the bloggers, the distributors, whatever the case may be. They can act naturally under observation because they're not acting. They're simply clocking in, getting to work, and doing what needs to be done, regardless of the technology, the interface, or how many people are watching.

What's more, and here's the biggie: the most highly recommended businesses know how to turn the magnifying glass around and use the transparency of social media to study, understand, interact with, and engage consumers on a consistent and quality basis. Some see transparency as a danger: "They'll learn all our secrets." Others understand it's an opportunity: "We'll learn all of theirs!"

The choice is yours: danger or opportunity, obstacle or freeway, failure or success. I can't divine your future anymore than you can, but I do know this much: you'll never know until you try.

Now it's time to try.

ENDNOTES

PREFACE

1. Malcolm Gladwell, *The Tipping Point: How Little Things Can Make a Big Difference*, Little, Brown, New York, 2000.

INTRODUCTION

1. Brian Solis, "How to Live a Recommendable Life," *Brian Solis* blog, July 5, 2012, http://www.briansolis.com/2012/07/how-to-live-a-recommendable-life/.
2. Graham Charlton, "How Many Bad Reviews Does It Take to Deter Shoppers?" *Econsultancy* blog, E-consultancy.com Limited, April 12, 2011, http://econsultancy.com/us/blog/7403-how-many-bad-reviews-does-it-take-to-deter-shoppers.

CHAPTER 3

1. Fournaise Marketing Group, London, 2011 Global Marketing Effectiveness Program.
2. Bill Lee, *The Hidden Wealth of Customers: Realizing the Untapped Value of Your Most Important Asset*, Harvard Business School Press, Boston, June 2012.
3. Bill Lee, "Marketing Is Dead," *Harvard Business Review*, August 2012, http://blogs.hbr.org/cs/2012/08/marketing_is_dead.html.
4. Richard Draycott, "'Marketing Is Dead' says Saatchi & Saatchi CEO," *The Drum* online, April 25, 2012, http://www.thedrum.com/news/2012/04/25/marketing-dead-says-saatchi-saatchi-ceo.

CHAPTER 5

1. Frederick F. Reichheld, "The One Number You Need to Grow," *Harvard Business Review*, December 2003, http://hbr.org/2003/12/the-one-number-you-need-to-grow/ar/1.
2. "The Economics of Buzz—Word of Mouth Drives Business Growth Finds LSE Study," 2005, The London School of Economics and Political Science, News Archives, http://www.lse.ac.uk/newsAndMedia/news/archives/2005/Word_ofMouth.aspx.
3. MotiveQuest, *Beyond the Dashboard: The Correlation Between Online Advocacy and Offline Sales*, December 3, 2011, http://www.motivequest.com/blog/index.php/beyond-the-dashboard-remarkable-implications/.

4. Carson Adley, "How Big Is the Coffee Industry?" *The Coffee
    Marvel* blog, May 17, 2010, http://www.coffeemarvel.com/blog/
    post/2010/05/17/How-Big-is-the-Coffee-Industry.aspx.
5. National Coffee Association, 2011 National Coffee Drinking
    Trends, press release, June 28, 2011, http://www.ncausa.org/
    custom/headlines/headlinedetails.cfm?id=762&returnto=778.

CHAPTER 6

1. Ed Keller and Brad Fay, *The Face-to-Facebook: Why Real Relationships
    Rule in a Digital Marketplace*, Free Press, New York, 2012.
2. Source: "Global Message Multipliers," *New York Times*, Thomson
    Reuters, and MediaVest.
3. Source: Peter Blackshaw, ConsumerGeneratedMedia.com blog,
    http://notetaker.typepad.com/cgm/.
4. Source: eMarketer.com.
5. Trevor Pinch and Filip Kesler, *How Aunt Ammy Gets Her Free
    Lunch: A Study of the Top-Thousand Customer Reviewers at
    Amazon.com*, http://www.freelunch.me/.
6. *Brand Advocates: Scaling Social Media Word-of-Mouth*,
    eMarketer report, October 2012, https://www.emarketer.com/go/
    brandadvocatesreport.
7. Source: Ed Keller, *Online vs. Offline Word of Mouth: A Special
    TalkTrack Analysis*, Keller Fay Group, New Brunswick, NJ, 2008,
    http://www.kellerfay.com/wp-content/uploads/2011/01/KellerFay_
    Online_vs_Offline_WOM_ARF_7-15-08.pdf.
8. Source: Josh Bernoff and Augie Ray, *Peer Influence Analysis:
    A Social Computing Report*, Forrester Research, Cambridge, MA,
    April 20, 2010, http://www.forrester.com/Peer+Influence+Analysis/
    fulltext/-/E-RES56766?objectid=RES56766.
9. Frito-Lay, *Snack Chat* blog, www.snacks.com.

CHAPTER 7

1. Malcolm Gladwell, *The Tipping Point: How Little Things Can Make a
    Big Difference*, Little, Brown, New York, 2000.
2. Josh Bernoff and Augie Ray, *Peer Influence Analysis: A Social
    Computing Report*, Forrester Research, Cambridge, MA, April 20, 2010,
    http://www.forrester.com/Peer+Influence+Analysis/fulltext/-/
    E-RES56766?objectid=RES56766.
3. Ibid.
4. Clive Thompson, "Is the Tipping Point Toast?" *Fast Company*,
    February 1, 2008, http://www.fastcompany.com/641124/tipping-
    point-toast.

5. Source: *Building Brands for the Connected World: A Social Business Blueprint by Facebook Based on a Commissioned Study by Forrester Consulting*, February 2012, as cited in "What Marketers Don't Get About Social Media Audiences," MarketingProfs, http://www.marketingprofs.com/charts/2011/6680/what-marketers-dont-get-about-social-media-audiences.

6. Mary Beth Kemp, *Match Word-of-Mouth Marketing to How European Consumers Share Opinions: A Social Computing Report*, Forrester Research, Cambridge, MA, May 2009, http://www.forrester.com/Match+WordOfMouth+Marketing+To+How+European+Consumers+Share+Opinions/fulltext/-/E-RES47307?docid=47307.

7. Ron Loch, *Embrace Critics to Drive Business*, American Management Association, New York, April 4, 2012, http://www.amanet.org/training/articles/embrace-critics-to-drive-business.aspx?pcode=xcrp.

CHAPTER 8

1. SocialMention.com.

2. Eric Swallow, "Dell to Launch Social Media Command Center [Exclusive]," *Mashable* Social Media, December 8, 2010, http://mashable.com/2010/12/08/dell-social-listening-center/.

3. "Dell-Commissioned Study Reveals Companies That Listen Realize Business Results," study conducted by Forrester Consulting on behalf of Dell, Dell press release, Round Rock, TX, July 13, 2011, http://content.dell.com/us/en/corp/d/secure/2011-07-13-dell-social-listening.

4. Susan Gunelius, "Listening and Discussing: The Social Media Success Imperative," *Corporate Eye* blog, May 5, 2010, http://www.corporate-eye.com/blog/2010/05/listening-and-discussing-the-social-media-success-imperatives/?wpmp_switcher=mobile.

5. Pranee Liamputtong, *Focus Group Methodology: Principle and Practice*, "Focus Group Methodology: Introduction and History," chap. 1, SAGE Publications, Thousand Oaks, CA, October 23, 2010, http://www.sagepub.com/upm-data/39360_978_1_84787_909_7.pdf.

6. Burns & Levinson, "Amazing Clients: Building Online Communities for Business," no date, http://www.burnslev.com/clients/amazing-clients-communispace.asp.

CHAPTER 9

1. "Sentry Safes Offer Versatility, Variety, and Peace of Mind," *The Survival Mom* blog, http://thesurvivalmom.com/2012/08/17/10059/.

2. "SentrySafe Giveaway and Review," *A Thrifty Mom* blog, June 6, 2012, http://athriftymom.com/sentrysafe-giveaway-and-review/.

3. Sara Lokitis, "3 Tips to Manage Your Social Media Reputation," SocialMediaExaminer.com, July 4, 2012, http://www.socialmediaexaminer.com/social-media-reputation/.

4. *Google Ranking Factors U.S. 2012, Searchmetrics SEO* blog white paper, http://www.searchmetrics.com/en/white-paper/google-ranking-factors-us-2012/.

CHAPTER 10

1. From the author's personal conversation with Christine Cea.

CHAPTER 12

1. Chris Matyszczyk, "Android Fanboys Rage at Microsoft's Droid Rage Hype," C|NET, December 9, 2012, http://news.cnet.com/8301-17852_3-57558083-71/android-fanboys-rage-at-microsofts-droid-rage-hype/.
2. Tom Warren, "Microsoft's #droidrage Campaign Results in #windowsrage on Twitter," The Verge, December 6, 2012, http://www.theverge.com/2012/12/6/3734852/twitter-droidrage-windowsrage-windows-phone-microsoft.

CHAPTER 13

1. https://twitter.com/farahanjuna.
2. https://twitter.com/Mondrayish.
3. https://twitter.com/doubletree.
4. Tricia Morris, "Social Customers' Great Expectations: 83 Percent Want a Response Within a Day," Parature, company blog, November 7, 2012, http://www.parature.com/social-customers-great-expectations-83-response-day/.

CHAPTER 14

1. "Pissed Off 'Employees' Bash Pretty Much Every Major Video Game Company," Kotaku.com, September 5, 2012, http://kotaku.com/5940672/pissed-off-employees-bash-pretty-much-every-major-video-game-company.

CHAPTER 15

1. "My Clorox!DEA.com," http://cloroxconnects.com/pages/08ef069c5d.

INDEX

Abercrombie & Fitch, 25
ABM (*see* Always Be Monitoring)
Active engagement, 166, 167
Activision, 169–171
Acxiom data broker, 116
Advertising, 53, 108
  broadcasting new form of, 23
  creepy, 27
  as interruptions, 16
  local, 7
  one-on-one communicators
    returning to, 23–24
  recommending and recognizing
    in, 17–18
  Super Bowl and, 131
  targeted involuntarily, 27
  traditional style dead in, 22
  unlearning one-way, 24
Advertising Hall of Fame, 29
Advocacy, 5–7, 40, 59–62
  brand and, 41, 42, 55–56, 59–62, 67,
    92, 116, 150
  business, 74–75, 122
  NPS not measuring, 42–43
Advocates, 48, 60, 67
AirTran Airways, 199
Alexa.com, 82
Altimeter Group, 206
Always Be Monitoring (ABM), 148
Amazon.com, 15, 17, 54–55, 58, 64,
  136, 156
American Express Global Customer
  Service Barometer, 159
The Anatomy of Buzz: How to Create
  Word of Mouth Marketing
  (Crown Business), 126
Android, 146
Angie's List, 9, 18–19
appinions.com, 120

Arena, Gary, 90
Audience, 16–17

Bad behavior, 140
Bain & Company, 40
Baltimore Gas and Electric, 206
Beastly, 39
Believe in Power of Marketplace,
  149–150
BenMark, Gadi, 159–160
Bennett, James, 63
Bennett's Newton, 63
Berry, Jon, 119
Best Offense Is a Good Defense,
  148–149
"Best Social Media Customer Service
  Award," 163
Beyond the Dashboard: The
  Correlation Between Online
  Advocacy and Online Sales, 42
Bing, 83, 98
Blackshaw, Pete, 51
Blogger.com, 83
The Book of Awakening (Nepo), 64
Booking.com, 153
Brand, 3
  advocacy, 41, 42, 55–56, 59–62, 67,
    92, 116, 150
  businesses use of, 7, 75, 136–137
  Consumer Decision Journey for,
    30–31
  content created by, 136
  conversations typical of, 50
  credibility of, 58
  Digital Footprint Analysis
    and, 91–93
  employees and, 176, 179–181
  endorsements explicit and implied
    of, 56–58

Brand, *continued*
 engagement and, 128–133,
  136–137
 fans of, 114–116, 133
 Influencer Ecosystem and, 66,
  69–70
 Internet users recommending,
  49–51
 key influencers identified
  by, 202
 loyalty, 50–51
 media and, 108, 109
 90/10 Rule sharing 10%
  time in, 129
 proactive protection tips for,
  147–150
 protection power of, 141–142
 recommendation for, 81–93, 97,
  102–103, 155
 Reputation Terrorists' destruction
  of, 144
 running ads realization of, 24
 search engine algorithms
  importance in, 98
 shareable story and, 96–97,
  103–106
 social business integral in, 14
 social media for, 52–53, 86,
  178–180
 strategies, 106–111
Branded merchandise, 137
Bruce, Michael, 63
Buffet, Jimmy, 70
Burger creating contest, 35–36
Businesses, 122
 consumers actions decided by,
  109–110
 Determined Detractor as beneficial
  to, 149–150
 model redefining of, 157–158
 recommendation used by, 3–8,
  13–14, 18–19, 36, 47–48,
  59–62, 75
 social care's prospects targeted
  by, 156

Buzz, 127
 engagement and, 128, 130, 132
 monetizing as challenge of, 126
 Super Bowl place for, 131

CAGR (*see* Compound annual
  growth rate)
Call of Duty: Black Ops II, 169
CareerBliss.com, 184
Cathy, Dan, 181
Cea, Christine, 118–119
Ceptara.com, 137
Chatter:
 employee monitoring and
  addressing of, 174–175
 Facebook and, 165–167
 Twitter and, 164, 166–167
"Checking In? Hidden Ways Hotels
  Court Guests Faster"
  (*Wall Street Journal*), 153
Chevy Volt, 122
Cialdini, Robert, 11
Ciardelli, Victor, 157
Cirque de Freak, 39
Clorox Company, 187–190
CLOROXCONNECTS, 188–189,
  196–197
CMO Council Co., 71
Co-creation:
 advantages of, 191–193
 charting own course for, 195–200
 companies and, 199–200
 customer engagement in,
  191–192
 feedback in, 198–200
 ideas in, 192
 social media using, 191, 196–197
Comment boxes, 15
Communications, 20, 23–24
Communispace Co., 90, 194
Companies:
 co-creation and, 191, 199–200
 employees' issues with, 169,
  175–176, 183–184
 recommendation and, 183–185

social media for, 171, 175–178
(*See also* Businesses)
Compete.com, 84
Competitive Destroyers, 145–146
(*See also* Determined Detractors)
Complaints:
consumer, 24, 26, 27
industry, 170–171
ComplianceAndSafety.com, 181–182
Compound annual growth rate
(CAGR), 169
Computer's cookies, 26–27
ComputerWord.com, 131
Consumer Decision Journey, 30–32
Consumer Pulse System, 114
Consumer Reports, 9
Consumers, 23, 25, 83–86
active engagement one-on-one
with, 166–167
brand Internet recommendations
helped by, 49, 51
businesses influenced by, 19, 60,
96, 109–110
co-creation's connecting
companies to, 191
complaints, 24, 26, 27
customer relationship, data and,
115–116
Highly recommended businesses
engagement of, 213
ideas, feedback and, 188–189
postpurchase and, 32–33
Recommendation Study (2013)
reviews by, 50
Content marketing, 130, 133–136
Conversation:
of brand, 50
Ground Control tracking web,
87–88
Listening for Leads in, 89
social media audience and sincerity
in, 167
volume, 44–45
word of mouth offline higher than
online, 56

Cookies, at check-in, 153–154, 157
Corporate, 170
Corporate Eye blog, 88
*Corporate Social Responsibility
(CSR) Report*, 180
CoveritLive, 75
Crimson Hexagon, 85–86
CRM (*see* Customer relationship
management)
Crowd Science, 52
CSR (*see Corporate Social
Responsibility Report*)
Customer care (*see* Customer service)
Customer relationship management
(CRM), 115–116
Customer service, 158, 160
marketing convergence of, 155–157
social media and, 153, 154, 155,
159, 164, 205
for Stew Leonard's, 5, 7
Customers, 7, 17–18, 160, 212
businesses relationship with,
113–114, 158, 162–163
co-creation engagement of, 191–192
recommendations and loyalty of,
40–41
relationship with, 32–34

Data brokers, 116
Davidson, Arthur, 137
Defensive action, 147–148
Defensive steps, 144–145
Dell Co., 87–88, 142–143
Determined Detractors:
businesses benefiting from,
149–150
Competitive Destroyers as, 145–146
defensive action and reach of, 147
Hear Me plea of, 142–143
Influencer Ecosystem, 72–74
protection and, 139–150
Reputation Terrorists as, 144–145
social media in, 141–142
Digg, 85
Digital Age, 181

Digital Footprint Analysis:
  brand in, 91–93
  safe sales conducted by, 96
  Zócalo Group performing, 90–93
Direct message (DM), 166
Disney, 170
Do Us a Flavor contest, 36, 191, 193, 199
Domino's Pizza, 73–76
DoubleTree, 153–154
Duxler Tire, 33–34

Earned media, 109
Easy Bake Oven, 131–132
Ebert, Roger, 58
eMarketer.com, 49, 72
Employee, 170
  brand and, 176, 179–181
  chatter monitoring and addressing of, 174–175
  companies working with, 169, 175–176, 183–184
  fans, 173–181
  recommendations/referrals, 171–172
  social media with, 173–178
Endorsements, 56–58
Engadget.com, 68
Engagement, 136
  of audience, 16–17
  brand and, 128–130, 132–133
  buzz and, 128, 130, 132
  90/10 Rule and, 129–132
  The Path to Recommendation phase in, 134
  social media and, 128, 130, 137, 168
Escalation plan, 148
Eurail Co., 162–163
Everyday Influencers, 119–122
Expedia.com, 153

Facebook, 9, 57–58, 74–75, 84–85, 98, 100, 108, 120
  businesses use of, 25–26, 35–36, 153, 180

chatter in, 165–167
fan page started on, 16–17
social media and, 50–54, 137, 147, 155, 159–161, 176–178
Fast and Furious 6, 131
Fast Company, 62, 67
Fay, Brad, 50
Federal Trade Commission (FTC), 108
Feedback, 198–199, 202
Fillion, Nathan, 11, 108
Fliptop Co., 115
Focus groups, 89–90
Food Politics, 70
Forrester Consulting, 87–88
Forrester Research, 65–66, 72
Fortune 500 companies, 204
Foursquare, 57–58
Fraud, 18–19
FriendFeed, 85
Frito-Lay Fan program, 59–62
Frito-Lay Co.:
  Do Us a Flavor contest of, 36, 191, 193, 199
  Fan program, 59–62
Full Contact Co., 115

Gaming Market: Global Industry Analysis, Size, Growth, Share and Forecast 2011 to 2015, 169
Gawker.com, 108
General Motors, 125–126
getlittlebird.com, 120
Gladwell, Malcolm, 64–65, 67, 126
Glassdoor.com, 170–171, 173
Global gaming market, 169
Google, 10, 85, 98–100, 153
  decision making in, 15
  features offered by, 83, 86
  influencers found in, 120
  information management priority of, 82–84
Ground Control, 87–88, 90
Guaranteed Rate, Inc., 157–158

Hands Free, 202–203
Harley-Davidson, 136–137
Harris, Neil Patrick, 11, 108
Hasbro, 131–132
Hear Me, 142–143
Hidden Valley, 189
The Hidden Wealth of Customers
(Lee), 21
Highly recommended, 36–37, 39, 46,
84, 202
being recommendable, 17–18
recruiting recommenders about,
19–20
Highly Recommended, Inc., 20
Highly recommended businesses:
adaptation allowance for, 209
becoming, 211–213
evolution and, 205–208
one customer at a time success
in, 212
one-on-one relationships in, 209
social media's impact on, 180,
204–205
vision of, 208–210
Hill, Kashmir, 139
Hilton Worldwide, Inc., 153–154
Hollister Co., 25–26
Holmes, Ryan, 178
Holthouser, Jim, 154
HooteSuite, 84, 178
HooteSuite.com, 178
*How Aunt Ammy Gets Her Free
Lunch* (Pinch and Kesler), 54
the Hub, 180
Human resources (HR),
173–183, 204
The Hunger Games, 8, 39

IBM, 88–89, 203
IceRocket blog search, 84
Industry eminents, 76
identifying, 116–119
Influencer Ecosystem tier in,
70–71

Nissan LEAF identifying
environmentalists for, 121
sales drive expanding expert list of,
117–118
Influence (Cialdini), 11
Influencer Ecosystem, 75, 76, 117
brand knowledge of, 69
crisis prevention in, 76
Determined Detractors doing
damage in, 72–74
industry eminents tier in, 70–71
information specialists as mavens
in, 65–67
Oprah Effect and, 63–65, 77
peer influencers as component of,
71–72, 77
recommendations driven by
engaging in, 68
Influencers, 76, 114, 119
identifying, 123
marketing power taken to the next
level by, 123
Nissan LEAF program not being
myopic as, 121
tools' search by topics and
categories in, 120
(*See also* Peer influencers)
The Influentials (Keller and Berry), 119
Information overload, 9–11
Interactive marketing, 22, 27, 35–37
"Interactive Media Award," 163
Internet, 10, 90
Consumer Decision Journey
influencing, 30
recommending brand users' reason
for, 49–51
search engines and, 83
Interruptions, 17–18
advertising caused by, 16
interactive marketing compared to,
22, 27, 34–35
Inventor network, 189
Iron Man 3, 131
iTunes, 136

Jack Morton Worldwide, 55
Jenest, Shannon, 3
Jezebel.com, 108
Jobvite.com, 171–173
Just Dance 4, 169

Keller, Ed, 50, 119
Keller Fay Group's TalkTrack data,
    56–58
Kesler, Filip, 54
Ketchum/FedEx Social Business
    Benchmarking Study, 206
Keywords, 86, 89, 96
    Digital Footprint Analysis and, 91
    Google alerts for, 83–84
    Recommendation Index's insight
        in, 43–44
Kimberly-Clark, 47
Kimpton Hotels & Restaurants, 154
Kindle, 136
klout.com, 120
Kotaku.com, 169–170
Kraft Foods, 90, 193–195
kred.com, 120
Kwikchex, 153

Landing page, 197
Lasker, Albert, 23
Lee, Bill, 21, 24–25
Leondakis, Niki, 153
Les Miserables, 156
Lever, Lord, 19
Li, Charlene, 206
Lightwedge, 63–64
Linde, Ed, 89
Lindegaard, Stefan, 190
LinkedIn, 177, 182
Listening for Leads, 88–90
Listening to and Acting on What
    Consumers Are Telling You,
    161–162
Lithium Co., 71
LLBean.com, 157, 158
Lok, Scarlett, 56

Lokitis, Sara, 98
London School of Economics (LSE),
    41, 42
Loyalty loop, 31–34

Mad Men era, 89
Management, 199
Market research, 89–90
Marketers, 21, 26–27, 46
Marketing, 28
    advocacy tidal wave in, 40
    blogs in, 27–28
    Buzz Marketing Period and
        campaigns in, 126
    campaign, 22, 27
    content, 130, 133–136
    customer service convergence and,
        155–157
    fans persuading fans in, 30
    influencers' power taken to the
        next level in, 123
    insights influencing, 45–46
    interactive, 22, 27, 35–37
    interruptions and interactive, 22,
        27, 34–35
    media streams essential pillar
        of, 107
    one-to-one, 113–114
    recommendation and, 25, 36–37,
        81–82
    social care gap in, 157
    social media, 3, 21, 119, 204–205
    (See also Word of mouth
        marketing)
"Marketing Is Dead" (Lee), 21–22,
    24–25
Marsden, Paul, 42
Marx, Erich, 122
Mashable.com, 181
McDonald, Robert, 113–114
McDonald's, 43, 139–140
McKinsey & Company,
    30–31
McNeill, Shirley, 35

Media (*see* Earned media; Owned media; Paid media)
MediaBistro.com, 178
Mehta, Manish, 87
Merchants, 22–23
Merton, Robert K., 89
Messages, 20
Microsoft, 53, 146, 169
Millennials, 185
Mission statement, 189–190
Moore, Ammanuel C., 206
MotiveQuest, 42
Motley Fool, 190

Nabisco, 194
Negative reviews, 141
Nepo, Mark, 64
Nestle, Marion, 70–71, 77
Nestlé Co., 51
Net Promoter Score (NPS), 40–43
Nike, 132
90/10 Rule, 129–132
Nissan LEAF, 121–122
Nissan North America, 122
NM Incite, 159
Nook, 136

Obama, Barak, 64
Obamacare, 181
O'Brian, Terence, 68
Old Navy, 64
OmniClean, 201–204
Omnicom Agency, 121
"One Number You Need to Grow" (Reichheld), 40
One-to-one marketing, 113–114
Online:
    communities, 90
    community, 201–202
    conversations, 164–165, 201
    influencers, 97
    privacy, 26–27
    recommendations, 50

Open innovation, 190, 196
Oprah Effect, 63–65, 71, 77
Oprah Winfrey Show, 63–64, 125–126
Oracle Open World, 203
Oracle Social Relationship Management Suite, 203
Owned media, 108

Pace, Tony, 74–75
Packaging and Design, 205
Paid media, 107–108
Papa John's, 181
Parature.com, 159
Party Bore, 127
The Path to Recommendation:
    content marketing and, 134–136
    mastering the four phases of, 134–135
Pattinson, Robert, 76
Peer influencers:
    community engaged Americans as, 119
    Influencer Ecosystem components and, 77
    influential consumers' small online presence of, 121
    tools available for finding, 120
Pellegrino, Adam, 35
People's Burger, 35–36
PepsiCo, 36
Percy Jackson and the LightningThief, 39
Peterson, Andrea, 153
P&G (*see* Procter & Gamble)
Philips Consumer Products Group, 3
Philips Norelco, 3
Piche, Greg, 189–190
Pilot groups, 194
Pinch, Trevor, 54
Pinterest, 52, 58, 196–197
"Pissed Off Employees Bash Pretty Much Every Major Video Game Company," 170

Pontiac G6, 125–126
Pope, Gavin, 131–132
Pope, McKenna, 131–132
Portion control, 194
Postpurchase:
   customer relationship beginning
      with, 32–34
   loyalty loop and experience of,
      31–32
Proactive:
   brand protection tips as, 147–150
   detractors as, 148
   marketplace power as, 149
Procter & Gamble (P&G), 113–114,
      116, 121
Product innovations, 201–202, 205
Protection, 139–150
Psychology of Selling and Advertising
   (Strong), 29
Purchase Funnel model, 29–30

Quintos, Karen, 88

Radian6, 85
The Radian6 Social Marketing
   Cloud, 204
Rankings:
   Amazon.com's system of
      reviewing, 54–55
   Recommendation Index, 43–44
   search engines raising, 99–100
Rapleaf data broker, 116
Ratings, 17, 58, 170
R&D capabilities, 188–189, 198
Recommendation:
   alignment terms wanted in, 102
   brand and, 81–93, 97, 102–103, 137
   businesses using, 3–8, 13–14,
      18–19, 36, 47–48, 59–62, 75
   companies' recommended
      by self, 183
   customer influencing, 17–18, 40–41
   employee satisfaction made easy
      by, 184

engagement leading to, 129–130
Guaranteed Rate, Inc.'s focus
   on, 158
Influencer Ecosystem driving, 68
Internet consumers helped by,
   49–51
listening to and acting on, 11–13
marketing, 25, 36–37, 81–82
merchants giving, 22–23
natural messaging and, 100–101
NPS questions in, 43
The Path to Recommendation
   phase of, 135
positive and negative, 40, 44–45
recognition in advertising and,
   17–18
relearning art of, 24–26
social media and, 52–54, 57–58,
   119, 202
strategies, 109–111
trustworthiness from, 9
wanting people's, 19–20
word of mouth marketing and, 8,
   40, 81, 107
(*See also* Highly Recommended;
   The Path to Recommendation;
   Word of mouth
   recommendation)
Recommendation age, 32, 40
companies keeping updated in,
   184–185
Ground Control benefits in, 87
powerful media mix evolving
   into, 28
shareable story monitoring in, 111
vocal majority of, 5–8
Recommendation Index, 43–45
Recommendation Study (2013), 50
Recruiters, 181–183
Red Robin Restaurant, 35–36, 191–199
RedHeadGrandma6, 187, 192, 199
Reichheld, Fred, 40, 41
Reputation Terrorists, 144–145
Return on investment (ROI), 122

Return on involvement, 22
Revenue growth, 41
Roberts, Kevin, 21–22
Roper, Elmo Burns Jr., 119
Roper Opinion Research
    Company, 119

Saatchi & Saatchi Worldwide, 21
Safe Food to Feed Your Pet Right
    (Nestle), 71
Sales department, 205
Sales drive, 117–119
Sales growth, 41–42
Salesforce, 85
SAS, 180
Satmetrix, 40, 41
Schnatter, John, 181
The Science of Becoming Highly
    Recommended, 203
Search engines, 83, 86, 98, 99–100
Search rankings, 98, 100
Searchmetrics SEO blog, 98–99
Sensei Marketing, 140
SentrySafe Co., 95–97
SentrySafe Shareable Story Map, 105
SEO Pyramid, 99
Shareable story, 100–101, 109, 115
    brand and, 96–97, 103–106
    map, 104–106
    person-to-person value in, 102
    powerful meaning conveyed in,
        101–103
    rankings rising and, 99–100
    recommendation age and, 111
    search rankings influenced by, 98
    vital link in, 97–99
    word of mouth success from, 106
Shared media, 109
Shares, 98
Siefker, Rob, 159
Simply Measured, 85
Siskel, Gene, 58
Slingshot study, 98
Smashwords, 136

Social business:
    brand integral in, 14
    framework of, 206
    influencers understanding and, 76
    resources spent on, 203–204
Social care:
    brand recommendation and, 155
    breakdown of known facts in, 160
    businesses' targeted prospects
        by, 156
    marketing gap in, 157
    protocols and procedures for,
        163–164
    social media for, 155, 159–161,
        167–168
    trend gaining momentum in, 161
    (*See also* Customer service)
Social gifts, 64–65
Social listening, 101
    businesses lagging behind in, 88
    focus groups' informational
        methods of, 90
    free tools for, 84–85
    mastering art of, 83–86
    recommendation marketing
        benefits of, 82
    search engine results from, 86
Social media, 212–213
    advertising wizards with, 24
    audience, 167
    backlash caused by consumer
        complaints in, 24
    bad behavior in, 140
    brands and, 52–53, 86, 178–180
    CEO's comment on, 181
    co-creation using, 191, 196–197
    companies using, 39, 87–90, 163,
        171–172, 175–178
    competitive opinion and power
        of, 14
    cookies, feedback and, 153–154
    counting of shares in, 98
    customer service on, 153, 154, 155,
        159, 164, 205

Social media, *continued*
  Determined Detractors in, 141–142
  employees and, 173–178
  engagement and, 128, 130, 137, 168
  Facebook and, 50–54, 137, 147, 155,
    159–161, 176–178
  feedback management and, 15
  filtering data for community
    activity in, 115–116
  highly recommended businesses
    impacted by, 204–205
  Human Resources using, 173–181,
    182–183
  infancy of, 11, 48
  information overload in, 10–11
  marketing, 3, 21, 119, 204–205
  mastering of, 12
  paid media advertising of, 108
  The Path to Recommendation
    transferable in, 135
  proper care and feeding of,
    158–162
  R&D capabilities increased
    through, 188–189
  recommendation and, 52–54,
    57–58, 119, 202
  recruiter becoming one on,
    181–183
  returns from involvement in, 22
  Searchmetrics SEO blog signals
    and, 98
  social care in, 155, 159–161,
    167–168
  Twitter and, 10–12, 84–85, 154,
    155, 156, 164, 166–167, 176–177
  Word of Mouth Marketing
    Association and, 106–107
*Social Media for Corporate
  Innovators and Entrepeneurs*
  (Lindegaard), 190
SocialMediaExaminer.com, 98
Social Mention, 85
Social networks, 181–182
Social platforms, 115

Social Proof, 11
SocialMediaToday.com, 164
Sonos, 68–69
Standard Oil Company, 119
Starbucks, 5, 43, 133, 135–136
STELLAService, 157
Stew Leonard's, 3–8
  advocacy and motivation detailed
    by, 6–7
  customer service of, 5, 7
  as 100 Best Companies to Work
    For, 4, 6
Subway, 74–75
Success, 161–162
Super Bowl (2013), 131
Superannuation, 170–171
Sustainable engagement, 136–137
Sysomos, 86

Taft, William Howard, 10
Taglines, 22–23, 96, 100, 102, 197
TBWA/Tequila/Shanghai, 56
TechJournal.com, 159
TechnoBuffalo, 142
Technorati, 84
The Thank You Economy
  (HarperCollins), 14
The Tipping Point (Gladwell),
  64–66, 126
"3 Tips to Manage Your Social Media
  Reputation" (Lokitis), 98
Toyota Prius, 122
Transparency-Market Research, 169
TripAdvisor.com, 13–14, 17, 153
Trump, Donald, 15
Tumblr, 115, 176, 192, 197
Twilight, 70, 76
Twitter, 52–55, 58, 61, 74–75, 98,
  120, 197
  businesses use of, 97, 139–140, 146,
    159–161
  chatter and, 164, 166–167
  customer service questions
    and, 157

social media and, 10–12, 84–85,
    154, 155, 156, 164, 166–167,
    176–177

*The Ultimate Question: Driving
    Good Profits and True Growth*
    (Reichheld), 41
Unilever Co., 117–119

Vaynerchuk, Gary, 14
Vazquez, Monica, 74–75
Vitamin Water, 197
Viva Divas, 48
Viva paper towels, 47–48
Vocal majority, recommendation age
    in, 5–8

Walt Disney World, 13–14
Watts, Duncan, 67
Website, 5, 133
Whole Foods, 132–133
Why Calories Count (Nestle), 71
Wikipedia, 10
Wilson, Jeff, 140
Wion, Rick, 139
Word of mouth (WOM), 41, 72, 95
    co-creation momentum of,
        192–193
    in Keller Fay Group's TalkTrack
        data, 56–57
    Nissan LEAF campaign for,
        121–122
    one-to-one marketing focus on,
        113–114
    as sales growth predictors, 41–42
    shareable story vital for success
        of, 106

Word of mouth marketing, 113–114
    Angie's List capturing wisdom
        of, 9
    global phenomenon in, 55
    as holy grail of marketing, 15–16
    Kimberly-Clark seeking, 47
    recommendation and, 8, 40, 81, 107
Word of Mouth Marketing
    Association (WOMMA),
    106–107
Word of mouth recommendation,
    3, 81, 123
    in Influencer Ecosystem, 69
    power exemplified by, 6
World War Z, 131

Yahoo!, 67, 83, 98
Yahoo! Small Business Advisor, 85
Yellow Dog Eats, 13–14
Yelp, 13–14, 17, 56–57, 148, 153,
    170, 212
YouTube, 50, 85, 142–143, 196

Zappos.com, 157, 158–159
Zócalo Group, 59, 66–67, 82, 86,
    110–111, 126
    brand advocacy platform launched
        by, 116
    Digital Footprint Analysis
        performed by, 90–93
    escalation plan of, 148
    Recommendation Index created
        by, 43–44
    Recommendation Study by, 50
    social business in, 206
    Viva paper towels and, 47–48
ZócaloNet, 71

About the Author

Paul M. Rand is the founder, president, and CEO of the Zócalo Group—an award-winning and highly recommended digital, social, and word of mouth marketing agency that represents some of the world's leading brands. Zócalo's mission is simple: to ensure that its clients become the most discovered, talked about, and recommended brands in their category.

In addition to his role at Zócalo, Paul is a partner at Ketchum—one of the world's largest and most awarded marketing and communications agencies. Both Zócalo and Ketchum are divisions of Omnicom Group.

Paul has been recognized as a visionary business strategist, entrepreneur, marketer, and public relations professional by a number of business and marketing publications, and he is a regular speaker at industry conferences. He is the past president and board member of the Word of Mouth Marketing Association (WOMMA), and he currently serves on the board of the Council of Better Business Bureaus (BBB). He is an adjunct faculty member and vice chairman of the dean's advisory board for DePaul University's Driehaus College of Business/Kellstadt Graduate School of Business, in addition to serving on the advisory board of Northwestern University's Spiegel Digital & Database Research Initiative.

Paul lives in Chicago with his wife and three children.